Japanese Game Studies

Fumihiko Ikuine • Kazufumi Fukuda
Akito Inoue • Nobushige Kobayashi
Editors

Japanese Game Studies

A Guide to Studying Japanese Games

Springer

Editors
Fumihiko Ikuine
Chuo Graduate School of Strategic Management
Chuo University
Chiyoda-ku, Tokyo, Japan

Akito Inoue
College of Image Arts and Sciences / Ritsumeikan Center for Game Studies
Ritsumeikan University
Kyoto, Kyoto, Japan

Kazufumi Fukuda
College of Image Arts and Sciences / Ritsumeikan Center for Game Studies
Ritsumeikan University
Kyoto, Kyoto, Japan

Nobushige Kobayashi
Faculty of Informatics, Department of Data Science
Tohoku Gakuin University
Aoba-ku, Sendai, Miyagi, Japan

ISBN 978-981-95-9856-4 ISBN 978-981-95-9857-1 (eBook)
https://doi.org/10.1007/978-981-95-9857-1

This Springer imprint is published by the registered company Springer Nature Singapore Pte Ltd.
The registered company address is: 152 Beach Road, #21-01/04 Gateway East, Singapore 189721, Singapore

Preface

Japanese games have always had a strong international presence, historically and contemporaneously. Consequently, they have attracted the interest of numerous researchers and students, leading to a growing number of international scholars who wish to conduct research in Japan.

Many of the editors and authors of this book are from the generation that grew up playing Japanese games on consoles like the Famicom. We were raised as gamers, later became academics, and have been involved in shaping the game studies scene in Japan. From this standpoint, while we strongly relate to the international discourse on Japanese games, we also observe epistemic gaps and contextual disjunctions. This issue does not stem from a one-sided lack of understanding; it is also rooted in the fact that the research backgrounds and contexts of Japanese game scholars are not sufficiently known abroad. Because Japanese game studies have circulated primarily in the Japanese language, they have formed a unique, and at times insular, academic ecosystem. To further invigorate this research, deepening international academic exchange is essential.

In fact, the inspiration for this book stemmed in part from a critical awareness of the asymmetry in academic discourse—a feeling of being on the periphery of the global canon. For better or for worse, there are palpable differences in the academic domains and research subjects between so-called global game studies and the research conducted in Japan. This volume is a collection of essays contributed by researchers affiliated with Japanese institutions, each writing from their own expertise. As such, it acts as a mirror, reflecting the current state of Japanese game studies, whether we like it or not. During the editing process, some expressed the critical view that "a collection like this might turn Japanese research further inward." Our intention, however, is precisely the opposite: by articulating our internal specificities, we aim to build a more robust bridge to the global community.

Therefore, this book has three main objectives: First, to reorganize and re-evaluate the fields of Japanese game research and game studies. Second, to serve as a practical guidebook for international students and researchers aiming to study at Japanese universities or conduct research in the country. Third, to catalyze international academic exchange.

As our title, *Japanese Game Studies*, suggests, this volume is grounded in the evolution of game studies itself. From the 1990s to the early 2000s, the field was centered on philosophical and theoretical debates concerning the essential characteristics of games, as exemplified by the narratology-ludology debate. Moving into the 2010s, the scope of inquiry expanded to include history, region, industry, and players—notably through research on player culture and the subsequent "material turn." In alignment with this shift toward materiality, Japanese research has increasingly focused on the preservation and analysis of paratexts, such as game manuals and packaging, recognizing them as vital cultural artifacts. Now in the 2020s, game studies is developing into an interdisciplinary field where diverse areas of study intersect, strengthening its connections to social issues while also incorporating methods from archival studies and digital humanities.

While loosely connected to these international trends, Japanese game studies has formed its own unique ecosystem due to its development primarily within the Japanese language. Its defining feature is not a focus on any single field, but rather a rich, unstructured diversity. The historical absence of an organizationally established field of humanistic game studies in Japan has made it difficult to group this work under a single "game studies" umbrella, but this has also been a source of its intellectual vitality. In recent years, guidebooks that organize and introduce game studies have been published in Japan (Matsunaga et al. 2017; Kobayashi 2020; Yoshida et al. 2023), indicating a growing movement toward research integration. This book builds upon that momentum, with a specific intention to present the depth and breadth of Japanese game research to an international readership.

This book is composed of three parts.

Part I: Understanding Japanese Game Studies provides an overview of the history and current state of game research in Japan and introduces academic societies, research institutions, and methods for accessing materials. Additionally, it addresses research subjects unique to Japan, such as media mix, arcade games, and doujin games. Part II: Joining Japanese Game Research deals with practical methods for conducting research in Japan. It introduces how to utilize archives, focusing on the Ritsumeikan Center for Game Studies (RCGS); analyzes fields that are easier or more difficult to research; and offers practical advice from those with experience studying in Japan. Part III: Accelerating Game Research in Japan offers a perspective on how Japanese game studies can contribute to the international field of game studies in the future. Through topics such as reconsidering "Japaneseness," re-evaluating game discourse from the 1980s, and business studies approaches, it re-examines games within their social, cultural, and business contexts. The final chapter emphasizes the significance of academic exchange and cross-disciplinary approaches, presenting proposals for future researchers.

This volume was structured based on key themes and a list of authors developed by the editors, who then commissioned manuscripts from the contributing researchers. The draft of each chapter was finalized after discussions in a workshop, a process that helped to clarify the book's overall concept. At the same time, the work of synthetically theorizing this field remains a task for the future.

We sincerely hope that by highlighting the specificities of Japanese game research, this book will spark international dialogue and serve as a catalyst for new collaborations and networks, turning these linguistic and conceptual "barriers" into opportunities.

This volume, *Japanese Game Studies*, has been co-edited by four editors, but the responsibility for writing this preface rests solely with me.

References

- Kobayashi, Nobushige. 2020. *Dejitaru gēmu kenkyū nyūmon: Repōto sakusei kara ronbun shippitsu made* [Introduction to digital game studies: From report writing to thesis drafting]. Kyoto: Minerva Shobo.
- Matsunaga, Shinji. 2017. Overall map of game research. In *Guide to game studies*, eds. Matsunaga Shinji, Inoue Akito, Kimura Tomohiro, Fukuda Kazufumi, and Roth Martin. Agency for Cultural Affairs. https://mediag.bunka.go.jp/mediag_wp/wp-content/uploads/2017/05/guide_to_game_studies_v2_public.pdf. Accessed 14 Jan 2026.
- Yoshida, Hiroshi. 2023. *Digital game studies*. Tokyo: University of Tokyo Press.

Kazufumi Fukuda, on behalf of the editors
Osaka, Japan
January 2026

Acknowledgments

This book, *Japanese Game Studies*, is the result of years of dialogue and collaboration among a diverse network of scholars.

First and foremost, we would like to express our deepest gratitude to all the contributors of this volume. Despite their busy schedules, they generously shared their expertise and engaged patiently with the editorial process. This book would not exist without their dedication.

Academic research involves more than just writing; it thrives on interaction. We would like to express our sincere appreciation to the numerous research communities that have served as the intellectual foundation for this project. We extend our gratitude to the vital hubs connecting many of us—starting with the Digital Games Research Association Japan (DiGRA Japan), the Ritsumeikan Center for Game Studies (RCGS), and the Replaying Japan conference series and extending to the members of various study groups, reading circles, and informal networks of scholars, students, and developers. The vibrant ecosystem of game research in Japan is built upon these collective efforts.

We also owe a debt of gratitude to the publishers who worked tirelessly behind the scenes.

It is our sincere hope that this volume will serve as a useful guide for future researchers and contribute to the further enrichment of global game studies.

The research presented in this book was conducted with the support of the following research grants, to which the authors express their sincere appreciation: JSPS Grants-in-Aid for Scientific Research (JSPS KAKENHI) grant numbers JP21H00753, JP22K18155, JP23K12555, JP23K25553, JP24K05119, and JP25K03667.

The studies are also supported by JST Moonshot R&D grant number JPMJMS2215 and grants from the Foundation for the Fusion of Science and Technology (FOST) and the Hayao Nakayama Foundation for Science, Technology and Culture. We would like to express our deep gratitude for this support.

January 2026

Akito Inoue, on behalf of the editors
Kyoto, Japan

Contents

Contributors

Kazufumi Fukuda College of Image Arts and Sciences / Ritsumeikan Center for Game Studies, Ritsumeikan University, Kyoto, Kyoto, Japan

Wei Huang Graduate School of Technology Management, Ritsumeikan University, Ibaraki, Osaka, Japan

Fumihiko Ikuine Chuo Graduate School of Strategic Management, Chuo University, Chiyoda-ku, Tokyo, Japan

Akito Inoue College of Image Arts and Sciences / Ritsumeikan Center for Game Studies, Ritsumeikan University, Kyoto, Kyoto, Japan

Yasuo Kawasaki Kinugasa Research Organization, Ritsumeikan University, Kyoto, Japan

Nobushige Kobayashi Faculty of Informatics, Department of Data Science, Tohoku Gakuin University, Aoba-ku, Sendai, Miyagi, Japan

Akinori Nakamura Ritsumeikan College of Image Arts and Sciences, Ritsumeikan University, Kyoto, Japan

Martin Roth Graduate School of Core Ethics and Frontier Sciences, Ritsumeikan University, Kyoto, Japan

Shinji Matsunaga Graduate School of Letters, Kyoto University, Kyoto, Japan

Hiroshi Yoshida Graduate School of Humanities and Sociology and Faculty of Letters, The University of Tokyo, Bunkyo-ku, Tokyo, Japan

List of Figures

List of Tables

Part I

Understanding Japanese Game Studies

Contents

Purpose and Structure of this Book

Fumihiko Ikuine

Contents

F. Ikuine et al. (eds.), *Japanese Game Studies*, https://doi.org/10.1007/978-981-95-9857-1_1

1

1.1 Purpose of the Book

Computer games originated in the United States and grew significantly in Japan. Since the 1980s, Japanese companies have created hardware such as the Family Computer, characters such as Mario and Sonic, and game content such as Dragon Quest and Final Fantasy. These products and works have captivated people around the world and remain popular in Japan and abroad. Even today, new games featuring Mario are popular worldwide, and Nintendo Switch 2 is in such high demand. Japanese games are one of the roots of computer games worldwide, and high-quality Japanese content and devices continue to have a significant influence today. Furthermore, the Japanese game business has grown into a large-scale market, where not only users but also business people are paying close attention to the trends in Japanese games.

With this history, current state, and the global expansion of computer games, Japanese games have become a subject of study within and outside Japan. At international conferences, such as Replaying Japan,[1] numerous presentations are conducted annually by researchers from Japan and abroad, addressing questions such as why Japanese games are attractive and what their characteristics are. The approaches employed are diverse, encompassing sociology, psychology, engineering, management studies, and economics. Collectively, such academic research can be regarded as studies about Japanese games.

Game studies in Japan are also thriving. Researchers in Japan incorporate global game studies into their unique perspectives, while also seeking to capture how Japanese games are influenced by other cultural domains, such as manga, animation, music, literature, and cosplay, and in turn exert a ripple effect on them. This area is an academic challenge that leverages the advantages of conducting research in Japan and seeks to understand games by considering Japan's cultural background.

This book was written to connect deeply and explicitly these two research trends related to Japanese games, thus the title "Japanese Game Studies." It introduces the intersection between "studies about Japanese games" and "game studies in Japan." Figure 1.1 illustrates this relationship below.

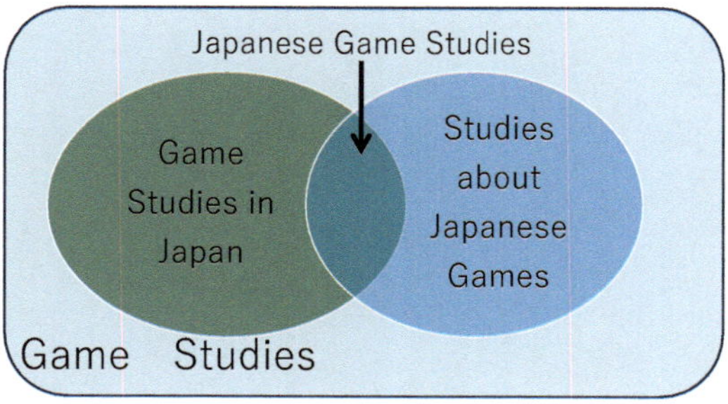

Fig. 1.1 Position of Japanese game studies

1 https://www.rcgs.jp/?page_id=200

This book contributes to the development of future game studies by summarizing the achievements and potential of researchers in Japan who have studied games while considering Japan's cultural background.

The issues we aim to understand as game researchers remain the same regardless of a research base in Japan. The discipline that researchers and aspiring researchers rely on is more important than the presence or absence of a research base. Awareness of one's discipline when conducting interdisciplinary research gives rise to diverse research results related to games. Regardless of the research base location, exchanging research findings and producing rich research results should be possible if the game research is conducted following the same discipline.

However, a "language barrier" exists. Research papers based in Japan are often presented in Japanese, with the international conference Replaying Japan being a rare exception. Furthermore, many game-related materials in Japan are written in Japanese, including interviews with developers and business people, articles, and books. Translation software and the Internet have recently reduced the language barrier significantly. However, research on historical events and those based on old materials shows that the language barrier still exists. Thus, students and researchers outside Japan who are interested in Japanese games face a challenge in reading literature and collaborating with researchers in Japan, resulting in a disconnect between researchers in Japan and those abroad. This book aims to bridge that disconnect.

What is the significance of conducting research using Japanese materials and Japanese game studies, which are mostly written in Japanese? One reason is the significance of internationalizing game studies in Japan. Game research in Japan has seen many studies published domestically. Consequently, the number of researchers in game studies in Japan has not grown significantly. Moreover, certain areas of research have not been sufficiently explored. By sharing the achievements of game studies in Japan with researchers worldwide through this book, we can contribute to the realization of advanced research. This objective not only promotes the development of game studies in Japan but may also have a ripple effect on game studies as a whole.

Another significance is the contribution to the development of Japanese game studies. Similar to other countries, games in Japan have been created and played within their cultural context. To understand Japanese games properly, knowledge of this cultural background can be helpful. The relationship between games and other cultural domains, such as manga, animation, movies, and music, must be examined. In addition, understanding the social context surrounding games in Japan, such as doujin, game centers, media mix, and corporate behavior, is necessary. In other words, Japanese games have been created from the culture and society of Japan and thus require an understanding of such culture and society. Furthermore, by using Japan as a case study, we can gain knowledge about the creation and development of culture, including games, as well as the influence of games on society and vice versa. Such knowledge about games will have a ripple effect on game studies, which aim to understand games in other countries and regions.

However, to understand the culture and society from which Japanese games have emerged, quantitative data and information obtained from the Internet are insufficient. Another effective approach is to stay in Japan, interact with researchers in Japan, and read primary sources to gain insights into phenomena that are not necessarily reflected in quantitative data. To this end, it is essential to identify the types of academic research accumulated in Japan, the primary data sources, and the relevant contacts in order to obtain reliable information about Japanese games. This information will also be useful for overseas researchers who plan to conduct research in Japan. This book will provide a guide for researchers in Japan and abroad in examining games in Japan and thus aims to enrich their game studies.

1.2 Target Readers

Based on the book's objectives, it is intended for two main types of readers. First, we have written this book for game researchers. This book provides game researchers around the world with information about where to go, who to contact, and how to engage in research exchanges to deepen their knowledge in collaboration with researchers in Japan. This book also introduces unique research results related to Japanese games (such as media mix, doujin, and game centers), as well as fields in which research has been accumulated in Japan and accessible research materials. Furthermore, it introduces game studies in Japan across multiple academic fields. By understanding these points, researchers can anticipate who to engage with in research exchanges and what type of research results are likely to be produced.

Second, this book is aimed at undergraduate and graduate students who aim to study games and pop culture in Japan. People outside Japan are increasingly interested in Japanese pop culture, including games. They have sent requests to the authors for study abroad and research guidance. However, studying games as a research subject beyond one's interest in Japanese games requires advanced preparation. Thus, this book introduces game-related research conducted in Japan for future researchers who aim to study abroad or receive research guidance.

Furthermore, this book provides detailed examples of game research in Japan, including interdisciplinary approaches. By referring to these examples, future researchers can gain insights into research-education institutions and academic societies that facilitate research, as well as the experiences and perspectives of researchers who have relocated their research bases to Japan from overseas. Along with these research examples, gaining the latest information on game research in Japan can help researchers identify the aspects of games they aim to explore and which research fields they align with. Such information will serve as a reference during the research planning. In addition, it can be useful during the research preparation in Japan, such as identifying what needs to be prepared in advance and selecting a study abroad destination and a faculty member for research guidance. These preparations can help aspiring researchers avoid the risk of discovering a mismatch between their research interests and institutions upon arrival in Japan.

1.3 Structure of the Book

This book was written with the above objectives and target readers in mind to provide a guide to researchers who aim to conduct game studies in Japan. By introducing Japanese game studies across multiple academic fields, this book is structured to help researchers find approaches that match their interests.

This book is divided into three main parts. Part I, "Understanding Japanese Game Studies", introduces an overview of game studies in Japan. After gaining an understanding of game studies in Japan, Part II, "Joining Japanese Game Research", explains how to participate in game studies in Japan. Finally, Part III "Accelerating Game Research in Japan", explains how game studies in Japan and around the world can develop through the efforts of researchers targeted by this book and who participated in game studies in Japan.

Part I provides an overview of game studies in Japan. Chapter 2 ("A Brief History of Game Research and Game Studies in Japan") provides an overview of past game studies in Japan. After reading Chap. 2, readers can gain a general understanding of the development of game studies in Japan. Chapter 3 ("Japanese Videogame Research Communities, Associations, Institutes, and Projects") introduces current game research in Japan. This chapter introduces the academic societies, educational and research institutions, research projects, and research communities that exist in Japan today. This information enables aspiring researchers to readily identify relevant researchers and academic societies they may wish to engage with. This chapter also introduces ways to obtain materials for conducting game research in Japan.

Those who have gained an overview of the previous and current game studies in Japan will learn about its originality in the following three chapters. Chapter 4 ("Media Mix and Digital Games") introduces media mix, in which games are developed alongside other content, such as animation, TV, and music. Chapter 5 ("A Study of Japanese Game Centers and Arcade Games") introduces research on arcade games and game centers, which have played an important role in the development of Japanese games and continue to influence current game content. Chapter 6 ("The History of Independent Game Production in Japan: Focusing on 'Doujin Games'") introduces doujin, the people, and communities that play an important role in Japanese culture, including games. An understanding of these three chapters, providing examples of game research that leverage Japan's cultural and social backgrounds, will provide readers with a concrete image of how to conduct game research in Japan.

Researchers who have developed an interest in participating in game research in Japan through Part I are encouraged to proceed to Part II to understand the preparations and methods necessary for engaging in game research in Japan. Chapter 7 ("Access Game Resources with Game Archives") introduces methods for obtaining the materials and data necessary for game research in Japan. In Japan, the Ritsumeikan Center for Game Studies (RCGS)[2] has been at the forefront of digitizing and archiving past games. By using RCGS as a starting point and combining it with other data sources,

2 https://www.rcgs.jp/

researchers will learn about Japanese games from various angles and utilize them in their research.

This book aims to introduce a wide range of research from multiple disciplines. However, when examining research in Japan, certain research areas are understudied. Chapter 8 ("Differences in Research Environments by Domain in Japan") introduces these areas. Because academic research values originality but individual achievements are inherently limited, collaborative research and participation in academic conferences play an important role. Understanding which types of research in Japan are conducive to group research and academic exchange, and which are difficult to find research partners for will allow researchers to advance their research activities.

Chapter 9 ("Field Research in the Japanese Game Industry: Developing an In-Depth Understanding from the Inside Out") is recommended for undergraduate and graduate students who plan to study in Japan in the future. A love for Japanese games or Japanese pop culture is an important research motivation, though it is not solely sufficient to conduct academic research. In particular, students who plan to study in Japan need to understand how to approach research on Japanese games and pop culture. Chapter 9 features a researcher who came to Japan from China, conducted empirical research, and earned a master's and doctoral degree. Based on his experiences, he explains the preparations he made before and after studying abroad. This chapter informs readers about research activities after studying abroad in Japan and provides hints for planning their research.

Understanding Chap. 9 helps readers to prepare for their participation in game research in Japan. They can plan how to participate in game research in Japan, including its characteristics, where to belong, and how to proceed with their research. We, who are engaged in game research based in Japan, look forward to seeing talented researchers with similar interests join us. Part III explains how researchers' participation in game studies in Japan will change this field of research and how it will contribute to global game studies.

Chapter 10 ("Japanese Game Studies Based on Management Studies") examines game studies in Japan in terms of the relationship between games and society. This chapter focuses on the relationship between games and business. In Japan, games and business have been closely related. By academically elucidating the relationship between the two, we can envision the type of research that has been possible in management and economics and will be possible in the future.

Another approach to deepen Japanese game studies is to link it closely to Japan's cultural context. This approach is attempted in Chap. 11 ("Reconstruction of Japanese Game History in the 1980s: Reconsidering Game as a Narrative Medium"). Games were a "new medium" that took advantage of the characteristics of computers in the 1980s. They have evolved to the present day through the interpretation of people who have been involved in culture since before that time. With their background in culture, society, and history, if Japanese games still possess "Japanese characteristics" today, then comprehensively understanding them will enable us to envision the future of games.

Chapter 12 ("Imagining Future Pathways for Japanese Game Studies") sketches one possible future direction for Japanese game studies. Similar to other countries and regions, Japanese games are caught between globalization and the narrowness of

Japan's local culture. In everyday life and academia, a de-politicized discussion of "Japan" or "Japanese-ness" is impossible. This chapter emphasizes the need to question the implicit assumptions underlying the national framing and consciously consider games and the cultural contexts in which they are produced. This also requires reconsidering our own positionality. Based on a short discussion of the complexity of the objects, phenomena, and processes that make up the field of Japanese game studies, the chapter explores ways toward a deterritorializing, play-based version of Japanese game studies that focuses on mutual knowledge creation rather than boundary maintenance.

In Chap. 13 ("For the Future of Game Research"), the final chapter of this book, we summarize the insights gained in this book and offer suggestions for students and researchers who will engage in Japanese game studies in the future. This book originally aimed to facilitate researchers' preparation to study in Japan or conduct joint research with researchers in Japan. Specifically, this book guides researchers in identifying fields and themes that are conducive to research in Japan in advance, thereby preventing mismatches in study abroad or research exchange programs.

Furthermore, it aims to assist researchers in exploring Japanese games freely based on their interests and preferences. If this book achieves its intended purpose, the number of researchers interested in Japanese games will increase within and outside Japan, and Japanese game studies will expand and develop. Consequently, international exchange and interdisciplinary research related to game studies will also become active. Looking ahead, this book concludes by considering what kinds of research may emerge and what new possibilities games may reveal as Japanese game studies continue to grow.

Fumihiko Ikuine is a Professor at Chuo Graduate School of Strategic Management, Japan. His research interests are management of technology and innovation. He received the Ph.D. degree from the University of Tokyo in 2006. He joined and taught at the IIR of Hitotsubashi University, Bunkyo Gakuin University, and the University of Tsukuba until 2020. He is the author of *Development productivity dilemma: The innovation pattern of the digital age*, Yuhikaku (in Japanese), which won the Takamiya Award (prize for books) from the Academic Association for Organizational Science of Japan.

A Brief History of Game Research and Game Studies in Japan

Shinji Matsunaga

Contents

F. Ikuine et al. (eds.), *Japanese Game Studies*, https://doi.org/10.1007/978-981-95-9857-1_2

Since the late 1970s, Japan has been a major force in both the production and the consumption of video games, alongside the United States. Many influential titles have been created in Japan, including the iconic *Super Mario Bros.* (Nintendo 1985). Nevertheless, studies on games written in Japanese remain surprisingly limited.

This chapter traces the development of academic research and critical writing on games written in Japanese from the 1950s, the period before video game culture emerged, to the 2010s, when game studies began to take shape in Japan as part of a broader global field. Referring to relevant cultural and historical contexts where appropriate, I examine representative cases across different periods and aim to clarify the kinds of research and discourse that appeared in each period.

2.1 Up to the Early 1970s: Before the Emergence of Video Game Culture

A search for the term *gēmu* [game] in CiNii, the bibliographic database of the National Institute of Informatics, returns more than 20,000 results. When these results are sorted from oldest to newest, studies with *gēmu* in the title from the 1950s to the early 1970s can be grouped into four main types.

(a) *Studies on Individual Sports in the Field of Physical Education.*
This category includes research that aims to identify general features of particular sports such as basketball or soccer. Examples include studies on how matches develop and what kinds of patterns they follow, what strategies are effective in each sport, what physical properties the balls used in these sports have, and how players respond physiologically during play.

(b) *Research in Game Theory.*
Game theory models human decision-making using mathematical methods. In economics and management studies, the works of John von Neumann and Oskar Morgenstern, along with John Nash's series of contributions, had already been introduced in Japanese by the 1950s. These introductions led to a significant amount of theoretical discussion and practical analysis.

(c) *Research on Business Games in Management Studies.*
From the late 1950s onward, studies on business games began to appear. A business game simulates corporate management as a kind of game, functioning as a structured form of "pretend management play" governed by explicit rules. Well-known business games in Japan at the time included the AMA Game developed by the American Management Association and the Andlinger Game (Gonō 1960). By participating in such games, players could experience, even in simplified form, what corporate management involves. In this sense, business games served educational and training purposes. In addition, observers could watch how players made decisions within the game, which linked business-game research directly to the broader field of gaming and simulation studies.

(d) *Research on Games in Computer Science.*
In computer science, games have often been used to explore what computers are capable of. For example, Claude Shannon, known as the "father of information

theory," discussed the conditions under which a computer program could solve chess problems. In Japan as well, research on having computers play games or solve puzzles increased around 1970, along with discussions of the significance of such work (e.g., Hitotsumatsu 1970). Naturally, this line connects directly to the field of artificial intelligence research.

These four types of studies each developed into firmly established fields that continued to grow beyond this period. However, topics that would later become central to video game studies—such as the nature of games, gaming culture, and the history of games—were rarely discussed under the heading of *gēmu* before the early 1970s. Instead, they were treated under the heading *asobi* [play]. In this sense, video game studies in Japan may be seen as having their most direct roots not in the fields listed above but in play studies. For this reason, I will briefly outline the state of play studies in Japan during this period.

2.2 Play Studies Up to the 1970s

Studies that examine the nature of play, asking what play is, had already appeared in Japanese as early as the beginning of the twentieth century. Education practitioner Wada Minoru (1908), for instance, introduced and discussed classical theories of play such as the surplus energy theory, the recreation theory, and the pre-exercise theory.

However, it was from the mid-1960s to the early 1970s that philosophical studies of play became more prominent in Japan. This surge was likely related to the publication of Japanese translations of major works in play studies during this period, including Johan Huizinga's *Homo Ludens* and Roger Caillois's *Man, Play and Games*. In particular, after the first Japanese translation of Caillois's book appeared in 1970, several special issues of philosophy and art journals devoted to the subject of play were published in quick succession (e.g., Jitsuzon-shugi 1971; Teatro 1971; Risō 1973).

Research on the culture of play also began to take more concrete shape during this time. For example, pedagogist Fujimoto Kōnosuke (1968) conducted fieldwork on children's behavior to show how particular forms of play emerge and what environmental factors contribute to their development. Cultural anthropologist Aoyagi Machiko (1977) drew on anthropological knowledge of play cultures around the world and offered a philosophical examination of what play means for human beings.

With respect to the history of games, Masukawa Kōichi, who would later become a central figure in the Japanese Society for History of Games, had already produced a substantial body of work during this period (e.g., Masukawa 1977). A little later, in 1984, *The World Encyclopedia of Play and Games* (Matsu'ura 1984), originally published in 1907, was reprinted. This work is an encyclopedia of indoor games and play traditions from both East and West. According to the commentary by the editor of the reprint edition, Hata Yoshie, the primary reason for its reprinting was its value as an important source for cultural history.

In sum, research on play from the perspectives of its nature, culture, and history took on a clear academic form from the 1960s through the 1970s. It was within this intellectual climate that arcade video game culture first emerged in North America and was then introduced to Japan.

2.3 Late 1970s to the 1980s: The Birth of Video Game Culture and the "Famicom Boom"

It is well known that the first commercially successful video game in the world was Atari's arcade game *Pong*, released in the United States in 1972. Throughout the 1970s, numerous titles followed, many of them produced by Atari, and playing video games gradually took hold as a cultural practice. In Japan, Atari's *Breakout*, known domestically as *Burokku kuzushi*, and its many imitators became highly popular.[1]

Within this context, a landmark Japanese arcade video game was born: Taito's *Space Invaders*, released in 1978 (Taito 1978).[2] The game triggered a nationwide phenomenon known as the "Invaders Boom" in late-1970s Japan. In the following years, a series of iconic works in video game history appeared one after another, including *Galaxian* (Namco 1979), *Pac-Man* (Namco 1980), and *Donkey Kong* (Nintendo 1981). In the global history of video games, this period is often called the "Golden Age of Arcade Video Games," and Japanese games played a major role in shaping it.

During the same period, personal computers, called *maikon* [microcomputers] in Japan at the time, also began to spread. Engineers and certain enthusiasts discovered the new pleasure of playing games on general-purpose computers.[3] By the early 1980s, adventure games and role-playing games, genres distinct from arcade games, were already widely played. Reflecting on this period, game journalist Tane Kiyoshi notes that a "big wave" of American computer RPGs reached Japan in 1983, and that Japanese-made computer RPGs "burst into full bloom" in 1984 (Tane 2014, 3–6). In this sense, one can say that the practice of playing and creating video games flourished in Japan from the late 1970s into the early 1980s.

What, then, was the state of discourse on video games at that time? A few journals and academic articles had already taken notice of video games before the Invaders Boom (e.g., Denshi Gijutsu 1978; Imamura et al. 1978). Guidebooks for creating games on personal computers were also published in the late 1970s. However, these works were limited to technical explanations and cannot be regarded as "research" on video games in any scholarly sense. Even in the early 1980s, although arcade games, computer games, and handheld electronic games (such as Nintendo's Game & Watch series) were all becoming established parts of everyday culture, there was still very little academic discourse on video games.

The situation changed dramatically around 1986. Nintendo's game console Family Computer (commonly referred to as the Famicom) had been released in 1983, but it was the enormous success of *Super Mario Bros.*, released in September 1985, that brought the console into Japanese households on an unprecedented scale. In parallel with this "Famicom Boom," the number of academic publications on video games and the Famicom increased rapidly.

1 For a detailed account of the emergence of arcade video game culture in Japan and its early history, see Kawasaki (2022).

2 For details on its production process, see Gorges (2018).

3 For the history of how personal computers were received and used in Japan, see Suzuki (2022).

Most game-related studies from this period were sociological or psychological investigations. Their topics included media reports and incidents involving video games, parents' and teachers' views on video games, and above all, the effects of video games on children's lives and development as players. Early examples include Jidō shinri (1986) and Kyōiku (1986), and other education journals published special issues on the Famicom Boom. Medical journals also featured articles on children's health, particularly the effects of video games on eyesight (e.g., Ganka 1987). These studies were largely motivated by public concern about the possible negative impacts of video games. Japanese translations of English-language books on video games from an educational psychology perspective also appeared during this period (Loftus and Loftus 1985; Greenfield 1986). In short, early academic interest in video games focused primarily on their effects on children.

Outside academia, new forms of writing began to treat video games as a distinctive and appealing contemporary culture. The first to take up this task were writers and game designers with critical perspectives. Horii Yūji, the designer of *The Portopia Serial Murder Case* and the *Dragon Quest* franchise, and Tajiri Satoshi, who would later become known as the creator of the *Pokémon* franchise, were both active as game critics during this period. Among these efforts, "Famicom shinken"—an irregular section of Shueisha's manga magazine *Weekly Shōnen Jump* for video game reviews, to which Horii partly contributed—is especially noteworthy as an early example of critical game reviewing in Japan.[4]

Yasuda Hitoshi (1986), who played a major role in popularizing tabletop RPGs in Japan, used his extensive knowledge about pulp fiction to trace the origins of video games incorporating elements of science fiction and fantasy. Although not an academic publication, his work can be seen as a precursor to video game history research. Tama Yutaka, who supervised the Japanese translation of Chris Crawford's game design book (Crawford 1988), discussed the history and nature of video games in several of his own works (e.g., Tama 1990). Akagiri et al. (1989), although focused on board games and card games, also offered sophisticated theoretical discussions of the nature of game rules and the pleasures of play. While these publications were commercial rather than academic, their content is rigorous enough to sustain scholarly attention.

Connections between literary criticism and video games also began to appear. One of the earliest well-known examples is Nakazawa Shin'ichi's essay "The Game Freaks Who Play with Bugs," which analyzes *Xevious* (Namco 1983) and its players' behavior (Nakazawa 1984).[5] In 1987, a dialogue book was published featuring the unusual combination of Nakazawa, Yasuda, *Xevious* designer Endō Masanobu, and philosopher Takeda Seiji (Endō et al. 1987). Takahashi Gen'ichirō, a leading figure in Japanese postmodern literature, examined the potential of literature "as a game rather than a narrative" through a comparison of *Dragon Quest II* (Chunsoft 1987) and *Dragon Quest III* (Chunsoft 1988).[6]

---

4 For Horii's activities during this period, see Kobayashi (2023).

5 An English translation of this essay, by Jérémie Pelletier-Gagnon and Tsugumi Okabe, is available; see Nakazawa (2015).

6 For Takahashi's criticism of *Dragon Quest*, see Ōnishi (2021).

Among the publications of this period, the most noteworthy is *The Complete Compendium of Video Games* (Terebi gēmu myūjiamu purojekuto 1988). This work is a comprehensive compendium of knowledge about video games at the time, fittingly described as "complete." It contains a dictionary of video games, developers, and companies; a history of video games; interviews with leading game creators; and several essays that offer cultural criticism of video games.

2.4 1990s: The Growth of Studies on the Video Game Industry

By the 1990s, academic research began to address more directly the actual experience of playing video games. For example, Nakatani and Yano (1993) analyzed how RPGs motivate players by breaking down the genre into its constituent elements. The perspective of clarifying the structure of a particular video game genre (in this case, RPGs) and examining how that structure affects players had not been present in research from the 1980s. The same authors also produced studies on video game interfaces. In psychology as well, discussions of the effects of video games on players were reorganized in ways that more closely reflected actual play experiences. A number of studies identified positive effects, such as the development of motor skills and spatial cognition (e.g., Yuji 1995), and research on the educational uses of video games also increased during this period.

Cultural approaches to video games also became more academically refined compared to the 1980s. Collections and monographs such as Shisō no kagaku (1991), Satō (1993), Fujii and Sawano (1993), and Yamashita (1995) examined phenomena specific to video games and the experience of play on the basis of identifiable theoretical frameworks. Although Tajiri Satoshi (1996) wrote from the standpoint of a game designer, his discussion of the nature of games, particularly, is noteworthy as an attempt to conceptualize the structure and function of video games.

In the English-speaking world, new media studies grounded in literary theory and narratology grew rapidly during this decade. In Japan, however, very few efforts paralleled this development. Rare exceptions include the Japanese translation of Brenda Laurel's *Computers as Theatre* (Laurel 1992) and Enomoto (1993).

What reshaped video game studies in Japan most significantly during the 1990s was research on the video game industry. The series of studies by Kohashi Reika (e.g., Kohashi 1996) was among the first to analyze the structure of the Japanese video game industry from managerial and organizational perspectives. Yada (1996) and Fujita (1998, along with subsequent works) offered objective analyses and descriptions of the history of the video game industry, including developments in North America.

More journalistic and nonacademic publications also appeared frequently during this period. *The University of Games* by Hirabayashi Hisakazu and Akao Kōichi (1996) provided an insider's account of the video game industry and its history, while Aida and Ōgaki (1997), a book version of a television program produced by The Japan Broadcasting Corporation (NHK), presented a dramatic documentary-style depiction of the industry through interviews and reporting. Although these publications cannot be considered reliable academic sources, they nonetheless offered broad and valuable overviews of the video game industry and its history at a time when scholarly research was still scarce.

By the late 1990s, project-based research initiatives began to emerge, including efforts to archive video games.[7] These projects would go on to produce sustained results in the decades that followed. Around the end of the decade, the Computer Entertainment Supplier's Association (CESA) began publishing the *CESA Game White Paper*, an annual report compiling various forms of data on the video game industry. Needless to say, such data serve as the foundation not only for market research and industry studies but also for any research that aims to establish objective facts about video games.

Another notable development during the 1990s was the emergence of new platforms for critical writing on video games, with the magazine *Gēmu hihyō [Game Criticism]*, launched in 1994, as a prominent example. Some articles in that magazine went beyond simple reviews or scoring systems and addressed questions such as what video games ought to be, what the nature of games is, and what makes a particular work good or bad. Although often presented in a relatively informal manner, these discussions clearly embodied what philosopher Noël Carroll calls "reasoned evaluation," a central feature of criticism.

The spirit of this kind of criticism was carried forward by personal websites that began to appear on the Internet in the late 1990s. Most of the video game criticism sites from that period have since closed, and access to their articles is now difficult. Even so, many people testify that from the late 1990s through the early 2000s, a wide variety of critical discourse on video games flourished on individual websites.

2.5 From the 2000s to the Present: Institutionalization and Diversification

In the field of video game industry studies, steady progress continued into the 2000s, as seen in works such as Shintaku et al. (2003). Research also began to appear on online games, which became a major industry during this period. Wi Jong-Hyun (2006) examined the structure of the video game industry in South Korea, one of the central hubs of online game culture. Nakamura Akinori (2005) provided an early report on the state of the video game industry in China. Nojima Miho (2008) analyzed how virtual digital assets such as in-game items acquire real-world value and how the markets that handle them are formed.

Meanwhile, game journalist Shin Kiyoshi (2002) produced a detailed account of the game development process using close-range reporting techniques. Although journalistic rather than academic, such work has clear scholarly value as case studies that reveal on-the-ground structures not visible from macro-level perspectives or quantitative data.

In the early 2000s, efforts to institutionalize researcher and developer communities also began to take shape. In 2002, the Game Amusement Society (GAS) was founded by researchers primarily in the Kansai region, while IGDA Japan, the Japanese chapter

7 For the background to the establishment of the video game archiving project at Ritsumeikan University, see an interview with its project leader, Hosoi Kōichi (CESA 2017).

of the International Game Developers Association, was formed as a community for game developers. In 2006, the Digital Games Research Association Japan (DiGRA Japan), a national academic society and the Japanese branch of the international organization DiGRA, was established, followed by the DiGRA international conference held in Tokyo in 2007. In 2009, the Content Culture History Society was founded as a scholarly organization that examines contemporary Japanese popular culture, including video games, from cross-disciplinary and integrative perspectives. These forms of institutionalization made it possible, at least in principle, to bring together research on video games, previously scattered across separate disciplines, into a more unified space for the study of games.

DiGRA, the international organization, originally grew out of the field of literature and new media studies and has a strong humanities orientation. By contrast, DiGRA Japan includes not only researchers in management and psychology who have long contributed to Japanese academic studies of video games, but also many game developers and researchers in engineering. As a result, DiGRA Japan features a considerable amount of game-design-oriented research. Its interdisciplinary character can be seen in publications such as Shibuya et al. (2016). Compared to DiGRA, the relatively limited presence of humanities-oriented research is a distinctive feature of DiGRA Japan.

From the late 2000s onward, empirical studies of video game culture by sociologists, virtually absent until then, began to emerge. Katō Hiroyasu (2011), using ethnographic methods such as on-site observation of behavior in Japanese arcades and analysis of the "communication notebooks" placed in arcades, examined the social relationships formed in these spaces and clarified the social dynamics of arcade game culture. Hichibe Nobushige (2012) analyzed the culture surrounding independently produced video games, most prominently known as *dōjin* games, focusing on questions such as what motivates creators and how these games circulate and are sold within particular industrial and market structures.

Important contributions to video game history also appeared both inside and outside academia. Akagi Masumi's *In the Beginning, There was Pong* (Akagi 2005) describes the history of the video game industry, especially arcade games, drawing on the author's extensive knowledge. Akagi had long served as an editor of arcade game magazines, and this background informed the detailed account presented in the book. In his review of the book, Koyama Yūsuke wrote that Japan had "finally produced a full-fledged historical study of the video game industry worthy of scholarly reference." Uemura Masayuki et al. (2013) presented a technological history of the Famicom from the standpoint of those involved in its development. Koyama Yūsuke's *A History of the Japanese Digital Game Industry* (Koyama 2016) is an empirical study based on rich data and can be regarded as a definitive account of the history of the Japanese video game industry. Historical writing characterized by the deep knowledge and enthusiasm typical of the *Gameside* mook series published by Micro Magazine Inc., also holds scholarly value, so long as its sources are clearly indicated. Tane Kiyoshi (2011) and Sayawaka (2013) examined video game genres and individual titles, along with the ways players received them, in historical narratives that incorporate a connoisseur's perspective. Nakagawa Daichi (2016) developed an original and exhaustive account of video game history from a broader cultural–historical viewpoint. Kawasaki Yasuo

(2022) clarified both the emergence of arcade video game culture in Japan and the historical background behind it.

Around 2010, practical and applied research that sought to incorporate video games into education and business contexts began to gain attention. Publications on serious games, especially video games designed for educational use, and on gamification, the application of game structures to various real-world contexts, subsequently emerged in Japan as these concepts spread from abroad. These included not only academic works but also business-related publications (e.g., Fujimoto 2007; Prensky 2009; McGonigal 2011; Inoue 2012). Although the term *gamification* has since declined as a buzzword, the educational use of video games continues to be an important research theme (Fujimoto and Morita 2017).

Beginning in the 2000s, and especially following the publication of Azuma Hiroki's *The Birth of Game-like Realism* (Azuma 2007), video games came to be a recurring topic in literary criticism and popular culture criticism.[8] Criticism magazines such as *Eureka* and *Planets* frequently published articles or special issues on video games. The special issue of *Eureka* on social network games (Eureka 2017) and volume 8 of *Genron* (Azuma 2018) represent notable examples of video game criticism in the 2010s. High-quality critical reviews of video games also appear regularly on online gaming media such as *Automaton* and *IGN Japan*.

Since the mid-2010s, humanities-oriented video game research has gradually increased in Japan (e.g., the Japanese Association for Semiotic Studies 2013; Obana 2016; Matsunaga 2018; Yoshida 2022). As discussed in the next section, this trend is closely related to the growing introduction and recognition of game studies as a global field within Japanese academia. In addition, Miyake Yōichirō (2016, 2018), a leading figure in the application of AI technologies to video games, offers an unusually stimulating perspective by connecting artificial intelligence with philosophical thought in both Western and Eastern traditions.

2.6 The Introduction and Development of Game Studies in Japan

The field now known as game studies, as established in the early 2000s primarily by scholars in the Nordic countries, had scarcely been introduced in Japan until the mid-2010s. As exceptions, Katie Salen and Eric Zimmerman's *Rules of Play* and Jesper Juul's *Half-Real* were already recognized as important works, but most other game-studies literature and journals were not only largely unread but also, in many cases, virtually unknown outside a very small circle of specialists. This situation was the result of the historical trajectory described above: Academic research on video games in Japan had developed largely independently of game studies.

Over the past decade, however, this situation has begun to change significantly. Several major works in game studies have been translated into Japanese: Juul's *The Art of Failure* in Juul (2015); *Half-Real* in Juul (2016); and Miguel Sicart's *Play Matters* in

8 For a catalog of Japanese-language video game criticism up to 2016, see Takai et al. (2016).

2

Sicart (2019). Around the mid-2010s, humanities-oriented scholars—including myself—also began actively engaging with and citing theoretical work from game studies. For example, Matsunaga Shinji's *The Aesthetics of Video Games* (Matsunaga 2018), based on his doctoral dissertation, inherits Juul's rule-fiction distinction and Grant Tavinor's theory of interactive fiction, and proposes a triadic model by introducing an additional level concerning the symbols on the screen that represent the ludic and the fictional. A new generation of scholars is now beginning to adopt and critically refine this framework (e.g., Namba 2020; Kurane 2024; Ueno 2024). Yoshida Hiroshi's *Digital Game Studies* (Yoshida 2022) is a rich and wide-ranging collection that brings together the author's previous writings on video games. Yang et al. (2024) offer an anthology of reflections on East Asian video game cultures by contributors from Japan, China, and Korea. In 2025, an introductory companion to game studies titled *Critical Words: Game Studies* was published (Yoshida et al. 2025). This volume is the first introductory work on game studies written in Japanese. Taken together, these works build on the accumulated scholarship of game studies while grounding their analyses in local Japanese cultural contexts. In this sense, they may be regarded, in the fullest sense of the term, as "Japanese game studies."

References

Aida, Yutaka, and Ōgaki Atsushi. 1997. *Shin denshi rikkoku 4: bideo gēmu kyofu no kōbō* [Towards the electronic nation II, vol. 4: the struggle for video game fortunes]. Tokyo: NHK Publishing.

Akagi, Masumi. 2005. *Sore wa pon kara hajimatta* [In the beginning, there was Pong]. Nishinomiya: Amusement Press.

Akagiri, Yuji, Nagumo Natsuhiko, Kusaba Jun, and Homma Haruki. 1989. *Gēmu tankentai: gēmu no shikumi o tokiakasu chiteki kōfun tokuhon* [The game explorers: an intellectually engaging guidebook to how games work]. Tokyo: Shoenshinsha.

Aoyagi, Machiko. 1977. *Asobi no bunka-jinruigaku* [The cultural anthropology of "play"]. Tokyo: Kodansha.

Azuma, Hiroki. 2007. *Gēmu-teki riarizumu no tanjō: Dōbutsuka suru Posutomodan* [Birth of game-like realism: Japan's database animals II]. Tokyo: Kodansha.

Azuma, Hiroki, ed. 2018. *Genron 8: the era of games*. Tokyo: Genron.

CESA. 2017. *Hosoi Kōichi sensei intabyū* [An interview with Professor Hosoi Kōichi]. https://www.cesa.or.jp/interviews/hosoi01.html. Accessed 9 Sep 2025.

Crawford, Chris. 1988. *Balance of Power dezaināzu nōto* [Balance of power: international politics as the ultimate global game]. Trans. Tama Yutaka. Tokyo: Ascii.

Denshi, Gijutsu. 1978. *Denshi Gijutsu* 18(12) (special issue: Exploring the possibilities of video games).

Endō, Masanobu, Yasuda Hitoshi, Nakazawa Shin'ichi, and Takeda Seiji. 1987. *Denshi gēmu no kairaku* [The pleasure of video games]. Tokyo: SoftBank.

Enomoto, Masaki. 1993. *Denshi bungaku-ron* [On electronic literature]. Sairyusha.

Eureka. 2017. *Eureka* 49(3) (special issue: The current state of social network games: beyond Pokémon Go).

Fujii, Masami, and Sawano Masaki, eds. 1993. *Hito wa naze gēmu o surunoka: dennō kūkan no firosofia* [Why people play games: the philosophy of cyberspace]. Tokyo: Yōsensha.

Fujimoto, Kōnosuke. 1968. Asobi bunka no seiritsu katei nitsuite [On the formation process of play culture]. *Jinbun kenyū* 20(4): 315–330.

Fujimoto, Tōru. 2007. *Siriasu gēmu: kyoiku, shakai ni yakudatsu dejitaru gēmu* [Serious games: digital games for education and social practices]. Tokyo: Tokyo Denki University Press.

Fujimoto, Tōru, and Morita Yūsuke. 2017. *Gēmu to gakushū* [Games and learning]. Kyoto: Minerva Shobo.

Fujita, Naoki. 1998. Beikoku ni okeru bideo gēmu sangyō no keisei to kyūgeki na hōkai [The formation and rapid collapse of the video game industry in the United States]. *Keizai ronsō* 162(5–6): 54–71.
Ganka. 1987. *Ganka* 29(12) (special issue: Video games and eyes).
Gonō, Tetsuya. 1960. "Bijinesu gēmu ronkō: bijinesu gēmu to gēmu no riron" [An essay on business games: business games and game theory]. *Kokumin keizai zasshi* 101(4): 52–66.
Gorges, Florent. 2018. *Space Invaders o tsukutta otoko Nishikado Tomohiro ni kiku* [An interview with Nishikado Tomohiro, the creator of *Space Invaders*]. Tokyo: Tokuma Shoten.
Greenfield, Patricia Marks. 1986. *Kodomo no kokoro o sodateru terebi, terebi gēmu, konpyūta* [Mind and media: the effects of television, computers and video games]. Trans. Mutō Takashi and Suzuki Toshiko. Tokyo: Saiensu-sha.
Hichibe, Nobushige. 2012. *Gēmu sangyō hatten no kagi toshite no jishuseisaku bunka* [The role of independent production culture in the development of the video game industry]. PhD dissertation, Tokyo Institute of Technology.
Hirabayashi, Hisakazu, and Akao Kōichi. 1996. *Gēmu no daigaku* [The University of Games]. Tokyo: Media Factory.
Hitotsumatsu, Shin. 1970. Keisanki niyoru gēmu no kenkyū o megutte [On research on games using computers]. *Johōshori* 11 (11): 689–691.
Imamura, Makoto, Takeuchi Hisaharu, and Ōsuka Hidemi. 1978. Bideo gēmu [Video games]. *Terebijon gakkai-shi* 32 (12): 1015–1022.
Inoue, Akito. 2012. *Gēmifikēshon: gēmu ga bijinesu o kaeru* [Gamification: Games Change Business]. Tokyo: NHK Publishing.
Japanese Association for Semiotic Studies, ed. 2013. *Gēmu-ka suru sekai: konpyūta gēmu no kigōron* [A gamified world: the semiotics of computer games]. Tokyo: Shin'yosha.
Jidō shinri. 1986. *Jidō shinri* 40(8) (special issue: How today's children play).
Jitsuzon-shugi. 1971. *Jitsuzon-shugi* 55 (special issue: Play).
Juul, Jesper. 2015. *Shikametsura ni saseru gēmu ha seikō suru* [The art of failure]. Trans. B-Sprount. Tokyo: Born Digital.
Juul, Jesper. 2016. *Hāfuriaru* [Half-real]. Trans. Matsunaga Shinji. Tokyo: New Games Order.
Katō, Hiroyasu. 2011. *Gēmusentā bunka-ron: media shakai no komyunikēshon* [Arcade gaming culture: mediated social communication]. Tokyo: Shinsensha.
Kawasaki, Yasuo. 2022. *Nihon no gēmusentā-shi: goraku shisetsu toshite no hensen to shakaiteki ichizuke* [The history of japanese game arcades: their changes as entertainment facility and their position in society]. Tokyo: Fukumura Shuppan.
Kobayashi, Nobushige. 2023. Furii raitā jidai no Horii Yūji no sōsaku katudō o sasaeta shakaiteki bunmyaku [The social contexts that supported Yuji Horii's creative activities as a freelance writer]. In *the Proceedings of the 2023 DiGRA Japan Summer Conference*, 90–94.
Kohashi, Reika. 1996. *Nihon no kateiyō terebi gēmu sangyō: sono kōzō to soshiki katei* [The Japanese console video game industry: its structure and organizational processes]. PhD dissertation, Kobe University.
Koyama, Yūsuke. 2016. *Nihon dejitaru gēmu sangyō-shi* [A history of the Japanese digital game industry]. Kyoto: Jimbun Shoin.
Kurane, Hajime. 2024. Bideo gēmu no sutōrii wa hiseigōteki nanoka [Are video game story incoherent?]. *Replaying Japan* 6:11–19.
Kyōiku. 1986. *Kyōiku* 36(11) (special issue: Game consoles, personal computers, and children).
Laurel, Brenda. 1992. *Gekijō toshite no konpyūta* [Computers as theatre]. Trans. Tōyama Takayuki. Tokyo: Toppan.
Loftus, Geoffrey R., and Elizabeth F. Loftus. 1985. *Bideo gēmu no shinrigaku* [Mind at play: the psychology of video games]. Trans. Nishimoto Takehiko. Tokyo: Companion Shuppan.
Masukawa, Kōichi. 1977. *Shōgi* (in Japansese). Tokyo: Hosei University Press.
Matsunaga, Shinji. 2018. *Bideo gēmu no bigaku* [The aesthetics of video games]. Tokyo: Keio University Press.
Matsu'ura, Masayasu ed. 1984. *Sekai yūgihō taizen* [The world encyclopedia of play and games], reprint edition. Hompō shoseki.

2

McGonigal, Jane. 2011. *Shiawase na mirai wa gēmu ga tsukuru* [Reality is broken]. Trans. Fujimoto Tōru and Fujii Kiyomi. Tokyo: Hayakawa Publishing.
Miyake, Yōichirō. 2016. *Jinkō chinō no tame no tetsugaku juku* [Philosophy lessons for artificial intelligence]. Tokyo: BNN.
Miyake, Yōichirō. 2018. *Jinkō chinō no tame no tetsugaku juku: toyō tetsugaku hen* [Philosophy lessons for artificial intelligence: eastern philosophy]. Tokyo: BNN.
Nakagawa, Daichi. 2016. *Gendai gēmu zenshi* [A complete history of modern games]. Tokyo: Hayakawa Publishing.
Nakamura, Akinori. 2005. *Chūgoku gēmu bijinesu tettei kenkyū 2005* [An in-depth study of the chinese video game industry, 2005 edition]. Tokyo: Enterbrain.
Nakatani, Tomoji, and Yano Yoneo. 1993. Rōrupureingu gēmu ni okeru yaruki no jizoku [Sustaining player motivation in role-playing games]. *Jinbun kagaku to konpyūta* 17 (6): 33–38.
Nakazawa, Shin'ichi. 1984. Gēmu friiku wa bagu to tawamureru [The game freaks who play with bugs]. *Gendai shisō* 12 (6): 190–203.
Nakazawa, Shin'ichi. 2015. The game freaks who play with bugs: in praise of the video game Xevious (trans. Jérémie Pelletier-Gagnon and Tsugumi Okabe). *Kinephanos* 5 (1): 175–201.
Namba, Yūki. 2020. Gēmu purei/ya no bigaku: purei, pureiya, perusona [Aesthetics of gameplay(ers): play, player, persona(e)]. *Replaying Japan* 2:111–121.
Nojima, Miho. 2008. *Hito wa naze katachi no nai mono o kaunoka: kasō sekai no bijinesu moderu* [Why people buy the intangible: business models of virtual worlds]. Tokyo: NTT Publishing.
Obana, Takashi. 2016. *Eiga ongaku kara gēmu ōdio e* [From film music to game audio]. Kyoto: Koyoshobo.
Ōnishi, Hisaaki. 2021. Dorakue suru Takahashi Gen'ichirō [Takahashi Gen'ichirō playing *Dragon Quest*]. *Kindai bungaku shiron* 59:81–92.
Prensky, Marc. 2009. *Dejitaru gēmu gakushū* [Digital game-based learning]. Trans. Fujimoto *Tō*ru. Tokyo: Tokyo Denki University Press.
Risō. 1973. *Risō* 478 (special issue: Play).
Satō, Takeshi, ed. 1993. *Jōhōka to taishū bunka: bideo gēmu to karaoke* [Information society and popular culture: video games and karaoke]. Tokyo: Shibundo.
Sayawaka. 2013. *Bokutachi no gēmu-shi* [Our shared history of video games]. Tokyo: Seikaisha.
Shibuya, Akiko, Hichibe Nobushige, Fujimoto Tōru, and Mikami Kōji. 2016. Kaku gakujutsu ryōiki no shiza kara mita dejitaru gēmu kenkyū ronbun [Research papers on digital games from the perspectives of various academic disciplines]. *Dejitaru gēmu gaku kenkyū* 8 (1–2): 17–23.
Shin, Kiyoshi. 2002. *Gēmu kaihatsu saizensen: "Samurai" wa koushite tsukurareta* [At the forefront of game development: the making of *Samurai*]. Tokyo: Shinkigensha.
Shintaku, Junjirō, Yanagawa Noriyuki, and Tanaka Tatsuo, eds. 2003. *Gemu sangyō no keizai bunseki: kontentsu sangyō hatten no kōzō to senryaku* [An economic analysis of the video game industry: the structure and strategies of content industry development]. Tokyo: Toyo Keizai.
Shisō no kagaku. 1991. *Shisō no kagaku* 136 (special issue: Cultures of games and computers).
Sicart, Miguel. 2019. *Purei matāzu* [Play matters]. Trans. Matsuanga Shinji. Tokyo: Film Art.
Suzuki, Mana. 2022. *1970 nendai kōhanki kara 1980 nendai zenhanki made no Nihon ni okeru kojin o taishō to suru konpyūta to yūza no kankei* [The relationship between personal computers and users in Japan from the late 1970s to the early 1980s]. PhD dissertation, Kyoto University. https://doi.org/10.14989/doctor.r13473.
Tajiri, Satoshi. 1996. *Shin gēmu dezain: TV gēmu seisaku no tame no hassōhō* [A new approach to game design: creative methods for making video games]. Tokyo: Enix.
Takai, Kurara, Fukuda Masatomo, and Yokoyama Kōsuke. 2016. Nihon no gēmu hihyō mokuroku from 1984 to 2016 [A catalog of Japanese game criticism, 1984–2016]. *Ecrit-o* 5:158–177.
Tama, Yutaka. 1990. *Konpyūta gēmu dezain kyōhon* [A guidebook for computer game design]. Tokyo: Ascii.
Tane, Kiyoshi. 2011. *Kyōyō toshite no gēmu-shi* [Cultivating the history of video games]. Tokyo: Chikumashobo.
Tane, Kiyoshi. 2014. JRPG no hassō no genten wa kokusan pc gēmu ni atta noka? [Did the Ideas behind JRPGs Originate in Domestically Developed PC Games?]. *Role-playng Gameside* 1:2–27.
Teatro. 1971. *Teatro* 341 (special issue: Play and theatre).

Terebi gēmu myūjiamu purojekuto. 1988. *Denshi yūgi taizen* [The complete compendium of video games]. Tokyo: UPU.
Uemura, Masayuki, Hosoi Kōichi, and Nakamura Akinori. 2013. *Famicom to sono jidai: terebi gēmu no tanjō* [The famicom and its era: the birth of console games in Japan]. Tokyo: NTT Publishing.
Ueno, Yū. 2024. Kojinteki na mono toshite no gēmu no purei: takuetsuteki purei, purei sutairu, jikojitsugen toshite no asobi [Game play as personal: exceptional play, play style, and self-realization]. *Replaying Japan* 6:85–95.
Wada, Minoru. 1908. Asobi towa nanzoya [What is play?]. *Fujin to kodomo* 8 (5): 14–17.
Wi, Jong-Hyun. 2006. *Kankoku no onrain gēmu bijinesu kenkyū* [A study of the online game industry in South Korea]. Tokyo: Toyo Keizai.
Yada, Mari. 1996. *Gēmu rikkoku no miraizō* [The future of Japan as a game powerhouse]. Tokyo: Nikkei Business Publications.
Yamashita, Tsuneo. 1995. *Terebi gēmu kara miru sekai* [A perspective on the world through video games]. Tokyo: JustSystems.
Yang, Junxiao, Deng Jian, and Matsumoto Kentarō, eds. 2024. *Nichi-chū-kan no gēmu bunka-ron* [Selected Essays on Gaming Culture in Japan, China, and South Korea]. Tokyo: Shinyosha.
Yasuda, Hitoshi. 1986. *SF fantajii gēmu no sekai* [The world of SF fantasy games]. Osaka: Seishinsha.
Yoshida, Hiroshi. 2022. *Dejitaru gēmu kenkyū* [Digital game studies]. Tokyo: University of Tokyo Press.
Yoshida, Hiroshi, Inoue Akito, Matsunaga Shinji, and Martin Roth, eds. 2025. *Critical words: game studies* (in Japanese). Tokyo: Film Art.
Yuji, Hiroki. 1995. Yōji no konpyūta gēmu asobi to undō kankaku ginō oyobi kūkan ninchi ginō tono kankei [How Preschool Children's Computer Game Playing Relates to Their Sensorimotor and Spatial Cognitive Skills]. *Nihon kyōiku kōgaku zasshi* 19 (3): 141–149.

Game Works

Chunsoft. 1987. *Dragon Quest II*. Family Computer. Enix.
Chunsoft. 1988. *Dragon Quest III*. Family Computer. Enix.
Namco. 1979. *Galaxian*. Arcade. Namco.
Namco. 1980. *Pac-Man*. Arcade. Namco.
Namco. 1983. *Xevious*. Arcade. Namco.
Nintendo. 1981. *Donkey Kong*. Arcade. Nintendo.
Nintendo. 1985. *Super Mario Bros.* Family Computer. Nintendo.
Taito. 1978. *Spece Invaders*. Arcade. Taito.

Shinji Matsunaga is an Associate Professor at the Graduate School of Letters at Kyoto University and a Visiting Researcher at the Ritsumeikan Center for Game Studies. His research interests include game studies, aesthetics, and philosophy of art. He is the author of "Bideo gēmu no bigaku" [The Aesthetics of Video Games] and the translator of several influential works, including Jesper Juul's *Half-Real,* Nelson Goodman's *Languages of Art,* and Miguel Sicart's *Play Matters*. Since 2015, he has been serving as a research coordinator for the game section of the Research Mapping Project within the Agency for Cultural Affairs' media arts initiatives.

Japanese Videogame Research Communities, Associations, Institutes, and Projects

Akito Inoue

Contents

F. Ikuine et al. (eds.), *Japanese Game Studies*, https://doi.org/10.1007/978-981-95-9857-1_3

3

3.1 Introduction

This chapter provides an overview of the research institutions, academic communities, and research projects that undertake videogame research in Japan. The aim is to offer valuable information for readers interested in identifying which academic communities in Japan include specific experts and determining suitable venues for academic presentations.

As a resource related to this chapter, Nobushige (2025) continuously updates the "List of Graduate Schools and Universities in Japan Where Game Studies Can Be Majored In." Regarding academic societies related to game research in Japan, there is a list compiled by the author (Akito 2014). For a general overview of global game research, including Japan, Shinji (2017) provides one, which is detailed in Matsunaga's section in ▶ Chapter 1 of this volume.

This chapter diverges from these resources by providing detailed descriptions of each academic institution and systematically outlining the distinct strengths of their respective scholarly activities. Furthermore, the latter half of this chapter illustrates overall trends within university organizations by utilizing the Kakenhi (Grants-in-Aid for Scientific Research) database for National Grants awarded in Japan and past presentation data from DiGRA Japan.

This chapter describes organized and prominent academic communities related to video games operating within Japan. However, as it is written based on the author's current scope of awareness, communities to which the author has had limited access may not be adequately described. Additionally, organizations primarily aimed at game developer education are not covered in this explanation.

Independent communities of hobbyists outside of universities have accumulated high-quality achievements in historical research related to video games. The activities of these hobbyists existing outside academia are often unorganized, making it difficult to grasp their full extent, and thus their description in this chapter is limited.

It should be noted beforehand that the author is, or has been at least temporarily involved in some capacity with, the majority of the videogame academic organizations and research projects described below, and therefore this is not a description from an entirely third-party perspective.

Although this chapter does not specifically introduce activities primarily focused on developer education rather than videogame research, the following sections will categorize the existing research landscape into four primary domains.

3.2 Interdisciplinary Activities

Video game research is, needless to say, an interdisciplinary field. Consequently, academic societies and research projects in the videogame research domain that bring together researchers from diverse fields such as the humanities, social sciences, and computer science are the most readily identifiable.

3.2.1 Research Societies, Associations (Gakkai)

DiGRA Japan (Digital Games Research Association Japan) (2006–)

Among interdisciplinary academic societies in Japan dealing with multiple areas related to video games, DiGRA Japan, established in 2006, would likely be the first to be mentioned. It has held annual conferences since 2010 and publishes an annual journal. The journal is linked with J-STAGE, making its articles accessible through searches on Google Scholar and other platforms. It has also been designated as an Academic Research Organization Cooperating with the Science Council of Japan since 2011, indicating its status as a society meeting certain standards within Japan. While its secretariat is in Tokyo, its academic conferences are not exclusively held there.

Furthermore, there are five Special Interest Groups (SIGs): Game Media SIG, Game Education SIG, Game Design SIG, Online Game SIG and Oral History SIG, each conducting its own activities (Kishimoto et al. 2023) (DiGRA Japan 2022).

Akira Baba (History), who led the game research project at the University of Tokyo, served as president from April 2006 to June 2010. Subsequently, Koichi Hosoi (Business Administration), who played a leading role at the Ritsumeikan Center for Game Studies, served as president for 6 years until 2016. Toru Iwatani, known as the creator of *Pac-Man* and a professor at Tokyo Polytechnic University, then served until 2018. Following him, Akinori Nakamura (Business Administration) from Ritsumeikan University served until 2022. From 2022, Masanobu Endoh, known as the creator of *Xevious* and a former professor at Tokyo Polytechnic University, took office, and from 2024, Koji Mikami (Engineering) from Tokyo University of Technology has been serving as president.

The international DiGRA (Digital Games Research Association) itself, without "Japan" in its name, has held conferences in Japan twice, in 2007 and 2019, with DiGRA Japan members supporting their hosting on both occasions.

When comparing international DiGRA and DiGRA Japan, some differences are apparent. A notable difference is that DiGRA Japan has significantly fewer presentations in humanities fields such as philosophy and cultural studies. Conversely, it features a higher proportion of presentations in computer science, social sciences, and education.

As of 2025, it can be considered one of the most active academic organizations related to video game research in Japan.

GAS (Game Amusement Society) (2002–)

This is an academic society related to video games, established in 2002. It was established earlier than DiGRA Japan and has seven Special Interest Groups (Game and Mathematics, Game and Education, Game and Society, Game and Art, Game and Health Science, Game and Human Science, and Game Industry).

The society holds annual conferences, but its journal is currently published irregularly.

The content of its journal predominantly features areas such as computer science, mathematics, and cognitive science, though presentations related to the humanities and social sciences are also seen.

The secretariat of the Game Amusement Society is located at Osaka Electro-Communication University, which conducts game developer education. The inaugural president was Katsuhide Tsushima (Information Engineering) from Osaka University. As of 2025, Toshihiro Hayashi (Educational Technology) from Kagawa University serves as president (Game Amusement Society n.d).

Replaying Japan (2012–)

This is a conference for discussing research related to Japanese video games. It was jointly started in 2012 by Ritsumeikan University in Japan and the University of Alberta in Canada, initially held alternately in Kyoto and Canada. It has since been held in various locations worldwide, including Leipzig University, The Strong National Museum of Play, The National Videogame Arcade, and the University of Liège. Since 2018, the *Journal of Replaying Japan* has been published annually, with the online version available on Ritsumeikan University's online repository, R-Cube.

Replaying Japan is often held outside of Japan, and conference presentations are generally in English. Therefore, it is positioned more as an international conference than a domestic one. However, journal submissions are accepted in both English and Japanese.

Submissions tend to be predominantly from the humanities and cultural studies fields.

Other Related Societies

Other interdisciplinary academic societies that frequently deal with content related to video games include: (1) The Academy of Content Tourism (ACT), established in 2011, and (2) the Creative Content Research Association, established in 2016.

3.2.2 Research Institutes and Projects

Ritsumeikan Center for Game Studies (RCGS) (2011–)

Established in 2011 and based on the activities of the Game Archive Project (GAP) started by Koichi Hosoi of Ritsumeikan University in Kyoto in 1998, this is the only dedicated academic institution in the field of game studies in Japan. The inaugural director was Masayuki Uemura (then a professor at Ritsumeikan University), formerly of Nintendo and the development manager for the Famicom (NES). As of 2025, Shuji Watanabe (Game Development) serves as the director.

In terms of organizational structure, it operates as a collective of researchers involved in game studies within Ritsumeikan, spanning the College of Image Arts and Sciences, College of Policy Science, Graduate School of Core Ethics and Frontier Sciences, College of Law, and College of Information Science and Engineering.

The topics it covers are diverse, including videogame preservation, videogame database construction, serious games, gamification, game design, game developer education, games and intellectual property law, game AI, game industry research, game criticism, and games and philosophy.

Among these, long-term collaborative research projects involving many researchers include, firstly, a group of projects on game databases, archives, and oral histories conducted jointly with entities such as Japan's Agency for Cultural Affairs. Secondly, the organization of the Replaying Japan Conference and the publication of the *Journal of Replaying Japan*, conducted jointly with the University of Alberta and others.

In addition to these, RCGS holds research meetings almost monthly and hosts academic conferences irregularly.

It should be noted that RCGS is a research institution and does not directly have an educational function. The acceptance of doctoral course researchers from overseas is handled not by RCGS itself, but by the faculty to which each researcher belongs (Ritsumeikan University n.d).

Tokyo University Game Research Project (2003–2016)

This project was jointly initiated in 2003 by the Historical Informatics Laboratory, Graduate School of Interdisciplinary Information Studies, The University of Tokyo, and the International Game Developers Association Tokyo (IGDA Tokyo) (Dengeki Inline 2003).

While several game research-related projects existed at the University of Tokyo, Akira Baba, then a professor at the Graduate School of Interdisciplinary Information Studies, played a central role, particularly in the establishment of DiGRA Japan and the hosting of DiGRA 2007. Game researchers such as Nobushige Kobayashi (Hichibe), Masataka Yoshida, Shinji Yamane, and Masahito Fujihara are alumni of Akira Baba's laboratory.

After Akira Baba left the University of Tokyo in 2016, there is currently no direct successor to this initiative. While there are game-related laboratories at the University of Tokyo's Graduate School of Interdisciplinary Information Studies, such as Toru Fujimoto's Ludix Lab@UTokyo, there is no direct line of succession.

For a list of other graduate schools and universities where videogame research can be pursued, please refer to the aforementioned list by Nobushige Kobayashi.

3.3 Humanities (Philosophy and Cultural Studies)

This section will focus on research projects and communities in the humanities related to video games, particularly those concerning philosophy and cultural studies.

3.3.1 Japanese Association for Contents History Studies (2009–)

This academic society was initiated in 2009 by Masataka Yoshida, who was then affiliated with the Graduate School of Interdisciplinary Information Studies at the University of Tokyo. It does not exclusively target video games; its primary objective is to comprehensively examine various content types such as anime, manga, games, film, television, music, and the Internet (Yoshida n.d).

The association holds annual conferences and publishes a journal. As its name, "Contents History Studies" suggests, presentations mainly focus on historical research of anime, manga, games, and other content.

3.3.2 RGN (Research on Game design and Narrative) Community (2006–2011)

In 2006, the author (Akito Inoue), then a member of Hiroki Azuma's (Critic) laboratory at the Center for Global Communications (GLOCOM), International University of Japan (IUJ), established this study group as its representative. However, Hiroki Azuma left GLOCOM in the same year the study group was launched, and activities were temporarily suspended after 2007.

Subsequently, with myself again taking the lead, the group was renamed RGN-u and held regular study meetings from 2010 to 2011. Following this, study groups and reading circles related to game philosophy and cultural studies, centered around a research group led by the author, were held intermittently until around 2015. Notably, Shinji Matsunaga (Analytic Aesthetics) and Hiroshi Yoshida (Aesthetics) were central members, both of whom have made significant contributions to game studies in the humanities in Japan. Currently, RGN operates as a closed research group, meeting irregularly.

As of 2025, Hiroki Azuma is not an active core member of these humanities-focused game research communities. He primarily focuses on activities addressing a wide range of social issues as a critic. His references to games are merely part of his cross-disciplinary activities. At the same time, he offers support to game studies in the humanities. In 2018, his critical magazine *Genron* Vol. 8 featured a special section on games, which became one of the most controversial texts on game criticism in Japan.

Other Related Societies and Communities:

1. **History of Play**

There are other academic societies conducting research in areas very close to videogame studies, even if they do not directly address videogames themselves. The Society of Game's History (Yūgishi Gakkai) (1988–2017), which was active until 2017, is a prime example. This society was dedicated to the historical study of a wide range of games, such as sumo and shogi, rather than digital games. The inaugural president was the late Isao Atsuta (Professor Emeritus, Kobe University). The second president was author Koichi Masukawa. In 2016, a joint research meeting was held with DiGRA Japan.

An academic organization concerning the history of play that is still active is The Institute of Amusement Industry Studies at Osaka University of Commerce, which continues its activities and has published its bulletin up to Vol. 23.

2. **History of Sports and Leisure**

In societies related to the history of sports and leisure, presentations closely related to video game research are sometimes made. For example, the Japan Society of Sport History (1986–), the Japan Society of Sport Anthropology (1998–), and the Association for Leisure and Tourism Studies (2012–) also conduct research related to play.

3. **Independent Critique Movement**

Authors such as Hiroki Azuma, Eiji Otsuka, Daichi Nakagawa, Sayawaka, and Kiyoshi Tane, who have published numerous works on Japanese videogames, engage in critical activities independently of these academic movements.

4. **Independent Videogame History Movement**

Historical research on video games is also actively pursued by nonacademics.

First, there are contributions from individuals within the video game industry. Masumi (2005) is a representative example of such achievements.

Second, there is the practice of commercial game media (e.g., Denfaminico Gamer) conducting interviews with key figures in the game industry. As popular content featuring interviews with many game developers, these are widely read in Japan. This has now merged with projects of the History of Content Industry Archives Research Center (HARC), established by Kadokawa in 2023 as a research center for Zen University.

Third, there is historical game research by independent hobbyists. The active presence of Comic Market since the 1980s, which provides an environment supporting the activities of hobbyists, is a characteristic feature of Japanese hobby culture. At Comic Market, research on game history has been conducted and disseminated through self-published works (dōjinshi). There are many diverse and high-quality achievements. Well-known activities include those by A.M.P Group, Haruhisa Tanaka (Hally), Zeku, Shoshin Kai, and Dento Teramachi. In addition, there are examples of game developers themselves committing to researching the history of games, such as the activities of Hiromasa Iwasaki.

Fourth, there are cases of companies or NPOs specializing in game preservation activities. Well-known examples include Project EGG and the Game Preservation Society, of which Joseph Redon is President (Game Preservation Society n.d). Details on preservation activities conducted in Japan are described in the report of the "Research Project on Collaboration Among Game Archive Collections," a project by RCGS and the Agency for Cultural Affairs.

Ritsumeikan Center for Game Studies and Agency for Cultural Affairs, Media Arts Projects

► https://www.rcgs.jp/?page_id=1316

5. **Reading Clubs/Study Groups**

Around the time of the pandemic in 2020, online reading group activities (using ZOOM, Discord, etc.) became prevalent. Various reading and study groups are conducted online, such as the "Philosophy of Games" Study Group (Organizers: Wakana Hirai, Hiroki Yamano), Kirigirisu no Kai (The Grasshopper

Association) (Organizer: Katsuhiko Shigeuchi), Game History Study Group (Organizer: Yasuo Kawasaki), the Discord server "Considering Games & Critique" (Chika Hitsujiya), and the Game Studies Reading Group (Organizers: Taito Sakai, Mirei Takahasi).

Furthermore, regarding the recent landscape of small-scale and informal videogame academic communities conducted via Zoom, the Ritsumeikan Center for Game Studies (RCGS) is actively working to make these informal communities more visible. This effort includes hosting joint events with DiGRA Japan, where representatives are invited to report on their respective community activities (Ritsumeikan Center for Game Studies 2025).

3.4 Social Sciences

3.4.1 Content Industries Research Project (2003–)

From 1998 to 2003, the TV-Game Industries Research Project was active, centered around Junjiro Shintaku (Economics Management) and Noriyuki Yanagawa (Economics) from the University of Tokyo, and Tatsuo Tanaka (Economics) from Keio University. The outcomes of this project were published as *Gēmu Sangyō no Keizai Bunseki: Kontentsu Sangyō Hatten no Kōzō to Senryaku* (Economic Analysis of the Game Industry: Structure and Strategy for the Development of Content Industries) (Toyo Keizai Inc., 2003). This research team changed its name in 2003 and has continued its activities as the Content Industries Research Project. It is a group that has continuously pursued research activities in the social sciences, particularly in the fields of business administration and economics.

Among this research group, members specifically focusing on the game domain separately launched the Game Industries Research Project in 2012 as a research project at IUJ, GLOCOM. The results of this were published in the book *Sōsharu Gēmu no Bijinesu Moderu: Furīmiamu no Keizai Bunseki* (Business Models of Social Games: An Economic Analysis of Freemium) (2015). In 2019, it changed its name again to the Digital Content Industries Research Project and continues its activities to the present.

*Note: Fumihiko Ikuine (Management), the main editor of this volume, has also been a member of this research group since its early stages.

3.4.2 Tagenka suru Geemu Bunka Kenkyu Kai (Diversified Game Culture Research Group) (2015–)

This was conducted with Hiroshi Matsui (Sociology) from Aichi Shukutoku University at its center, and managed by Takanori Iguchi (Sociology) from Kansai University, Masumi Oishi (Media Studies) from The Graduate University for Advanced Studies (SOKENDAI), and Mikako Hata (Comic Studies) from Hanazono University, among others. This study group was conducted with a significant gathering of sociology and humanities researchers, particularly from the Kansai region, and its outcomes were published as *Tagenkasuru Gēmu Bunka to Shakai* (Diversifying Game Culture and Society) (2019).

3.4.3 Other Trends

Separately from the aforementioned trends, many authors frequently present their work in interdisciplinary communities. For example, prominent authors in the social science field of game studies, such as Yusuke Koyama (Economics) and Nobushige Kobayashi (Hichibe) (Sociology), present their findings at DiGRA Japan and replaying Japan, among other venues.

3.5 Natural Sciences/Computer Science

3.5.1 Information Processing Society of Japan (IPSJ), Research Groups

As for research communities in this domain, those operating as individual research groups within the Information Processing Society of Japan (IPSJ), Japan's largest academic society in this field, are particularly active. Among these, I would like to describe the research groups in particularly relevant areas.

IPSJ, Game Informatics Research Group (1999–)

This research group primarily focuses on issues such as algorithms for computer Shogi and Go, and game AI. In addition to holding research conferences twice a year, it also hosts an annual Game Programming Workshop. As of 2025, Kiminori Matsuzaki (Game Informatics) serves as the Organizer. The name "Geemu Jyohogaku" (Game Informatics) was decided by Jin Matsubara and Koichi Hashida (Jin 2012). As mentioned earlier, it is the name of a Kakenhi application category and can be considered an organization that has led computer science-based game research in Japan.

IPSJ, Entertainment Computing (EC) (2005–)

Established as an IPSJ SIG in 2005, Mitsunori Matsushita (Interactive System Design) serves as the organizer as of 2024. While not a research community focused solely on digital games, this SIG is likely where the most presentations related to digital games are found among IPSJ SIGs.

The overall goal of the SIG, as its name suggests, is to broadly accept research in computing fields related to entertainment, and presentations span many areas including VR, UI, robotics, and music. It holds four research presentation meetings annually and one EC symposium per year.

IPSJ, Digital Contents Creation (DCC) (2012–)

Established in 2012, Takefumi Ogawa (Sensitivity Informatics) serves as the organizer as of 2025.

This is also not a SIG targeting digital games exclusively, but it is one where presentations related to digital games are frequently made.

As a SIG, it features presentations in various technological fields related to promoting the creation, distribution, and utilization of digital content.

IPSJ, Interaction (1997–)

This is a symposium jointly hosted by five IPSJ SIGs and held annually in winter. The participating SIGs are Human–Computer Interface, Groupware and Network Service, Ubiquitous Computing System, Entertainment Computing, and Digital Contents Creation. Various presentations related to interaction are given, and a considerable number of them concern digital games (Kimura 2022).

3.5.2 Global Game Jam (GGJ, 2009–)

The Global Game Jam, where games are developed intensively over a few days, is positioned as an important event in game development education and is held jointly by multiple universities in various regions of Japan, including Kanto and Kansai.

The first GGJ was held in 2009, organized by the International Game Developers Association (IGDA). The scale of participation has expanded each year. Since 2013, its operation has been transferred to the international nonprofit organization Global Game Jam, Inc.

Universities and vocational schools that provide game developer education collaborate across institutions for these activities, and research related to GGJ is reported annually at venues like DiGRA Japan. A particularly central university in these activities is the Tokyo University of Technology, which has a faculty specializing in game developer education. Koji Mikami is actively involved.

3.6 Serious Games, Gamification

In the context of the social and educational application of games, trends can be divided into two main streams: those existing before the rise of video games, such as the Japan Association of Simulation And Gaming (JASAG), and those that emerged after the rise of video games, such as serious games and gamification.

3.6.1 JASAG (Japan Association of Simulation And Gaming, 1989–)

As a Japanese academic society with "game" directly in its name, it is one of the academic communities with a considerably long history. It is not primarily focused on digital games but has mainly conducted research related to Gaming Simulation. Therefore, it is characterized by many presentations on analog board games and the use of game-like frameworks in education, although presentations on the use of digital games in education are also seen (Kato & Arai 2004).

3.6.2 Serious Games Japan Community (2004–)

Launched by Toru Fujimoto, a leading researcher of Serious Games in Japan. It was originally established and operated as the Japanese hub for the Serious Games Initiative in the United States. In 2013, Ludix Lab was established as a research unit on games and learning within the NPO "Educe Technologies," which is involved in educational activities. Currently, activities are primarily conducted under the Ludix Lab name. Toru Fujimoto serves as the director of Ludix Lab, with Yuki Fukuyama, Ryohei Ikejiri, Koji Takahashi, and Hiroyuki Tameda as fellows (Serious Games Japan n.d).

3.6.3 Serious Game Jam (2014–)

Centered around the Nihon University Serious Game Design Studio (Masakazu Furuichi Lab), a Serious Game Jam has been held annually since 2014.

3.6.4 Other Trends

Although not an academic community, the Japan Gamification Association, established by Yoshihiro Kishimoto in 2019, is an organization in Japan related to gamification. It operates domestic awards related to gamification, among other activities (Japan Gamification Association n.d).

3.7 Critique Communities

Communities involved in game criticism can be broadly divided into two main streams: one consisting of game writers working in commercial media, such as game magazines, and another stemming from humanities research focused on "critique." As there is no single central focus in this section, I will briefly outline community trends.

3.7.1 Game Writer Communities

Regarding the former stream of game criticism by commercial game writers, detailing important magazines on a media-by-media basis would deviate from the purpose of this chapter, so I will only briefly mention their names.

The point at which game criticism is considered to have emerged in Japan varies depending on the criteria, but in terms of simply publishing some discourse on digital games, examples include the magazine *Game Machine*, first published in 1974, and descriptions in technical journals like *Denshi Gijutsu* (Electronic Technology) and the *Journal of the Institute of Television Engineers of Japan* in the late 1970s. However, these publications mostly dealt with industry trends and purely technical issues rather than critiques of individual works.

Subsequently, in the mid-1980s, as market demand for game strategy information intensified, numerous game magazines were launched. From these, discussions emerged that adopted a meta-perspective on the nature of the gaming experience. In particular, texts by writers such as Hitoshi Yasuda, Akira Yamashita, and Yutaka Tama in serializations in magazines like *ASCII*, *Login*, and *Micom BASIC Magazine* can be considered valuable critical texts of that era.

In the 1990s, the formation of a "devoted fan" base for games progressed, and in 1994, magazines focusing on game critique, such as *Game Kaigi* (Game Conference) and *Game Hihyō* (Game Criticism), were launched one after another. Magazines with a strong critical aspect, such as *gM*, *CONTINUE*, *USED GAMES*, and *Game Gene*, followed.

However, since the mid-2000s, due to declining sales of print media, this role has now shifted to web media outlets such as *4Gamer.net*, *Denfaminico Gamer*, *AUTOMATON*, and *IGN Japan*.

There are several discussion communities for game writers. One is the Game Media SIG, held irregularly since 2010 as a DiGRA Japan SIG, and another is the "Game Writer Community," started in 2015 by former *Game Hihyō* editor-in-chief Kenji Ono and others. However, both are communities focused on the profession of game writers and the nature of game media rather than critique communities per se.

3.7.2 Game Criticism as Cultural Critique

The origin of cultural criticism of games in Japan can be traced to Shinichi Nakazawa's "Game Freaks Play with Bugs: A Theory of the Video Game 'Xevious'," published in the magazine *Gendai Shisō* (Contemporary Thought) (vol. 12-6) in 1984. Nakazawa subsequently developed game-related critiques such as *Denshi Gēmu no "Kairaku"* (The "Pleasure" of Electronic Games) (Nippon SoftBank, 1989), co-authored with Seiji Takeda, Masanobu Endoh, and Hitoshi Yasuda, and *Poketto no Naka no Yasei* (Wildness in the Pocket; Iwanami Shoten, 1997). The situation surrounding video games in the 1980s and 1990s is described in more detail in Hiroshi Yoshida's manuscript in this volume.

Later, Hiroki Azuma published works such as *Dōbutsuka suru Posutomodan* (Otaku: Japan's Database Animals) (Kodansha Gendai Shinsho, 2001) and *Gēmu-teki Riarizumu no Tanjō: Dōbutsuka suru Posutomodan 2* (The Birth of Game-like Realism: The Animalizing Postmodern 2; Kodansha Gendai Shinsho, 2007) from the context of *otaku-ron* (discourse on otaku) as something that updates the modern concept of the human. These generated considerable discussion in the game criticism community. Hiroki Azuma's work is likely known to some extent in the Anglosphere as well.

As of 2025, it cannot be said that media or communities dedicated solely to cultural criticism of games currently exist. However, this does not mean there are no venues for discussion. Comprehensive cultural criticism magazines such as *Yuriika*, *Genron*, and *PLANETS*, which cover topics from literature to pop culture, periodically publish special issues on games. Consequently, a situation exists where several individuals, including the author, frequently write critical texts about games for these cultural criticism media.

Writers who repeatedly appear include humanities-oriented writers (including the author, Shinji Matsunaga, and Hiroshi Yoshida), writers active in critical media (Daichi Nakagawa, Naoya Fujita, Sayawaka, and Takamitsu Yamamoto), or writers who span both categories (Akito Inoue, Yusuke Oiwa, Dominique Chen, and Yuuki Namba).

3.8 Business Conferences

While not research clusters per se, organizations within the game industry for exchanging knowledge and fostering the industry have often developed in mutual support with Japan's game research community.

Although there are numerous game business conferences in Japan, this section will describe CEDEC and IGDA Japan, which have particularly strong ties with the game research community.

3.8.1 CEDEC (Computer Entertainment Developers Conference)

This is a conference for the game industry organized by the Computer Entertainment Supplier's Association (CESA), which also hosts events like the Tokyo Game Show, and has been held since 1999. It is similar in nature to the Game Developers Conference (GDC) and is one of the largest events of its kind for the game industry in Japan.

There are seven session categories, one of which is "Academic and Foundational Technology," where game researchers make presentations every year. University-affiliated individuals such as Takuji Narumi (VR researcher), Hironori Mitake (CG researcher), and Koji Mikami (CG researcher) are also part of the event's executive committee.

In 2007, CEDEC 2007 and DiGRA 2007 were co-hosted at the University of Tokyo.

3.8.2 IGDA Japan (International Game Developers Association Japan)

Game journalist Kiyoshi Shin launched it as IGDA Tokyo in April 2002 (IGDA Japan 2022), and it was renamed IGDA Japan in April 2004. As of 2025, Katsuteru Takahashi serves as its chairperson. It provided full cooperation when the game research project at the University of Tokyo began in 2003 and has significantly contributed to the growth of Japan's game research community.

Several Special Interest Groups (SIGs) are active, with the following being particularly relevant to academic activities:

1. SIG-Academic: Managed by Shinji Yamane, this SIG aims to foster industry-academia collaboration and support game developers.
2. SIG-Independent: Managed by Nobushige Kobayashi (Hichibe) of Tohoku Gakuin University, this SIG aims to expand the base of independent game developers.

3.9 Frameworks Related to Videogame Research Funding

This section introduces research funding frameworks that play a particularly important role in relation to video games.

As a National Budget, Kakenhi (Grants-in-Aid for Scientific Research) from the Japan Society for the Promotion of Science (JSPS), under the jurisdiction of the Ministry of Education, Culture, Sports, Science and Technology (MEXT), can be mentioned. This is not limited to video games but exists as a competitive funding system for all academic fields in Japan. Researchers apply within their respective academic fields to obtain funding. For video game research in information engineering, an application category called "Game Informatics" exists. Conversely, researchers in humanities and social sciences focusing on video games do not have a dedicated application category, so they apply under categories such as business administration, education, sociology, or philosophy.

Numerous investigative and research projects are also conducted by Japanese governmental bodies such as the Ministry of Economy, Trade, and Industry (METI), the Ministry of Health, Labour and Welfare, and the Agency for Cultural Affairs, involving many researchers. However, these projects differ in nature from grants for researchers like Kakenhi.

As private budgets, the Hayao Nakayama Foundation for Science & Technology and Culture, established in 1992 by former SEGA President Hayao Nakayama, and FOST (Foundation for the Fusion Of Science and Technology), established in 1994 by KOEI President Yoichi Erikawa, annually conduct grant-making programs for the fields of videogames and play.

In addition, projects related to game research are carried out under funding frameworks for ICT-related research grants, cultural studies, and interdisciplinary research.

3.10 Final Remarks

The preceding sections have provided a brief overview of various research clusters related to games in Japan. However, I would like to conclude by mentioning points not fully addressed in this chapter.

3

First is the mutual cooperation between industry, government, and academia. Video game research is a matter of significant interest for both the game industry and the nation. Besides SEGA and Koei Tecmo, which were briefly mentioned in this chapter, numerous companies such as Nintendo, Sony, Bandai Namco, Konami, Square Enix, Cygames, DeNA, COLOPL, Akatsuki, Capcom, and Kadokawa have provided support and cooperation for videogame research at various times. Cooperating with research from a corporate standpoint often involves more constraints than for university researchers. Researchers' approaches to people working in companies can sometimes be burdensome. I am deeply grateful for their cooperation under such challenging conditions, taking time out from their primary work.

Second, the establishment of academic research clusters is often based on informal relationships among concerned parties, preceding formal institutionalization. The author myself has been publishing critical and research texts related to games online since 2001, and through this, have formed connections with various research colleagues. Some of the friends I have debated with over these 20 years work within universities. Others are not affiliated with universities. And I have been greatly influenced by my friends outside academia as well.

As mentioned at the beginning, this chapter has only partially described the uninstitutionalized research-related activities of such individuals. However, these informal and formal spaces for discussion are intricately intertwined. Insofar as game research is cultural research, it goes without saying that the exchange of folk discourse extending outside the "institution" of the university is extremely important. Many of these important informal activities do not have names.

I would like to conclude this chapter by expressing my deep respect for these endeavors outside the university.

References

Akito, Inoue. 2014. List of digital game related journals & academic societies. http://www.critiqueofgames.net/2014/07/post_9.html. Accessed 08 Oct 2022.

Dengeki Online. 2003. Industry-academia collaboration "University of Tokyo Game Research Project" to hold first public lecture on December 12. https://dengekionline.com/data/news/2003/12/3/fa54684a1ba2e0532bd2985fe2c2ac6d.html. Accessed 24 Aug 2022.

DiGRA Japan. 2022. What is DiGRA JAPAN? https://digrajapan.org/?page_id=206. Accessed 08 Oct 2022.

Fumitoshi, Kato, and Yusuke Arai. 2004. The past, present, and future of JASAG. *Simulation & Gaming* 14 (1): 19–27.

Game Amusement Society. n.d. About Game Amusement Society. http://old.gameamusementsociety.org/about/. Accessed 08 Oct 2025.

Game Preservation Society. n.d. About Game Preservation Society. https://www.gamepres.org/. Accessed 08 Oct 2022.

IGDA Japan. 2022. About IGDA and IGDA Japan. https://www.igda.jp/igda%e6%97%a5%e6%9c%ac/. Accessed 08 Oct 2022.
Japan Gamification Association. n.d. https://www.jgamifa.jp/. Accessed 08 Oct 2022.
Jin, Matsubara. 2012. The current state of game informatics: has game research ceased to be marginalized in Japan? *Joho Shori (Information Processing)* 53 (2): 102–106. Information Processing Society of Japan.
Kimura, Asako. 2022. Message from the conference chair. INTERACTION 2022. https://www.interaction-ipsj.org/2022/message/. Accessed 08 Oct 2022.
Kishimoto,Yoshihiro, Kenji, Ono, Goto, Makoto, Kawano, Yoshihiro Zaitsu Kosuke, Kawamura Keigo, Aibara Megumi, and Furuichi Masakazu 2023 Game education SIG activity report: lessons learned from 8 study sessions and think about the future of games, digital games research association JAPAN. In *Proceedings of 13th annual conference.*
Masumi, Akagi. 2005. Sore wa "Pon" kara Hajimatta: Ākēdo TV Gēmu no Naritachi [In the beginning, there was Pong: the origins of Arcade TV games]. Amusement Tsushinsha.
Nobushige, Hichibe. 2025. List of graduate schools and universities in Japan where you can major in game studies. https://chimarisan.wordpress.com/university_list/. Accessed 08 Oct 2025.
Ritsumeikan Center for Game Studies. 2025. Shōkibo/infōmaru na bideo gēmu no gakujutsu komyuniti jōhō kōkankai [Information exchange meeting for small-scale/informal videogame academic communities]. https://www.rcgs.jp/?p=3117. Accessed 05 Sep 2025.
Ritsumeikan Center for Game Studies. Journal "REPLAYING JAPAN". https://www.rcgs.jp/?page_id=200. Accessed 08 Oct 2022.
Ritsumeikan University, Ritsumeikan Center for Game Studies. n.d. https://en.ritsumei.ac.jp/research/organizations/ritsumeikan-center-game-studies/. Accessed 08 Oct 2022.
Serious Games Japan. n.d. About us. https://seriousgames.jp/about. Accessed 08 Oct 2022.
Shinji, Matsunaga. 2017. Overall map of game research. In Matsunaga Shinji, Inoue Akito, Kimura Tomohiro, Fukuda Kazufumi, & Roth Martin (Eds.), Guide to game studies. Agency for Cultural Affairs. https://mediag.bunka.go.jp/mediag_wp/wp-content/uploads/2017/05/guide_to_game_studies_v2_public.pdf. Accessed 18 Jan 2022.
Yoshida, Masataka. n.d. About the Japanese Association for Contents History Studies. http://www.contentshistory.org/about/. Accessed 08 Oct 2022.

Akito Inoue is a Game Researcher and Associate Professor at the College of Image Arts and Sciences, Ritsumeikan University. In addition to his faculty role, he serves as a Steering Committee Member for the Ritsumeikan Center for Game Studies (RCGS). His current research focuses on the essence of game experiences, a theme explored in his ongoing series, "On Games as Phenomenon without Center." He is also actively engaged in game archiving and database initiatives. He is the author of "Gamification" (NHK Publishing, 2012). As a game designer, he developed #denkimeter, an electricity-saving game released following the 2011 earthquake which received the CEDEC Award for Excellence in Game Design, and The Tragi-Comedy of the Commons, which won the Grand Prize at the 19th Game Society of Japan Game Competition.

Media Mix and Digital Games

Akinori Nakamura

Contents

F. Ikuine et al. (eds.), *Japanese Game Studies*, https://doi.org/10.1007/978-981-95-9857-1_4

4

4.1 Introduction

This chapter examines digital games in the broader context of media franchises. In the Japanese media industry, media mix (wasei-eigo, mediamikkusu, henceforth media mix) refers to an approach of media business strategy developed in Japan, in which various elements of the intellectual properties (henceforth IP) are dispersed and or extended across multiple media platforms, such as broadcast media, mobile technologies, location entertainment sites, and even to non-media related products like collectibles and other types of the franchise" (Ito 2005; Jenkins 2006, 289).[1]

It is a common practice among various IPs to maximize customer value by increasing the number of touchpoints, including those of digital games. This chapter provides an overview of the development of the media mix in Japan and its integration into digital game business strategies. Furthermore, this chapter examines the implications of this phenomenon for digital games and identifies areas for future research.

4.2 Overview of Previous Studies and Approach of this Chapter

This section discusses previous studies on Japan's media mix and related concepts, providing an overview of the approaches adopted. This chapter examines media mix practices related to digital games as extensions of both existing and emerging IPs from the perspective of digital games.

4.2.1 Previous Studies on Media Mix

The term "media mix" was first used by major publishers such as Kadokawa,[2] Tokuma,[3] and Kodansha[4] during the early 1980s. However, similar media deployment strategies were in use even before the term appeared in the literature. Such media strategies were then usually named after the names of particular authoritative figures, such as Kikuchi Mono (Shimura 2013), referring to Kan Kikuchi, and specific names of companies, such as Tsuburaya Shōhō (Noboru 1972), Tōei Shōhō (Yamaguchi and Watanabe 1978), and Kadokawa Shōhō (Yamaguchi and

1 This is based on Jenkins summarized version (Jenkins 2006, 289) of Ito's article (Ito 2005).

2 Nikkeisangyōshinbun (1982, December 2). Ponī to Kadokawa ga teikei; Kadokawa eiga sakuhin o ponī ga bideo sofuto-ka shi hatsubai [Pony and Kadokawa forms partner: Pony releases video software based on Kadokawa films]. *Nikkeisangyōshinbun,* 4.

3 Nikkeisangyōshinbun [Nikkei Sangyo Shimbun] "Tokumashoten Tokuma Oto kō, animeno 'bunko' 'rekōdo' dōji hatsubai: Sōjō kōka nerau" [Tokuma Shoten/Tokuma Onko Releases Anime "Bunko" and "Record" Simultaneously: Aiming for Synergy]. Dec 7, 1982: 4

4 Nihonkeizaishinbun [Nihon Keizai Shimbun] "Kōdansha, MGM UA to teikei shi Amerika ni anime urikomu: Kyarakutā hanbai ni mo shinshutsu." [Kodansha Cooperates with MGM and UA to Promote anime to the United States: Entering into Character Merchandize]. Feb 15th, 1983: 11

Watanabe 1978).[5] Thus, various media-related companies and publishers adopted media mix strategies even before the war began.

The academic exploration of media mix began with Eiji Ōtsuka, a former manga artist, manga plot designer, novelist, manga magazine editor, and social critic. He analyzed the social phenomenon of *Bikkuriman* chocolates in the children's market. He pointed out that the real reason children wanted *Bikkuriman* chocolates was their desire to find and interpret the grand narratives and hidden meanings in the fragmentary information and stories on the back of Omake stickers,[6] calling this phenomenon "narrative consumption" (Ōtsuka 1989). He also pointed out how the *Astro Boy* series differed from the *Bikkuriman* media mix projects. While the *Astro Boy* franchise and other licensed products were derived from the original work, the *Bikkuriman* stickers were created from their own mythos (concept) at the top, deriving content such as stickers, manga, TV anime, and games with equal weight (Ōtsuka 1989, 63).

In contrast, Azuma (2001) highlights the effects of rapid globalization, the database nature of the world, and the emergence of computer adventure games, in which consumers deconstruct the components that make up the software. In this environment, some enthusiasts developed a desire to consume every piece of information in a given media product, reconstruct the product later, and appreciate alternative combinations. Azuma coined the term "database consumption" to describe this consumption behavior. Furthermore, Azuma (2001) noted that in media mix, where the authoritative nature of the original work could be ambiguous, the simultaneous production of multiple components only collates characters, mecha designs, and worldviews across various media products. Branding causes fans to naively consume content without considering that no narrative meaning is attached to it (Azuma 2001).

When the book was published, Azuma (2001, 57) assumed that although consumers no longer sought grand narratives, both those who preferred grand narratives and those who appreciated a variety of data sets coexisted. Consumers may also adjust their preferences based on the type of media content they consume. Thus, both concepts are equally significant for examining the media mix strategy. With the *Pokémon* craze and the export of other cultural products such as the Nintendo Entertainment System, numerous Western scholars also began to examine Japanese pop culture and its transmedia nature. For example, Allison examined Japan's exports of cultural products to other countries in the mid- to late 1990s and concluded that odorless strategies on the part of producers led to large-scale, multifaceted multimedia campaigns, resulting in the worldwide success of media products (Allison 2000, 75). In a later study, Allison (2006) examined the social phenomenon of global consumption of Japanese pop cultural products such as

---

5 Nikkeisangyōshinbun [Nikkei Sangyo Shimbun] "Kadokawashoten shachō kadokawa harukishi: "Kadokawa shōhō" kotoshi no senryaku (sokogashiritai)" [Mr. Haruki Kadokawa, President of Kadokawa Shoten: "Kadokawa Method" This Year's Strategy (We Want to Know About It)]. Jan 31st, 1978: 3

6 Omake means an extra or a freebie. For Bikkuriman chocolates, such a freebie is a sticker. For kids' snacks, small toys are attached to entice the buyers.

Godzilla, *Astro Boy*, *Sentai Hero*, *Sailor Moon*, *Tamagotchi*, and *Pokémon*, and considered the Japanese tendency to combine reality (technology) and spirit (animism) in all phenomena, including pop culture (2006).

Furthermore, Ito (2001) introduces the concept of media mix as a characteristic of the Japanese media franchise, citing the case of *Yu-Gi-Oh*. In subsequent studies, she shows that media mix goes beyond mere diversification, "increasingly designed to sustain intertextual referencing across different media" (Ito 2005, 5). Tanaka (2009) examines the Japanese media mix from an organizational perspective. A horizontally disintegrated organizational structure, characterized by production committees, is one of the key characteristics of an organization. In such an organization, every committee member is treated equally, thus encouraging media products to create synergy rather than allowing one to dominate another hierarchically. However, Tanaka posits that Hollywood transmedia productions occur within a vertically integrated organizational structure, such as a media conglomerate, in which all related IP is concentrated within a single organization. Tanaka concludes that a trade-off occurs: Diversity is often compromised in transmedia storytelling. This is consistent with the definition of transmedia storytelling as convergence to a single worldview, which is the most essential feature of this narrative structure. Several Western scholars now compare the Western transmedia production with the Japanese media mix. Steinberg (2012) is one of the most recognized analyses in this regard. By comparing the media mix practices of the Astro Boy and Suzumiya Haruhi franchises, Steinberg explained the evolutionary step taken by the Japanese media and entertainment industry in implementing media mix practices and analyzed the differences in concepts of transmedia storytelling, which is defined by Jenkins (2007) as follows:

> Transmedia storytelling represents a process where integral elements of fiction get dispersed systemically across multiple delivery channels for the purpose of creating a unified and coordinated entertainment experience. Ideally, each medium makes its own unique contribution to the unfolding of the story.

Steinberg (2015a, 20) asserts that Jenkins naturally inherited the concept of transmedia storytelling from the direct inspiration of the Matrix franchise creators and media mix practices prevalent in Japan. Patrickson and Young (2013) further examine the media mix projects of the Japanese media industry and transmedia productions in Hollywood, emphasizing their mutually influential relationship. Ōtsuka (2014) asserts that the business models that constitute the Japanese essence of media mix strategies were inspired by their Western counterparts. In their initial collaborative investigation of the *Mobile Suit Gundam* franchise, Nakamura and Tosca (2019) conclude that it embraces both the convergent approach of transmedia storytelling and the divergent approach of media mix strategies. Therefore, media mix and transmedia storytelling are distinct from the Japanese or Hollywood models and should be viewed as complementary strategies. In-game studies, scholars have addressed Japanese games and their place within the broader franchise media ecology. Kinephanos' special edition on Geemu and media mix is a notable effort in this regard (Picard and Pelletier-Gagnon 2015). This edition includes Schedules (2015), which focuses on the downloadable cross-cover contents of The

Tales series, expounding on their game-centric traits in the media mix ecology. Steinberg (2015b) examines the *Madara* project, which lasted from 1987 to 1996. He asserts that incorporating the battle system into the manga's narrative before the game's release was due to the involvement of game designer Nobuhiro Aga in the project's early stages. The organizers wanted to place games at the center of the media mix ecology at the DiGRA 2019 conference, as the conference's theme was "game, play, and the emerging Ludo Mix.

The findings included *Final Fantasy XV* Universe (Bjarnason 2021) and the *Fire Emblem* franchise (Blom 2021). Scholars have attempted to historicize media mix practices, focusing on the era preceding the term's widespread adoption (Ōtsuka 2017, 2018; Nakamura and Tosca 2021). However, none of these studies exclusively focused on digital games.

4.2.2 Strategic Mode of Japanese Media Mix

As a director, producer, and world-setting designer of digital games and other creative works, Jiro Ishii classifies intellectual property (IP) according to their long-term sustainability, categorizing it as Story IP, Character IP, and Worldview IP. He argues that for an IP to endure over time, it must transcend individual ownership and become organizationally managed property. An IP can continue to thrive across generations only by evolving beyond Story IP into Character IP and ultimately Worldview IP (Ishii 2020). While further examination is necessary to generalize Ishii's claim, his work contributed to the categorization of media franchises. This concept is vital for capturing the core strategy: The media mix orchestrates a wide range of media deployment strategies under a unified umbrella.

This chapter introduces three strategic modes of the Japanese media mix, defined by degree of divergence/convergence with the original work and worldview, and by narrative structure: variation media mix (VMM), worldbuilding media mix (WMM), and storybuilding media mix (SMM). As defined by Ito (2001), the concept of "media mix" itself has no fixed rules beyond the expansion of a specific work (or IP) across multiple media platforms and related merchandise. Furthermore, a media franchise may shift its media mix strategies from one category to another or employ multiple patterns across its overall portfolio. If a particular expansion strategy attracts a larger audience, it can be legitimized. Within these practices, the most prevalent approach is creating a variation within a franchise. From one adaptation to another, including simple licensing practices, the attempts to create more touchpoints for consumers with a variety of interests in an IP can be categorized as VMM. In this sense, VMM is the most fundamental media mix strategy from the perspective of divergence expansion: It prioritizes accessibility over the structural integration of the media franchise.

Unlike the more flexible approach of VMM, both WMM and SMM focus on building tighter connections across a media franchise, even as their goal of creating new content remains the franchise's expansion. Thus, both modes closely align with convergent strategies. The difference between the two lies in emphasis. WMM is less sensitive to narrative integration so long as there is consistency in worldview.

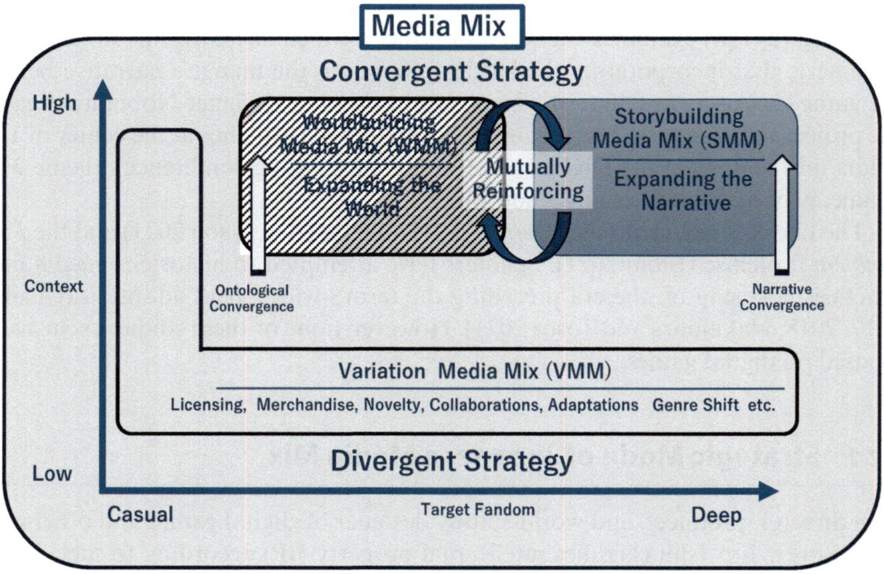

Fig. 4.1 Overall positions of three strategic modes of media mix in Japan

SMM, on the other hand, stresses narrative integration the most. Thus, WMM is considered an ontological convergence approach; the convergence is achieved among stories within the SMM. However, because these two categories are closely associated, both characteristics may appear simultaneously within a single media franchise. Additionally, strategic shifts from one mode to another may occur due to changes in the vision of internal creators and producers, or due to market research. This dynamic illustrates one of the core challenges of convergent approaches: The more creators and producers adhere to the structural constraints imposed by worldview coherence or narrative integration, the less creative freedom they can explore. The following diagram is intended to clarify the overall relationship of the strategic modes within the media mix. The strategic modes are not "clear-cut" as in typical categorizations, but they provide helpful guidelines for understanding how strategies within the media mix are designed, extended, and integrated into the overall media franchise (Fig. 4.1).

Variation Media Mix (VMM)

This leading media mix strategy aligns most closely with the definition of media mix strategies presented by Ito (2001) at the beginning of this chapter. The idea behind this approach is to disseminate a range of original works, thereby establishing points of contact that allow fans to have a more varied experience of the franchise while simultaneously drawing new audiences from every point of contact. Internal documents from anime studios, publishing, and merchandizing industries demonstrate awareness of the positive effects of media mix strategies. For example, while introducing the proposal for the anime TV program *Mazinger Z*, which began broadcasting on December 3, 1972, the producer analyzed the *Masked Rider* boom, highlighting the potential benefits of the media mix as follows.

> Capitalizing on the popularity of the TV show ... the commercialization of the characters, and their use in events, novelties, and premiums, has been highly successful, creating a synergistic effect in which the popularity of the characters is reflected in the popularity of the TV program, resulting in a long-lasting Rider boom with sustained high viewer ratings (Dengeki Hobby Web 2018, 38).

Considering such a strategy, it can be referred to as a variation media mix (VMM). ◘ Figure 4.2 presents such a media mix strategy. The primary objective of this strategy is to generate more variations of the original IP. This would create touchpoints for potential users to become aware of the IP, introduce a new item that core fans desire to collect, and foster synergy among IP holders, content creators, and related product developers.

Worldbuilding Media Mix (WMM) and Storybuilding Media Mix (SMM)

Some IPs focus on building fictional worlds to attract consumers. Various media franchises have attempted this before, such as the *Ultraman* franchise, superhero legends in DC and Marvel Comics, and the *Dr Who* franchise, to name a few. However, the method implemented by the *Record of Lodoss War* franchise, which originated from replaying record sessions of the tabletop role-playing game (TRPG) *Dungeons & Dragons* featured in Comptiq magazine from September 1986 to 1989 (Steinberg 2015b), is one of the prime examples of the WMM approach.[7] This pioneering work and other similar media mix consider producers as sort of game master in TRPG (Ōtsuka 1989) and provide a playfield to collaborative creators where the worldview, ranging from a mythological system to TRPG rulebooks, in which each element is established. A group of stories is then created in parallel to the media mix in the framework governing the fictional world (Ibid). Narrative consumption theory (Ōtsuka 1989) focused on how consumers are motivated to discern a grand narrative by combining fragmented stories. Such grand narratives are termed *Sekaikan* (worldview) in Japan. It is a trend aimed at maintaining and expanding the established worldview. The expansion of the work occurs according to the internal logic or worldview (Sekaikan) that governs it. However, narrative inconsistencies or discontinuities within the broader story network are tolerated; direct connections between narratives are not required. In such a case, the IP holder or producer may claim that these inconsistencies are legitimate due to the parallel-world framework. However, no explicit narrative connections are intentionally designed among these works.

Storybuilding media mix, on the other hand, requires narrative coherence across media. Even if parallel worlds are created in the universe, efforts are made

7 Steinberg (2012) coined the term "Kadokawa Media Mix Strategy." But others have used this type of approach, and Kadokawa also uses Variation Media Mix and Story building Media Mix, and thus, I would separate this particular approach and call it the Worldbuilding Media Mix to clearly indicate where this strategy fits within the overall media mix strategy for a franchise, as shown in ◘ Fig. 4.1.

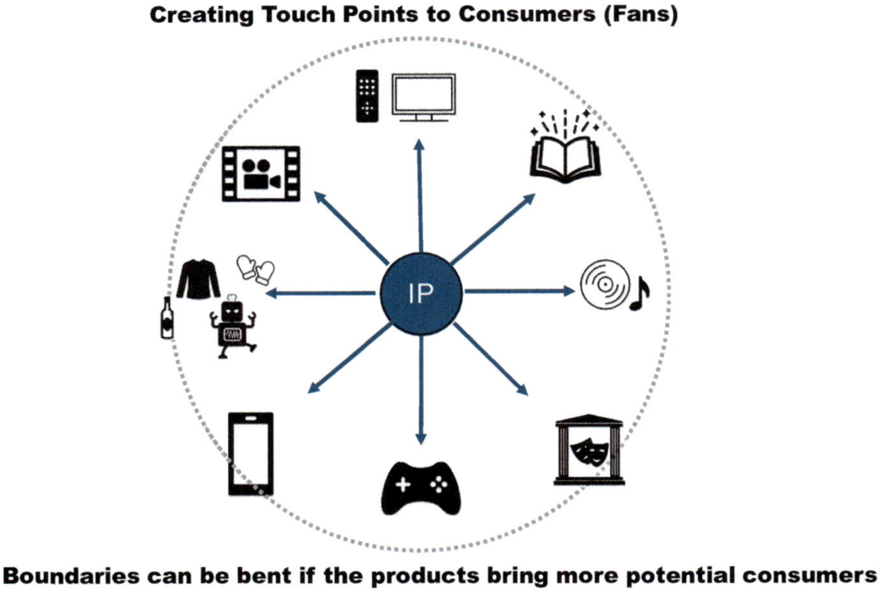

Fig. 4.2 Variation media mix (VMM)

to construct a legitimate narrative framework that allows the coexistence of multiple universes within the IP. Figure 4.2 presents such a strategy.

Enthusiasts enjoy diverse story experiences when the narrative elements align with the established framework. These participants often analyze their connection to the story and sometimes create their own versions, such as fan fiction, to address perceived narrative gaps. This phenomenon is referred to as the worldbuilding media mix (WMM), which centers on defining the world's rules underlying the creation of these narratives. In contrast, the Western media-franchise approach to transmedia storytelling, as introduced by Henry Jenkins in 2003, emphasizes more rigorous unification. Jenkins (2007) and Pratten (2011) argue that narratives in this category ought to provide interconnected stories across various media. Figure 4.3 depicts this model. This model is quite close to the definition of the shared-universe model, in which original work serves as the foundation for subsequent variations developed by single or multiple authors (Tran 2024).

Unlike the category presented in this section, the original works are often categorized within the public domains, and in majority of cases, ownership of each derivative works, are retained by respective authors, which prevents all the works known as the shared universe genre from fitting into this category. Trans also define corporate shared world model,[8] but he defines the term to incorporate Marvel Cinematic Universe (Tran 2024, 8), or IPs that implemented transmedia storytell-

8 Trans defines it as "Film Shared Universe" or "Cinematic Shared Universe" (Tran 2024, 116–117), but the IPs are owned by corporate, thus the term corporate is also accurately depicting what he conveys in the text.

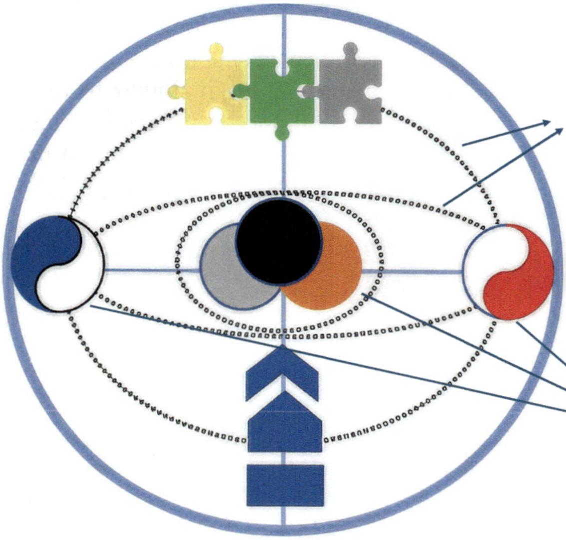

Fig. 4.3 Worldbuilding media mix (WMM)

ing also fall into this category, which I coin the term storybuilding media mix (SMM) in this chapter. Thus, the definition of shared universe is more broader and more ambiguous compared to the categorization suggested in this chapter.

Following careful consideration of the interconnectivity of each work, the stories are linked in meaningful ways in SMM as shown in Fig. 4.4. Furthermore, an epic event occurring in the final phase ties all the threads together. Consumers of these media projects focus on scrutinizing various details, which may foreshadow what is yet to come in the untold portion of the experience, leading to more buzz and speculation among fans. Nakamura and Tosca (2021) demonstrate that certain aspects of the Gundam franchise exhibit similarities to transmedia storytelling. These characteristics suggest that it can be categorized as the storybuilding media mix (SMM). Thus, in this study, the media mix projects considered will be categorized into VMM, WMM, and SMM.

Acknowledging Similar Media Deployment Strategies to Japan's Media Mix

It is important to acknowledge that several terms exist in both industry and academia to describe similar practices of deploying multiple media around an IP. Transmedia storytelling, introduced in an earlier chapter, is a representative example. The characteristics of transmedia storytelling are similar to those of SMM. However, SMM functions as a strategy implemented within the broader context of an overall media franchise.

The concept of a shared world, on the other hand, is much broader. Tran (2024) provides the following working definition: "a transfictional textual environment

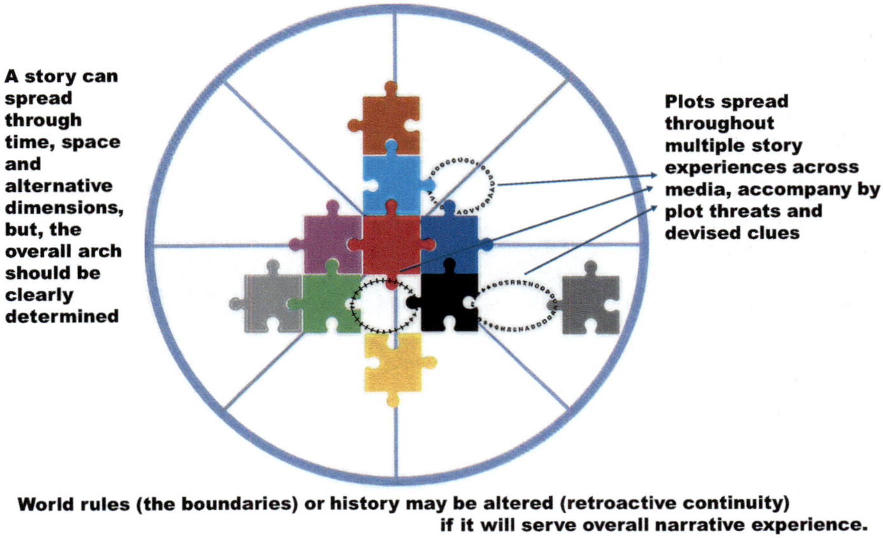

Fig. 4.4 Storybuilding media mix (SMM)

occurring across two or more discrete texts, following different characters or settings that attempt to become realized and believable" (p. 2). In other words, it does not limit whether these texts in the shared universe belong to the public domain or IPs owned by a company, nor does it mandate that the texts share only the world rules or adhere to narrative consistency. Thus, it faces issues identical to those of the term *media mix*, which is too broad to determine strategic positioning when deploying various narrative experiences across media within a media franchise.

This chapter, therefore, argues for the importance of establishing strategic modes within the media mix strategy of a media franchise. The terms primarily used in Korea, such as Once Source Multi-Use (i.e., Kim 2007), Pan-Entertainment in China (Nakamura 2018b; Wang 2021), are very similar concepts to Japan's media mix, but the extensive scrutiny of this terminology should not be included in this volume, for it should be a major undertaking.

4.2.3 Japan's Digital Game Media Mix from a Historical Perspective

Next, this chapter attempts to historicize the Japanese media mix practices from a digital game perspective. As it is virtually impossible to trace every single case of media mix practice, the chapter attempts to describe how the media mix ecology developed by the time digital games became one of the major indoor entertainment and media activities in Japan, and how it embraced digital games and evolved over time, using the comparative case study method. Cases were selected based on the following criteria: (1) titles that took advantage of a particular media platform, (2) titles that exhibited a new model or an alternative to an existing business model,

(3) titles that had a significant impact on succeeding generations, and (4) titles that survived the highly competitive environment. The selected titles were further categorized by type in accordance with ▶ Sect. 4.2.2. The information about media products presented in this chapter, such as release dates, is taken from the Media Arts Database[9] unless otherwise noted in the footnotes.

4.3 Digital Games and Japan's Media Mix

This section presents various examples of media mix related to digital games. First, the section presents several examples of the golden age of arcade games, then explains how the media mix ecology surrounding digital games developed in Japan.

4.3.1 Media Mix During the Arcade Era

Even before media mix projects related to digital games gained popularity in Japan, some games had already appeared in other media formats. The manga Game Center Arashi, which initially appeared in the November 1978 issue of CoroCoro Comic, was created at the request of editors (Sugaya 2009, 172) who noticed the popularity of arcade games among children. It began with Breakout in the first issue, followed by Space Invaders (Taito 1978) numerous times as Arashi competed with his rivals for a high score. Besides Space Invaders, several other games, such as *Galaxian* and *Pac-Man*, were featured. However, this did not constitute a media mix in the strict sense because digital games were not the main feature of this project; the focus of the project was the narrative surrounding Arashi, an avid game player.

For actual media mix projects surrounding digital games, the notable example is *Pac-Man* (1980), released in North America. First, the music album *Pac-Man Fever* was released by Buckner & Garcia, ranked No. 9 on the ARC Weekly Top 40 chart in the Single category,[10] and sold 1.2 million copies by April 1982.[11] These developments were unprecedented in the history of games. An animated TV show (Hanna-Barbera Products) was first aired in the United States on September 25, 1982, and then telecast across several other countries, including Japan (Terpstra and Lapetino 2021, 192–193).

Pac-Land was released in 1984 (Namco 1984) as a side-scrolling action game. It was designed for North American fans who had already seen the cartoon (Ibid). Starting with cases like *Pac-Man Doodle*, with the original version played on a browser, the game was later adapted to multiple incarnations on various platforms,[12]

9 Media Arts Database Agency of Cultural Affairs, Japan. ▶ https://mediaarts-db.bunka.go.jp/
10 The ARC Weekly Top 40, March 20, 1982 Archived on ▶ *RockontheNet.com*: ▶ http://www.rockonthenet.com/archive/1982/03-20.htm
11 Based on Billboard (April 24, 1982).
12 Created as a part of the 30th-anniversary project. Pacman Doodle homepage ▶ https://www.google.com/logos/2010/pacman10-i.html

while maintaining the original rules, such as "Pac-Man eats dots while avoiding ghosts" and "consuming large flashing dots called 'Power Pellets' temporarily grants Pac-Man the power to consume ghosts." Such new titles were continuously released to meet the changing needs of the game-playing population.[13] *Pac-Man and the Ghostly Adventures* was broadcast as a computer-generated (CG) animation program in 2013 in North America, and in 2014 in Japan.[14] The game also appeared in the film Pixels and the CG animated feature *Wreck-It Ralph*, and has been an icon of digital pop culture with unique crossovers since the 1980s.

4.3.2 Digital Games in the Media Mix Ecosystem

By the time the term media mix became a media product deployment strategy used by major publishers, the business ecosystem related to media mix was already organized among manga magazine publishers, animation studios, TV stations, merchandize-related companies such as toy and stationery companies, and even major advertisement agencies, with collaborative efforts surrounding certain IP.[15]

It was during this era that the Family Computer (Famicom) was introduced to the Japanese market in 1983 articles, a supplement booklet, and extra issues of computer magazines (Uemura et al. 2013, 208). This trend eventually led to the launch of game-dedicated magazines one after another, beginning with Beep, published by Softbank Japan (then) in December 1984. Editors of the manga-dedicated magazine published by Shueisha also noticed this trend. Kazuhiko Torishima, who was in charge of Janpu hōsōkyoku (Jump Broadcast Station), a group of editors and writers of infographic articles for Weekly Shonen Jump, asked Yuji Horii to write an article on computer games; this was published on September 20, 1982. Horii then became an official member of the group, and the feature articles on computer games gained strength. Then, when the Famicom was booming,

13 The official website provides a chronological description of the various incarnations of Pac-Man through 2009.

2Pac-Man Official Website (Nov 29th, 2022, Accessed. ► https://www.pacman.com/en/

14 Dengeki Online. TV anime "pakkuwārudo" ga 4 tsuki 5-nichi yori hōei kaishi! Shudaika wa hyadain-shi ga tegakeru "pakku THIS WORLD! ! !" [The TV anime "Pacworld" will start airing on April 5th! The theme song is "PAC THIS WORLD!!!" by Hyadain] March 6, 2014. ► https://dengekionline.com/elem/000/000/817/817016/

15 Testimonies of cooperation between publishers (mainly manga editorial departments), animation studios, toy companies, advertising agencies, and TV stations can be found in various industry-related sources. For example, Shonen Gaho (2001) discusses the partnership between manga publishers and movie studios in the early Showa period. Miyahara (2005) discusses the approach to the manga industry from the TV drama production side, from the editorial side, Hirayama (2012) from the video studio side, and Sugaya (2022) from the manga artist's point of view. As for the manga artist's viewpoint, Sugaya (2022) has shown this. Furthermore, Nishimura (2004) writes about media mixing by new manga artists and elaborates on their roles with magazine editors. The development of projects developed by animation studios is detailed by Kimura (2020). As for research books and articles, the prewar situation was organized by Nakamura and Tosca (2020). See Masuda (2007) for a discussion of the formation of production committees and the synergies that result from them.

the first feature article on the console game appeared in their September 3, 1984, issue, titled "MSX VS Family Computers." Thereafter, from August 18, 1985 to January 7, 1989, the issue Famicom Shinken, a section dedicated to the Famicom, appeared in serial form (Famikon denshō iinkai 2016). The success of this unique feature eventually led to the creation of the monthly manga and game magazine VJump in July 1993 (Famikon denshō iinkai 2016, 78–80). The years 1985 and 1986 were the heydays for game-related books and magazines. The strategy games for Super Mario Bros. ranked the best-selling books consecutively for these 2 years. With the publication of Shōnen manga magazines, several publishers began publishing magazines dedicated to console and handheld games. Starting from the Family Computer Magazine (Famimaga) published by Tokuma Shoten in July 1985, three magazines followed in 1986: Famicom Hisshobon Magazine by JICC (at the time) in March, Marukatsu Famicom (hereafter Marukatsu) by Kadokawa in April, and Famicom Tusushin (hereafter Famitsu) by ASCII (at the time) in June. Thus, an environment was created in which information on game-related issues was readily available to fans and the target group. Bestsellers created using game strategy books demonstrated the marketability of digital game information. *Super Mario Bros.: The Complete Mario Bros. Strategy Guide* was a bestseller in 1985 and 1986 (Yamamoto 2011, 36).

Furthermore, the media industry is increasingly incorporating games into its media mix. Shogakukan Boys Manga, Hobby Magazine, and CoroCoro Comic began featuring Family Computer as a special article in their January 1985 issue, and the serialization of the manga Famikonrokkī began in their April 1985 issue. Enix, a game publisher, launched the manga magazine Monthly Shonen Gangan on March 12, 1991, with manga adaptations of digital games released by its Digital Entertainment division. The manga business continued to grow even after Square merged with Enix in April 2003, forming Square Enix. The group that produced the famous manga *Fullmetal Alchemist* currently has five monthly manga magazines and three online manga services. The rise of these publishers has enabled game makers to offer a variety of media mix strategies.

4.4 Digital Games as Part of Existing IP

This section analyzes the development of existing IPs into digital games based on the three classifications given in ► Sect. 4.2.

4.4.1 Variation Media Mix (VMM)

Digital games based on existing IP began appearing in the early days of arcade games, personal computer software, and some console games, before Nintendo's Family Computer; for example, Arcadia by Bandai was released in March 1983. These digital games began by simply adding graphic motifs to existing game mechanics and then using the titles of existing IP to increase their appeal, particularly among fans of media franchises. Thus, games became a part of the variation media mix (Picard and Pelletier-Gagnon 2015). This was also true for games developed for the Family Computer. For example, *Popeye* (1982), developed by Nintendo for Arcades in December 1982, was released in 1983 as a launch title for the Family Computer (1983a). Additionally, *Popeye's English Play*, which incorporated the Popeye character for English language learning, was released a few months later in the same year (1983b).

Furthermore, as indicated in the previous section, a media mix business ecosystem materialized among publishers, animation studios, and toy companies. Several games based on manga and anime works were created around this period, starting with Bandai's *Kinnikuman Muscle Tag Team Match/Tag Team Match: MUSCLE* (1985), released on November 8, 1985. Many manga and anime games were later ported to digital platforms, though with some technical limitations. However, some companies found the characters and narratives to be disconnected from the original work (Ito 2019). Still, amidst these challenges, some works were released effectively. Konami, in collaboration with Kadokawa Publishing, released the digital game *Hinotori:hōō-hen: Gaōnobōken* (Phoenix Chronicles: Gaou's Adventure) (Kadokawa 1987), which formed part of Kadokawa's new media mix project centering around the animated feature film *Hi no tori hōō-hen,* to sell half a million copies (Sato 2021, 70). Other companies added value by using the RPG mechanics to develop crossovers, connecting multiple worldviews that would typically be impossible to connect. *Famikonjanpu eiyū Retsuden (Famicom Jump: Hero Retsuden)* (Bandai 1989) was released by Bandai on February 25, 1989. In this game, the main characters from the Jump manga join hands to defeat Demon King Piccolo, a villain from the *Dragon Ball* universe, in a world ruled by him. Gundam was released the same year. The same year also saw the development of a simulation game featuring *SD Gundam*, a deformed toy version of the *Gundam* series. This created a Gundam world unique to the anime, though constrained by technological limitations (Nakamura and Tosca 2019). This concept was further developed in 1991 into a crossover, bringing together popular robot anime in a Game Boy software. Since then, the *SD Gundam* and *Super Robot Wars* series have evolved into distinct product lines from their originals. As for the aforementioned media mix based on games and manga, technological improvements in game consoles and changes in the attitudes of development studios led to the release of several works that were more faithful to manga and anime IP. The game media thus began to play an important role as a destination for the development of manga and anime IP.

4.4.2 Worldbuilding Media Mix (WMM)

As previously mentioned, the development method used in TRPGs inspired media creators and producers to conceive and develop the worldbuilding media mix (WMM). This trend coincided with the rise of digital games as mainstream entertainment, which inevitably led to their inclusion in media franchise projects alongside manga and anime from the early stages of development. Media mix projects that incorporated digital games later still treated them as works of equal importance to those developed earlier.

The Record of Lodoss War Franchise

One of the early examples of worldbuilding media mix involving digital games is *the Record of Lodoss War* franchise (hereafter referred to as *the Lodoss War* franchise), which was introduced in ▶ Sect. 4.2.2.2. Although novels, manga, OVA, and TRPG kit are positioned in a horizontal relationship (Mizuno 2018), the novel was released first, on April 1, 1988, followed by the OVA in 1990, which ran for 13 episodes and covered volumes 1–4 of the novel. Then the *Lodoss War* franchise made its debut with *Hajimari no Boukenshatachi: Legend of Crystania*, distributed by Toei on July 29, 1995, and expanded into three OVA episodes from 1996 to 1997 as sequels to the film. Finally, in 1998, the television series "*Chronicles of the Heroic Knight*" aired from April 1, 1998 to September 30, 1998, comprising 27 episodes. From Episode 1 to Episode 8, the story arc from the original OVA was retold, though its storyline aligns more closely with the novels. For the remaining episodes (Episodes 9–27), the *Holy War of Kings* arc, which comprises Volumes 6 and 7 from the novels, was adapted. The subsequent light novels then continued the saga from where the anime ends, expanding the storyline across six volumes published between 1998 and 2006. The latest canonical novel was published in 2019 and set 100 years after the last novel. Among these novels, the first and latest arcs were adapted into manga. As for digital games, several adaptations and licensed products have been developed. The first digital games were developed for console games, such as the PC Engine.

The Moryo Senki Madara Franchise

The MADARA project, as Ōtsuka claimed, was inspired by the media mix method from the *Lodoss War* franchise (Ōtsuka 2014; Steinberg 2015b). Unlike the *Lodoss War* franchise, which was initiated as a play session of the Dungeons and Dragons tabletop Role-playing game, the MADARA project was conceived and evolved by Ōtsuka himself, along with narrative consumption theory (Ōtsuka 2014). *Moryo Senki Madara* originated as a manga serialized in the Marukatsu Famicom Magazine, followed by video game adaptations and OVA releases. Ōtsuka also deliberately contradicted the main storyline depicted in the official manga, leaving some parts untold so that fans could actively participate in "dōjin" activities.[16] A chronology with a world setting was also released, leading to the creation of several dōjin manga, which eventually prompted Kadokawa to publish a series of dōjin anthology comics and recruit artists to draw an official spin-off manga. In terms of other media such as OVAs and digital games, both OVA and the initial digital games approached the manga as source text, incorporating some variations. This diverged from Ōtsuka's intended approach, which was to allow new versions as long as they remained within the established *MADARA* universe (world setting and character premises) frameworks (Ōtsuka 2020). The second role-playing game (RPG) installment for the Super Nintendo was developed in line with Ōtsuka's vision. It featured a story set in contemporary Japan, with distinct plotlines that retained the core premise and character concepts of the original setting, including reincarnation.

16 Dōjin literally means "people who share the same interests," but it is often used by those actively engaged in creating fan fiction.

The Mobile Police Patlabor Franchise

Another early example of worldbuilding media mix emerged from the science fiction genre as well. It is the *Mobile Police Patlabor* franchise, developed by HEAD GEAR, a creative group formed by manga artist Masami Yuki, mechanical designer Yutaka Izubuchi, character designer Akemi Takada, animation director Mamoru Oshii, and screenwriter Kazunori Ito. The original idea was submitted to several animation publishers but was ultimately developed when HEAD GEAR members invited Shin Unozawa of Bandai Visual to a Christmas party in 1985 and proposed the project (Akiyama and Myst 2013, 186). As the initial proposal submitted to the Model Department of the Bandai Group was rejected, as the Department had a TV anime in mind, it was decided to begin with a small-scale OVA project. The reason was that if the project succeeded, it could be developed later into an animated television series. Six episodes were initially proposed for production, with a budget of JPY 60 million. Funds were raised by selling the video software rights to Tohoku Shinsha and the laser disc software rights to Warner. The video software and laser disc were released simultaneously on April 25, 1988 (Akiyama and Myst 2013, 187). Serialization of the story began the same year in issue 17 of Weekly Shōnen Sunday by Masami Yuki, who presented the original idea for the standard. While the work was serialized until issue 23 in 1994, the first animated feature film directed by Mamoru Oshii was released on July 15, 1989. The television anime series aired for about a year, from October 11 of the same year. A revised version was published in the July issue. This is one of the early works in which a full-scale media mix was conducted, leveraging various settings and characters, yet the IP ownership is clarified among the team, as it is already credited as HEADGEAR in collaboration with various studios and creative units for each project. These works spanned from OVAs, television anime series, animated film features, manga, novels, video games, and live-action films, to name a few, from 1988 to the present day, with a new animated feature released in 2026. As for digital games, while most are licensed to reach a diverse consumer base, the PlayStation game *Mobile Police Patlabor: Game Edition,* released on November 30, 2000 (Production IG 2000), featured a completely original story created by HEAD GEAR. The stories told could fill a void connected to either the anime TV program or film versions. Thus, fans can enjoy various aspects of the Patlabor Universe through multiple narrative experiences and simultaneously compare and contrast slightly different universes.

4.4.3 Storybuilding Media Mix

Projects in the storybuilding media mix (SMM) category are often observed in games published by American and European companies. *Blade Runner* (1997), published by Virgin Interactive, was developed as a "sidequeal" because the events are set to occur almost simultaneously with the first film. *Enter the Matrix* (2003), an action game published by Infogrames under the Atari Brand and developed by Shiny Entertainment, was part of the canonical episodes set between the second and third films in the Matrix Franchise. Similar examples include *The Thing* (2002), launched by Vivendi Universal Games, and *James Cameron's Avatar: The Game* (2009), launched by Ubisoft, both set in timelines after the events depicted in the film. All the Star Wars console video games released after Lucas Entertainment became part of the Disney Group; their story modes were considered canon. Unlike digital games published in the West, it is challenging to find licensed games that align with the storybuilding media mix model. However, there are some exceptions. The most obvious exception is the licensed Hollywood IP, The *Nightmare Before Christmas: Oogie's Revenge*, developed by Capcom in 2004, which set the timeline 1 year after the incident depicted in the original *The Nightmare Before Christmas* film (2004). The story was expanded to depict all the film's incidents in the games. In other cases, the story mode in the games expands the existing stories. Notable examples are Bandai Namco's *JoJo's Bizarre Adventure: Eyes of Heaven* (2015) and Aniplex's first 3D action-adventure game *Demon Slayer—Kimetsu no Yaiba—The Hinokami Chronicles* (2021), both developed by Cyber Connect 2. More extensive efforts were required for the *Mobile Suit Gundam* franchise games. They began with *Mobile Suit Gundam F91 Formula Wars*, which was preceded by the events depicted in the film *Mobile Suit Gundam F91*. Several other Gundam games focused on spin-offs of the main story depicted in anime television programs, original video animations, and films. Nakamura and Tosca (2019, 2021) and Tosca and Nakamura (2025) provide a major list of such efforts.

4.5 Digital Games as Original IP Extended to Other Media

This section examines nine examples of digital game IP media mix development, encompassing approaches that range from conventional media mix to media mix extensions that include regional revitalization. The section first examines six cases that can be classified as variation media mix, then considers three cases of storybuilding media mix, and two cases of worldbuilding media mix.

4.5.1 Variation Media Mix (VMM)

As with other IPs, digital games were extended into original IPs by leveraging a media mix to create variations and attract broader audiences. Thus, this category presents a variety of deployment examples in digital games, as reflected in the analysis performed in this section.

The Super Mario Bros. Franchise

The first signature work of game-related IP in the media mix was *Super Mario Bros* (Nintendo 1985). About a year after the console version of *Super Mario Bros.* was released, its anime version premiered in theaters on July 20, 1986. The film cleverly incorporated sounds from the original game in the background music. The film was produced by Sūpāmarioburazāzu Seisaku Jimusho (Super Mario Bros. Production Office) under the sponsorship of Hori Kikaku Seisaku, Hori

Production, Vap Nippon Television Music, and others, adopting the production committee method at this stage. Keibunsha published *Super Mario Bros.* Gaiden in 1986 (Rikio and Shiina 1986). This was an adventure gamebook in manga format. The story differed completely from the main game. In addition, *Super Mario Bros.* was also published in various Shōnen manga magazines. One of the best examples is *Super Mario-Kun*, a gag comic that has been serialized since 1990.

The franchise for this game evolved as the platform changed. The sidekick character Yoshi first appeared in *Super Mario World* (Nintendo 1990) for the Super Famicom and eventually appeared in their own spin-off games. Mario also appeared as a major character in several crossover titles, including the *Super Smash Bros.* franchise, *Mario & Sonic at the Olympic* Games, and *Mario + Rabbids: Kingdom Battle* (Ubisoft 2017). Therefore, the aforementioned *Super Mario*-Kun manga became a long-running series by focusing on everyday gags and mirroring the content of each new installment of the game series. However, not all the media products developed in franchises have been successful. Universal Studios featured *Super Mario Bros.: The Movie,* in the summer of 1993 marked the first Hollywood video game adaptation in both North America and Japan. The film received extremely low user ratings, even among video game film adaptations.[17] However, Shigeru Miyamoto responded that it was "interesting to see works that can be interpreted differently by the artist."[18] Thus, for this franchise, the media mixes that emphasized a diversification strategy were tolerated, including those that deviated from the original Hollywood film adaptation. The current media mix strategy for the *Super Mario Bros.* franchise is to increase diversity while preserving the integrity of the original worldview's aesthetic. For example, *Super Nintendo World,* which opened at Universal Studios Japan on March 18, 2021, was directly based on the *Super Mario Bros.* franchise, with Miyamoto supervising the world.[19] Miyamoto was also heavily involved in the animated film, the *Super Mario Bros.* movie, from the planning stages in collaboration with Illumination and Nintendo.[20] Regarding efforts, Chris stated the following:

> We had a conversation with Miyamoto and the Nintendo team about virtually every aspect of the movie, from design, animation, story, music. We went through the entire process with the great filmmaking team… really came together, looking at even the small details of the movie. So it was really a wonderful partnership (FamitsuTUBE 2023).

---

17 For example, see Rotten Tomatoes ► https://www.rottentomatoes.com/m/super_mario_bros

18 Based on a report in CinemaToday. Mario no uminooya miyamoto shigeru, hatsu animēshon o tegaketa kikkake ya, jissha-ban Mario e no omoi o kataru! [Mario creator Shigeru Miyamoto talks about what inspired him to create his first animated feature and his thoughts on the live-action version of Mario!] October 26, 2014. ► https://www.cinematoday.jp/news/N0067574

19 Based on a Press Release by Universal Studio Japan. June 8, 2017. ► https://www.usj.co.jp/company/news/2017/0608.html

20 Based on a joint press release between Illumination and Nintendo. October 7, 2022. ► https://www.nintendo.co.jp/corporate/release/en/2022/221007.html

The collaborations between Universal Studios and Illumination seem to be more aligned with what this chapter defines as a worldbuilding media mix. Yet Miyamoto's emphasis on "not to betray those who love the games" (Ibid) suggests that the true purpose was not merely a matter of media mix strategy, but rather a focus on the Value Co-Creation model on a global scale—particularly in the case of major theme park attractions or Hollywood animated features destined for worldwide distribution. Meanwhile, other media, such as comics and smartphone games, continue to expand the franchise's touchpoints.

Street Fighter Franchise

The *Street Fighter* franchise was another media mix project that eventually led to Hollywood films. This franchise was aggressively developed through a media mix after *Street Fighter II: The World Warrior* launched in Arcades in March 1991 (Capcom 1991), adding a fighting match mode. Following the release of an anthology manga in September 1992, the *Street Fighter* franchise was published in a wide range of media, including American comics by Malibu Comics in 1993, a serialized four-panel manga published in CoroCoro magazines, and by other publishers. *An animated film* was released on August 6, 1994, and a 29-episode anime television series was produced by Yomiuri Television and broadcast by Nippon Television Network, starting on April 10, 1995. Furthermore, Universal Pictures in Hollywood released a live-action film in North America on December 23, 1994, and in Japan on May 6, 1995. The movie merely used the characters' names and did not follow the original story setting. However, Capcom was involved in the film's production, rather than in licensing it out. Moreover, an arcade game based on the film was launched in May 1995. Although it took over ten years to recoup the cost of making films, films contributed to increased publicity as they (often pirated copies) were distributed in countries where neither arcade games nor game software were available (Haruhiki 2010, p. 45). While expansions across different media are not as active as they were before, UDON Entertainment has continued publishing comics since *Street Fighter IV* in 2009.

The *Street Fighter* franchise continues to innovate by releasing numbered titles, with the latest installment, *Street Fighter 6,* released on June 2, 2023. Despite the absence of the next series, spin-offs, or any other derivatives, the core experience that still engages fans to this day is esports competitions featuring the *Street Fighter* series as the main title. Capcom initiated this movement in 1992, when it hosted the *Street Fighter II* Championship '92 at Kokugikan, drawing 4000 competitors in collaboration with local toy shops and arcades (Capcom eSports 2021). Such initial attempts had spread and evolved, and finally, in 2013, Capcom USA hosted the Street Fighter 25th Anniversary World Tournament. This initiative had evolved into CAPCOM CUP, initiated in December 2013 by CAPCOM USA. Since 2014, the point-based professional circuit competition system, CAPCOM Pro Tour, has been in operation, and in November 2019, the Street Fighter League was established in Japan (Ibid., 51). Currently, CAPCOM hosts CAPCOM CUP for individual competitions, and the World Championship for Street Fighter Leagues spans the USA, Japan, and Europe; CAPCOM hosts both competitions and uses Street Fighter 6. Thus, fans continue to irk the franchise, whether as esports players or spectators. This shows that so long as the media mix is aimed at expanding the franchise, the realm, such as brain sports, becomes an essential part of the entire franchise.

Dragon Quest Franchise

The Dragon Quest (Enix 1986) franchise is an early example of a game developed in synergy with games, anime, and manga from its inception. This franchise is also considered a milestone in Japanese role-playing games (hereafter JRPG). The director, Yuji Horii, one of the members of the Famicom Shinken feature article writing team for Weekly Jump, as described in ► Sect. 4.3.2, wrote game development progress reports even before its release. These feature articles promoted the RPG genre, which was not well established in Japan at the time, to raise awareness of *Dragon Quest* (Famikon denshō iinkai 2016). Thus, this title became one of Japan's most popular RPG series. The serialized manga *DRAGON QUEST: Dai no Daiboken* first appeared in Weekly Shonen Jump Volume No. 45 in 1989; it ran until 1996, volume No. 52. *DRAGON QUEST* was an anime television series with the same worldview and setting as the game version; part 1 was broadcast from December 2, 1989 to September 22, 1990, and part 2 aired from January 11 to April 5, 1991. The game's core team was directly involved in the anime's production.[21] Akira Toriyama is credited for the original character, and Yuji Horii is credited for the original ideas. Part 1 aired during a period when the synergistic effects could have been affected by the launch of *Dragon Quest IV: Chapters of the Chosen* (Enix 1991, hereafter, *DQ IV*), which was released on February 11, 1990. By maintaining high-frequency touchpoints, such as weekly television visibility precisely at the moment when *DQIV*'s peak performance is expected, it ensured maximum exposure for the driving component of this media franchise.

The anime adaptation of the *Dai no Daiboken* manga series ran from October 17, 1991 to September 24, 1992. Furthermore, during this time, Enix made a pivotal decision that would influence the Dragon Quest franchise. The manga magazine Monthly Shōnen Gangan was first published on March 12, 1991. Along with this, the serialized manga *Dragon Quest: Emblem of Rotowas* featured.

These are good examples of gap-bridging approaches. It ended just before the release of *Dragon Quest V: Hand of the Heavenly Bride* (September 27, 1992).[22] The publication of monthly manga magazines would also play a vital role for the company, even after Enix merged with Square to become Square Enix. Comic magazines are later diversified to target narrower audiences, becoming a prime source for fans to retrieve the latest information about various intellectual properties created by them, including the *Dragon Quest* Franchise. They are an early form of Owned Media strategy. This additional strategy continues to emphasize the impor-

21 First season referred simply as Dragon Quest ► https://mediaarts-db.bunka.go.jp/id/C8599, and the second season being referred as Dragon Quest Dainikii (the second term) from 33 to 43. ► https://mediaarts-db.bunka.go.jp/id/M24637

22 Based on the Square Enix Dragon Quest 5 page. ► https://www.jp.square-enix.com/game/detail/dq5/

tant part of the *Dragon Quest* franchise from then on. The position of the newly featured *Dragon Quest: Emblem of Roto* is also interesting. The story takes place within the Roto trilogy universe and is set in the time between *Dragon Quest III*[23] and *Dragon Quest. So, this particular work,* along with *the initial Dragon Quest trilogy,* forms Storybuidling Media Mix (SMM). This indicates the dynamic nature of Japan's Media mix strategy.

During the time between and around the launch of *Dragon Quest VI: Realms of Revelation* on December 9, 1995, a new addition to the media mix was a spin-off video game title, *Torneko's Great Adventure,* released on September 19, 1993. This was the first time delivering roguelike dungeon action role-playing games, using the popular character, the shopkeeper, *Toruneko in Dragon Quest IV* as its protagonists. Although the characters are adapted from the *Dragon Quest* franchise, the game mechanics and main narrative have little connection to the numbered titles, making it an additional variation of the franchise. Providing different ludic experiences within the franchise is a vital feature for the media mix originating from video game IP.

The deployment of derivative works during the interim between *Dragon Quest VI: Realm of Revelation* (December 9, 1995) and *Dragon Quest VII: Warriors of Eden* (August 26, 2000) has undergone significant changes from previous strategies. Unlike previous titles, it took over 4 years and 8 months to release, as the game's volume continued to grow in tandem with the ongoing innovation of game platforms. The media mix strategies were quickly adapted to these changes. By this time, the manga series *Dragon Quest: The Emblem of Loto* continued its storyline, and the animated feature film *Dragon Quest: The Emblem of Lot* was released in theaters on April 20, 1996. The timing was positioned approximately four and a half months after the release date of *DQ VI*, about 4 years and 4 months before the launch date of *DQ VII* (Enix 2000).

The absence of nongame-related works is supplemented by spin-off video games and the porting of classic games to handheld devices. *Dragon Quest Monsters* is a game that collects monsters, breeds them, and pits them against opponents' monsters was released on September 25, 1998. The second installment of the *Toruneko* series was also released on September 15, 1999. Subsequently, the dragon quest franchise allowed diverse types of games to be a part of the franchise, which includes but not limited to trading card game version (2000), casino collection game on mobile phone (2000), a game with a motion-sensor-equipped sword toy (2003), its adaption to console game, using Wii game controller (2007), action adventure games, having a slime as protagonist (2003), card battle arcade game (2007), a turn based strategy game (2009), MMORPG as official numbering title, *Dragon Quest X* (2012), and quest-driven crafting building as *Dragon Quest Builders* series (2016).[24] It does not end here. The franchise explores new game experiences in collaboration with other game studios that already have a strong presence in a

---

23 Although released later (hence III), Dragon Quest III is considered a prequel to Dragon Quest and Dragon Quest II.

24 Release years are based on (Square Enix and Studio BentStuff 2011).

specific genre. For example, they collaborated with Omega Force, a part of Koei Tecmo, to release a warrior hack-and-slash game titled *Dragon Quest Heroes* (2015). In collaboration with Colopl, a Japanese mobile entertainment company renowned for its enormous success with location-based games, the augmented Reality location-based game *Dragon Quest Walk* began service in 2019. To develop a smartphone-based turn-based tactical battle game, they collaborated with Aiming to release *Dragon Quest Tact* in 2020. When VR entertainment became enormously popular, *Dragon Quest VR* operated in collaboration with Bandai Namco Amusement from 2018 to 2020, when these facilities ceased operations due to the pandemic. For non-game expansion, the 3DCG animated film *Dragon Quest: Your Story,* helmed by Takashi Yamazaki, produced by Robot with SHIROGUMI, one of Japan's acclaimed VFX/CG studios, opened in Japan on August 2, 2019. This was followed by the serial anime, *Dragon Quest: The Adventure of Dai* (*Dai no Daibōken*; hereafter "*Dai*"), full readaptation of the manga, which initially aired from October 3, 2020 to October 22, 2022, covering the entire saga. The *Dai* series was further strengthened by the addition of spin-off Manga, the Dai, Avan the *Brave and the Demon King of Hellfire* (Yusa Avan to Gokuen no Maō). It began serialization in V Jump, starting with the November 2020 issue, and is ongoing. The story is positioned as a prequel to the Dai. As for smartphone games, *Tamashii no Kizuna (Connection of Souls)* was in service from September 28, 2021, until April 27, 2023, in collaboration with DeNA.

Additionally, an action game for Console and PC, based on the Dai series, titled *Infinity Strash: Dragon Quest, The Adventure of Dai,* was released on September 29, 2023. In other words, the *Dai* series was treated as a separate media franchise from the main *Dragon Quest* line.

Pokémon Franchise

The *Pokémon* franchise culminated in a media mix practice developed in cooperation with various media companies, as described in the previous section. Although Game Boy, the platform for this software, was not the latest generation of game consoles, the decision was made at CoroCoro Comic to feature Pokémon Special articles in an extra issue of CoroCoro Comic just 1 day after the release of the first Pokémon games, *Pokémon Green* and *Pokémon Red* (Feb. 27, 1996). Shogakukan's decision was based on marketing research indicating that the Game Boy was the most-played game hardware among primary school children. Masakazu Kubo, then deputy editor of CoroCoro Comic, believed that exchanging one's monsters with friends via a network adapter could attract more children over time (Kenji and Kubo 2000, 178–179). Rumors then spread among readers about the existence of additional, secret Pokémon within the game's program. After discussions with the developers at Game Freak and confirming that such rumors were valid, Shogakukan decided to launch a Pokémon giveaway campaign starting from the May issue of CoroCoro Comic.

This campaign was successful, and 78,000 applications were received. While promoting the gift campaign, an attempt was made to sell 600,000 copies of *Pokémon Blue*, starting with the November 1996 issue, which was released on October 15, 1996. A *Pokémon card game* was then released on October 20, 1996, and the *Pokémon TV anime* program was launched on April 1, 1997. The proposal for the TV anime series came from Shogakukan to Nintendo, and Nintendo gradually approved the proposal. The success of the anime television series was followed by *Pokémon the Movie: Mewtwo Strikes Back,* released on July 18, 1998, in Japanese movie theaters (Kenji and Kubo 2000, 387–388). Thus, the total number of Pokémon games shipped exceeded ten million units in March 1998. The Game Boy, the platform for this title, sold 18.11 million units in Japan in 1996 and 1998, even though 8 years had passed since its release. In 1999, with Pokémon's overseas expansion into North America and other countries, global Game Boy sales surpassed 100 million units, 52 million of which were sold after 1996, the year *Pokémon* was released (Kenji and Kubo 2000, 383). With the enormous success of the *Pokémon* franchise across multiple media products and merchandise, Nintendo, Game Freak, and Creatures formed Pokémon Center Co., Ltd. through a joint investment in April 1998. The company initially focused on managing its retail outlets. However, it later changed its name to Pokémon Company, expanding its responsibility to manage everything related to the *Pokémon* franchise and brand management. Since then, the Pokémon brand has continued to thrive for a strong linkage between theatrical anime, televised anime programs, digital games, and trading card games. Such media mix strategies of the *Pokémon* franchise are characterized by a business ecosystem in which anime studios, game studios, and publishing companies form an almost coextensive relationship, centered on the IP. Recently, in further developments, *Pokémon GO* (2016) a location-based game, was developed in collaboration with Niantic, Inc., a Google-affiliated company. This has been in service since July 6, 2016.[25] Furthermore, a Hollywood live-action movie, *Detective Pikachu*, based on the 3DS game (The Pokemon Company 2016) of the same name, was co-produced by Warner Bros. Pictures, Legendary Pictures, and Pokémon, and released on May 3, 2019. It was distributed by Warner Bros. Pictures and Toho Co.[26] In addition, *Pokémon UNITE* (The Pokemon Company 2020), a Pokémon version of MOBA games, a genre often used in e-sports, was co-developed with TiMi Studios at Tencent Games and began global distribution on Nintendo Switch on July 21, 2021. This was followed by the launch of iOS and Android device versions in September 2021,[27] and *Arceus* on January 28, 2022, further expanded the ludic experience, accompanied by the *Pokémon* franchise: Open World within the Pokémon universe. Initially, a turn-based action game, the next installment of the Legend series, *Pokémon Legends: Z–A*, released on October 16, 2025, on the other hand, focused on real-time action at its core game mechanic while retaining the strategic layer of team-building, considering the synergy of selected Pokémon regarding type balance, role distribution, and move coverage. This represents an ever-expanding of the company's media mix strategy, both

25 Niantic Press Release, "Break out the sneakers and Poké Balls!" Nianticlab. July 6, 2016 ▶ https://nianticlabs.com/news/launch/?hl=en

26 Based on Detective Pikachu's official home page ▶ https://meitantei-pikachu.jp/

27 Based on a Press release by the Pokemon Company, "Pokémon UNITE Launches on Nintendo Switch on Jul 21st. Jul 15th, 2021"▶ https://www.pokemon.com/us/pokemon-news/pokemon-unite-launches-on-nintendo-switch-on-july-21

across media and forms of play. Such horizontal alliances among companies can be realized only when there is room for creativity, with a high degree of freedom for each employee. The success of Pokémon's media mix practices became the benchmark for numerous IPs, but none could reach that level.

The Game IPs Strategically Incorporating Live Stage Entertainment

In the licensed practice of media mix strategies, there have been cases of intellectual properties originating from digital games adapted for live performance since the 1980s.[28] Nevertheless, one of the most distinct examples of an IP holder successfully integrating live stage entertainment within a varied media mix strategy is the *Sakura Wars* franchise. The game was released on September 27, 1996 (Sega 1996).[29] As software for the Sega Saturn, it is an IP that actively incorporated the live stage into its media mix strategies. Kosuke Fujishima, a well-established manga artist, was recruited as the principle character designer; thus, media mix strategies were broadly outlined at this stage. The game was divided into adventure and battle segments and involved a turn-based war simulation. After the game was released, its light novel adaptation started in May 1997. The anime was released as an OVA on December 18, 1997, and broadcast on TV from April 8 to September 23, 2000. Songs and drama CDs were released in succession; the stage *Sakura Wars Song Show: Imperial Kagekidan Hanagumi Special Performance: Because of Love* was premiered on July 19, 1997. Subsequently, stages, both big and small, were held regularly until 2006. Café Taishō Roman-dō (Sakura Cafe) opened at the Sega amusement facility, Ikebukuro GiGO, on Jun 13, 1998. The concept of the Café was "a specialty store themed around *Sakura Wars* and its fictional historical background." This allowed fans to visit the location, enjoy the atmosphere, and learn the latest information about the *Sakura Wars* franchise. These endeavors played a pivotal role in pioneering 2.5D live entertainment based on games.

Koei's Neo-Romance franchise followed a strategy of incorporating stage events into its media mix. *Neo Romance* is the brand name for romantic adventure games mainly targeted at female audiences, produced by Koei (at the time). It began with *Angelique* (Koei 1994) for the Super Famicom, released on September 23, 1994. The game initially had no voiceover, but a drama CD based on the game was released the next day, September 24, 1994, before a sequel was developed. Since then, all the Neo-Romance series, including the *Angelique* series, have featured voice acting. These series have been developed into comic book series, animated OVAs, animated TV series, and other media formats, adopting strategies similar to those of conventional media mixes. However, Koei attempted a voice actor stage performance in 1995, but due to various complications, the franchise's

---

28 The earliest known example is the Super Mario Brothers segment in *The Ice Capades* (The Ice Capades with Jason Bateman and Alyssa Milano, 1989).

29 All the dates are based on the official timetable of the Sakura Taisen franchise as archived in Internet archive on April 7, 2022. ► https://web.archive.org/web/20220407120842/https://sakura-taisen.com/archives/history.html

production team decided not to hold such events until 2000.[30] Many voice actors took the stage at the *Angelique Memoire 2000* event held in Yokohama on February 27, 2000.[31] The event featured public readings, skits, concerts, and other performances related to the work. Although these were not full-fledged stage performances, they were pioneering events that brought together all the male voice actors. Along with the *Sakura Wars* series revue, they also created content that was a precursor to 2.5D musicals.

Rise of Game IP Involving the Regional Public Sector as Media Mix Collaborators

The culture of enjoying variety without regard for the uniformity of story worlds enabled loose collaboration among entities in implementing media mix strategies. Moreover, this culture extended to local public institutions. The *Sengoku BASARA* franchise—whose first game was released by Capcom on July. 21, 2005 (Capcom 2005)—illustrates this. A sequel to the same title was released on July 27, 2006 (Capcom 2006), and an arcade game version was launched in April. 2008. The first season of the anime adaptation aired from April 5 to June 21, 2009, precisely coinciding with the release of the PlayStation Portable game *Sengoku BASARA Battle Heroes* on April 9, 2009 (Capcom 2009). The second anime season aired from July 11 to September 26, 2010. In this case, the season overlapped with *Sengoku BASARA 3*, which was released on July 29, 2010 (Capcom 2010). In addition, the film version of the anime *Sengoku BASARA—The Last Party*—was released on June 4, 2011, followed by the console game Sengoku BASARA 3 UTAGE released on November 10, 2011 (Capcom 2011). These release strategies are consistent with the typical media mix strategies implemented by Japanese entertainment companies. Comic book adaptations were also released regularly after the launch of the first game, in line with the traditional media mix strategy.

This franchise was unique because it leveraged the warlords and warriors associated with various locations throughout Japan. For example, the city of Shiroishi in Miyagi Prefecture, associated with warlord Katakura Kojuro, who appeared in *Sengoku BASARA 2*, ran a special bus featuring illustrations of the warlord on the back and sides for a limited period in 2008.[32] Production IG, which oversaw the anime adaptation at the time, visited Miyagi Prefecture. This region, associated with the warlord Date Masamune, the anime's main character, held a meeting in February 2009 to explain the commercialization plans and sales strategy for the series. Consequently, local beer, rice, hot noodles, Tamamushi-dyed picture postcards, sake, miso, mentsuyu, beef tongue curry, daifuku, and other products featuring characters from the works were sold

30 Based on the interview with Keiko Erikawa by Famitsu (2015).

31 Based on the official homepage. "Event Report." (Feb 27th, 2000) ► http://www.gamecity.ne.jp/angelique/EVENT/000227/mem2000.htm

32 Based on the news article by IT media. "Miyagi ken shiraishishi no shibasu ni `sengoku basara' no `ki ~yassurukun kojūrō basu' ga tōjō" ["Cassuru-kun Kojuro Bus" from *Sengoku BASARA* Appears on City Buses in Shiroishi City, Miyagi Prefecture] IT media. (Mar 21st, 2008) ► https://nlab.itmedia.co.jp/games/articles/0803/21/news067.html

from April to June 2009, during the anime's broadcast period. Additionally, sales of these products were initially limited to the Hobby Shop, which opened in May 2009. The special sales corner at Radio Kaikan and the *Sengoku BASARA Café* at the Akihabara Cure Maid Café had a substantial economic impact (Nakamura 2009). Since then, in addition to the aforementioned regional development roles, anime characters have been utilized in collaboration with local governments to raise awareness of voting and public safety, as well as to attract tourists through posters. These endeavors have been featured on special sections of CAPCOM's official homepage.[33] Other examples of regional collaborations involving game characters include various historical games by Koei Tecmo, *Kantai Collection -KanColle* by Kadokawa Games and DMM Games (2013), and *Touken Ranbu -ONLINE-*(2015) by Nitro Plus and DMM Games (Nakamura 2021).

Traits of Digital Game Media Mix: Creating Variants to Original IP

The examples shown in Sect. 4.5.1 emphasize the Japanese consumer culture of enjoying variation without considering the integrity of the narratives across multiple media forms. This tendency enables loose coordination between entities when implementing a media mix, thereby creating more diverse touchpoints and increasing the likelihood of reaching a broader audience of potential users. Additionally, this lack of restriction enables a broad network of partnerships. The examples shown in subsection Rise of Game IP Involving the Regional Public Sector as Media Mix Collaborators, however, are closer to Steinberg's definition of marketing media mix. They are included in this section to demonstrate the uniqueness of the strategy adopted in Japan, where regional promotions using pop culture characters are commonplace. Project-based connections with the public sector are a perfect example.

4.5.2 Worldbuilding Media Mix (WMM)

Worldbuilding media mix (WMM) projects with digital games functioning as the primary IP source are widely regarded as challenging to execute. This type of media mix, which was a format conceptually derived from TRPG production methods, generally refers to a media franchise in which all media products center on a shared "worldview." Therefore, when planning a worldbuilding media mix project, it is more efficient to begin with a medium that facilitates content expansion once the world and its principles are established. However, with digital games serving as original IP, there are several compelling reasons to develop a worldbuilding media mix from a game-based IP. These include generating meaning that exceeds simple variation by integrating multiple IPs. This section analyzes the *Kingdom Hearts* franchise as an example of the former and the *Fate* franchise as an example of the latter.

33 CAPCOM, 2016. "Ninki kyarakutā o katsuyō shita chihō sōsei" [Regional revitalization utilizing popular characters] ▶ https://www.capcom.co.jp/ir/feature/2016_regional.htm

Kingdom Hearts Franchise: Mediating the Separate Disney Story Worlds by the Kingdom Hearts World System

The *Kingdom Hearts* franchise was first released on March 28, 2002, as an action RPG for the PlayStation 2. Three officially numbered titles have been released over the past 20 years, all of them action RPGs developed using the latest consoles of the time.

However, stories that could not be told in the main storyline, such as foreshadowing anecdotes and the origins of major characters and villains, were often developed into spin-off games. In such cases, the games were developed for portable game consoles, smartphones, and other platforms. Various challenges were addressed through game mechanics, including card battles, rhythm, and action sequences, utilizing the command deck system.

Thus, the franchise used different game mechanics to tell its stories. This transludic experience is the hallmark of the series.

However, this franchise sets itself apart by incorporating various Disney-branded story universes into each game stage. Furthermore, the story universe includes fantasy live-action films, classical animation, contemporary animated features, CG animation, and animated television programs. Thus, the dimension in which the main protagonists and villains advance the story can be considered a medium uniting the various story worlds within the Disney brand as separate. Moreover, the world of the protagonists is a world of light, darkness, in-between, and a fourth space, the quadratum. That is, the world lacks a clear concept of life and death. Although the narrative worlds of the Disney characters are diverse, the narrative settings, as mentioned earlier, allow the various worlds of the Disney brand to be deconstructed through game mechanics and rules, constituting what Hutchinson calls "an inner transmedia text" (Hutchinson 2018, 68).

The Fate Franchise: Connecting Game Branches as Multiverse

The *Fate* franchise is a unique media mix property that incorporates branching storylines and adventure game mechanics into its narrative structure. Branching storylines constitute a typical game design feature in adventure games, usually with good, normal, and bad endings. A player's mission is to reach good endings while avoiding bad ones. The *Fate* franchise, however, is characterized by this feature, depicting various possible worlds as separate, fully independent commercial works. Another critical element of the franchise is its premise, established with the release of *Fate/Stay Night* on January 30, 2004 (TYPE-MOON). A group of sorcerers called *Masters,* who can summon heroes and heroines from history, mythology, and folklore from all ages and cultures as *Servants* to fight over the Holy Grail, is said to grant any wish. This unique worldview, which arbitrarily incorporates historical figures and even enables gender transformation, allows the narrative to extend beyond the *Stay Night* story arc. It expands the *Fate* universe without adhering to a unified continuity, while retaining the franchise's unique brand identity. Thus, this franchise can be categorized as a WMM. The story of the *Stay Night* series is based on a novel by Kinoko Nasu, TYPE-MOON's prominent scenario writer, written as a teenager, inspired by the novel Makai Tensei, where a swordsman from the past is reincarnated into the story world. By release, the game included three routes. Nasu, the franchise's scenario writer, states that each scenario should be treated equally, with the same protagonist, but that each branch should feature a different heroine.[34] Consequently, all the branches eventually become spin-offs of the anime.

First, the protagonist, Shirou Emiya's, scenario was adapted into an anime TV series from January 7 to June 17, 2006. *Unlimited Blade Works*, however, is an anime adaptation of Rin Tohsaka's scenario, which was shown in two seasons, one starting on October 5, 2014, and the other starting on April 5, 2015. *Fate/Stay Night [Heaven's Feel],* adapted and produced as an animated movie trilogy from 2017 to 2020, was based on Sakura Matou's scenario. Furthermore, the main scenario was adapted into a manga that preceded the 2006 anime, thereby following conventional media-mix strategies (Sakagami and TYPE-MOON 2017, 70–98). Besides the *Fate/Stay Night* series, a prequel light novel series was launched by renowned author and scenario writer Gen Urobuchi. According to Sakagami and TYPE-MOON (2017), this step was the beginning of a new era for the *Fate* universe. External scenario writers, novelists, manga artists, and others began to join endeavors to expand the *Fate* universe (Sakagami and TYPE-MOON 2017, 144). In an interview, Gen Urobuchi stressed that, although Nasu Kinoko supervised the Holy Grail War and the existing characters, 90% of his ideas were approved.[35]

Urobuchi's *Fate Zero* was based on Nasu's original plot. The degree of freedom given in the creative process should be noted. As for the first volume of the *Zero* series, it was sold as a dōjinshi in December 2006. Then, a drama CD was released in 2008. The anime TV series ran for two seasons, in the fall of 2011 and the spring of 2012. Manga has also been adapted several times.

These efforts led to the establishment of a system in which multiple writers collaborated to produce works under Nasu's creative direction. The *Fate/Kaleid liner Prisma Illya* series by Hiroshi Hiroyama followed this path, with a series spanning three seasons on monthly *Comp Ace* beginning with the September 2007 issue, where the story was set in the parallel world of Fuyuki City, with Ilya as the main character.[36] The story's premise is similar to dōjin works, but note that, despite a far-fetched worldview, as the title suggests, it can still be part of the Fate universe.

Furthermore, 2010 saw the release of the cyber RPG *Fate/EXTRA* (Marvelous Entertainment 2010), while its sequel, *Fate/EXTRA CCC,* was released in 2013 (Marvelous AQL 2013), set in another parallel world. The *CCC* setting is the lunar surface in the 2030s. In contrast, the light novel *Fate/Apocrypha* was released in

34 Based on the interview with Nasu by ► Dengeki.com. 2006. "Type—Moon sutaffu ga kataru, PS 2-ban feito\ Stay Night no ima" ► Dengeki.com. ► https://dengekionline.com/soft/interview/fate/

35 Mendez and Uehara "Interview: Fate/Zero Screenwriter Gen Urobuchi Animenewsnetwork Oct 21st, 2011. ► https://www.animenewsnetwork.com/interview/2011-10-21/interview-fate-zero-screenwriter-gen-urobuchi

36 Based on the interview by the website Comic Nataly "`Feito/kaleid rainā purizuma ☆ Iriya'`feito/stay night [Heaven' s Feel]' tokushū hiroya ma Hiroshi × tasukuōna taidan"["Fate/kaleid liner Prisma☆Illya" "Fate/stay night [Heaven's Feel]" Special Feature Hiroshi Hiroyama x Task Owner Interview] July 26, 2018. ► https://natalie.mu/comic/pp/prismaillya-hf

2012 by Yuichi Higashide, an established novelist and game writer. These works depicted yet another parallel world, in which the Holy Grail War took place in Romania in the 2000s, in a timeline altered during World War II, with the system altered.

Another major turnaround after *Fate/Zero* was the launch of the smartphone game Fate/Grand Order on July. 30, 2015 (Aniplex). This is the only work in the *Fate* series in which the players themselves become Masters who summon historical heroes and set out on a journey through time and space to save humanity, which is doomed to extinction due to a timeline altered by historical singularities. While Kinoko Nasu was the original author and supervising editor of the game, several scenario writers contributed to various chapters; Nasu explained the specifics as follows:

> I make a plot outline of the entire book and give the writers a document showing what needs to be done in each chapter, along with which foreshadowings will be paid off. After that, I ask the writers to develop the plots for the different lost belts they are in charge of, and if there are no problems with my judgment, I leave the rest to them. Finally, we add foreshadowing elements related to the overall story arc while supervising the written scenario (Nasu 2019, 122).

Like other series, *Fate Grand Order (FGO)* was developed as an anthology of manga, novels, an anime TV program, and a theatrical animated film based on the game. The premise of *FGO*, where the protagonist travels to a particular place in the world in a specific historical period, allows external writers to work on creating various types of stories on different scales without conflicting with one another's works. This "system" enabled the work to proceed for a while even without Nasu's support (Nasu 2021, 96).

Thus, the *Fate* franchise is characterized by a media mix structure based on a world-building system that expands the story worlds across timelines and regions into an alternative universe, embracing the multiverse concept. Moreover, once the original work is adapted into novels or manga, it is subsequently converted into anime television programs or theatrical animated films and, following traditional media-mix practices, functions as a hybrid adaptation that contributes to world-building.

4.5.3 Storybuilding Media Mix (SMM)

As mentioned in the previous sections, RPGs are characterized by a detailed and immersive worldview. Once completed, these games can inspire the production of various media works, such as manga and anime TV shows, through transmedia storytelling techniques that incorporate elements of the games' world. The Japanese media industry fosters a loose alliance between publishing companies and animation studios, enabling the creation of transmedia narratives that are coherent across multiple media platforms. This has led to the emergence of several story-building media mix projects in Japan that offer unique and intricate narratives on a smaller scale. Three examples of such cases are presented below.

Resident Evil Franchise

In terms of IP originating from digital games, the *Resident Evil* franchise is among the most advanced to emerge from Japan, with global expansion and the maintenance of narrative integrity and consistency across the game series. Even if all the games were organized chronologically and geographically, the content would still be consolidated (Capcom n.d.). Chris Redfield appears in the first game (Capcom 1996) and subsequently in all but a few, and his character development is depicted in each game in which he appears. The storyline expands from Raccoon City to various locations, including France and Rockfort Island, a cold village in Europe, Africa, Eastern Europe, North America, China, and other global locations. Similarly, the scale of incidents traces the evolution from a virus leak at a secret Umbrella Corporation laboratory to the company's collapse and, ultimately, to bioterrorism worldwide. However, *Resident Evil 7 biohazard* (Capcom 2017) and *Resident Evil 8: The Village* (Capcom 2021) focus on ordinary people, with the former main characters appearing only in cameos. The *Outbreak* series also focuses on civilians, enabling online cooperative gameplay. In contrast, the *Chronicle* series emphasizes gunplay, allowing players to relive scenes from Resident Evil 0 through 3, as well as a Russian Umbrella facility, and introduces new elements to the storyline. The *Revelations* series, meanwhile, selects a story development more appropriate for FPS action than horror expression; it sometimes takes place between the *Resident Evil 4* and *Resident Evil 6* time periods, but in regions entirely different from the story universe.

The full CG feature films, released in October 2008, August 2012, May 2017, and July 2023, in October 2008, August 2012, May 2017, and July 2021, and four full CG animated dramas released on Netflix also fit into the story universe, allowing spectators to further deepen their understanding of the *Resident Evil* universe. Manga adds depth to the understanding of this world. Biohazard: *The Marhawa Desire*, by Naoki Serizawa, was serialized in Weekly Shonen Champion from February 23, 2012 to September 26, 2013.[37] It was set in Asia, depicted events at the Marhawa Academy, a prestigious school, and depicted the transition from *Resident Evil 5* to *Resident Evil 6*. The story was scripted by the Biohazard production team and serialized by Serizawa. The second official manga, *Resident Evil: Heavenly Island,* was serialized from January 15, 2015 to February 2, 2017. This was the story of a survival program set on an isolated island in the Caribbean Sea, where celebrities and staff are caught in a bio-terror attack.[38]

The franchise returns to the video game *Resident Evil 7: Biohazard.* The main story takes place at the Baker House, a swampy region located outside the town of Dulvey, Louisiana, where the protagonist, Ethan Winters, searches for his missing wife. From a game mechanics perspective, the series returns to the franchise's roots: survival horror, as the protagonist is severely limited in how they can use their arse-

37 Based on Akita Shoten Home Page. Biohazard: Marhawa Desire. ► https://www.akitashoten.co.jp/comics/425313291X

38 Based on Akita Shoten Home Page. Biohazard: Heavenly Islands. ► https://www.akitashoten.co.jp/comics/4253131212

nal. Furthermore, the game is fully compatible with VR mode, allowing for a fully immersive experience. *Resident Evil 8: Village* continues the harrowing journey of Ethan Winters, a civilian. After his daughter was mysteriously taken by the former protagonist of the franchise, Chris Redfield, and he was thrown into the isolated village in Eastern Europe, he was forced to fight against the creature as he sought to uncover the mystery behind Chris Redfield's actions. The latest installment in the *Resident Evil* franchise is *Resident Evil: Requiem.* The game will take players back to Raccoon City thirty years after the incident, in which the player assumes the role of Grace Ashcroft, who investigates a series of mysterious deaths at the Wrenwood Hotel, located near the now-ruined Raccoon City. The game system now combines the immersive First-Person View of *RE7* and *RE8* while also allowing players to switch to an over-the-shoulder third-person view, which is better suited for tactical combat. From a canonical perspective, Requiem is planned as the concluding chapter of the main plot, centering on the collapse of the Umbrella Corporation and its aftermath. The story of Ethan Winters in RE7 and RE8 is considered a mini-episode within the larger Resident Evil canon, while Requiem pushes the entire canon further.

Six theatrical films starring Milla Jovovich were released, all set in parallel universes, allowing Hollywood creators to exercise their creativity with a high degree of freedom and non-gamers to experience the "Resident Evil" world. The reboot of the film franchise incorporates elements of the original game series' survival-horror aesthetic, and its sequel is also scheduled for release later in 2026. These films are also considered parallel universes that will never interact with the narrative of the original canonical universe. This is consistent with Capcom's media mix (one-content multi-source) strategy, as exhibited in the *Street Fighter* franchise.

The .hack Franchise

The *.hack* franchise is a project developed for the PlayStation 2 (PS2), the first video game console that could play DVDs as well as games (Bandai 2002). Nakamura (2018a) conducted a case study of this franchise using a transmedia storytelling (TMS) analysis framework to validate its development. This section summarizes the analysis results.

The *.hack* franchise was developed for the PS2, the first video game console that could play both DVDs and games. Nakamura (2018a) confirmed that the franchise could create an entertainment experience that connects the timeline, reality, and virtual space in a consistent, unified story world across series in multiple media.

This franchise was born when Hiroshi Matsuyama, President and CEO of Cyber Connect 2, proposed to Shin Unozawa of (then) Bandai that Cyber Connect 2 fund the development of a new IP for the PlayStation 2. The IP was conceived as a project to be developed simultaneously in multiple media. PS2 was on the market, but the killer content during the initial era was DVDs. The idea was to enhance the user experience by offering anime and games as bundles. This was an idea that only Unozawa, who had already successfully launched the OVA business at Bandai, could have conceived.

With these games and OVA-bundled products as the core, the media mix experience was designed around manga, anime television series, and light novels, as in other media mix projects. Each story in the *.hack* franchise was carefully crafted to connect with or deepen the understanding of the franchise's fictional world, rather than merely serving as a simple adaptation or reinterpretation.

For example, the anime television program *.hack//Sign* ran from April 4 to September 25, 2002, before the events depicted in the game and OVA bundle products went on sale on June 20, 2002, with *.hack//Infection Vol. 1* and the first series continuously sold until the final volume, volume 4, was sold on April 10, 2003. All the volumes depicted incidents in the fictitious MMORPG, the WORLD, with the players assuming the role of Kite, the protagonist of the first series. Player data could be transferred across the volumes. The OVAs bundled with .hack//Liminality took place around the same time as the games. Each episode coincided with the game's volume but was set in the real world, rather than within the games. Thus, both works complemented each other in unraveling the secrets of the story universe.

The anime television series *.hack//Sign* continued until the second volume was released. When the third volume was released on December 12, 2002, the serial novels and manga were featured simultaneously. The fourth game was released on April 10, 2003, immediately after the broadcast of the manga adaptation of the *.hack* anime TV series, *Legend of the Golden Bracelet,* ended. Thus, the manga, anime television series, and light novels were featured before and after the launch of the driving content (in this case, the four volumes of Games and OVA-bundled products). However, they were not merely supplementary products for bundled offerings, but a vital segment of the series' fictional world.

After the first season, *the .hack* franchise spanned several seasons. The second season positioned digital games as primary products, with each title sold as a standalone console game without accompanying anime. However, transmedia strategies were implemented following the success of the first season. The first special infographic magazine dedicated to the *.hack* franchise began publication with the November 2005 issue. Then the anime series *.hack//Roots* began airing in April, a month before the release of the first volume of the season, *.hack//G.U.* The anime *.hack/Roots is* a prequel to *.hack/G.U.* As the second season introduces a new protagonist, the anime effectively tells the origin story of how he became a part of *.hack* universe. The third season, however, is mainly composed of multiple media types, including a handheld game, OVAs, a feature-length animated film, two smartphone apps, and web novels and comics. Each title essentially delved into various aspects of the *.hack* universe, expanding the story world without contradicting or introducing inconsistencies into the worldview. In other words, for the first and the second seasons, the *.hack* franchise rolled out its production lines in line with storybuilding media mix, but the final season diverged from these strategies. This diversion warrants further examination.

Final Fantasy VII Franchise and "Polymorphic" Content

One large-scale project adapting the storybuilding media mix model was Square Enix's *Final Fantasy* franchise. The *Final Fantasy* franchise, like the *Dragon Quest franchise described* in ► Sect. 4.5.1.3, was developed as a variation of media mix. However, at the fiscal year-end briefing on March 31, 2004, the company announced that it would implement the polymorphic content strategy. This strategy involves creating a more comprehensive fictional universe that would not merely tell a single story in one medium but could be expressed in many different forms. *The Compilation of Final Fantasy VII* (hereafter *The Compilation*) was announced with this vision. The compilation was based on the world of *FINAL FANTASY VII* (hereafter, the *original VII),*[39] released on January 31, 1997 (Square). The series was then expanded into anime, full-length 3D CG animation, mobile games, console games, and handheld games. Products based on this concept were released in sequence from 2004 to 2007. First, before the *Crisis: FINAL FANTASY VII* (Square 2004), a networked action RPG for cell phones, was released on September 24, 2004. It was set 6 years before *VII* from the perspective of the enemy's elite forces. This was followed by a full-length CG *Final Fantasy VII: Advent Children (*hereafter *Advent Children),* which was released on September 14, 2005.

An OVA, *Last Order—Final Fantasy VII*, which was inserted as a bonus disk into *ADVENT CHILDREN*, depicted a 5-year-old story. The anime was created by MADHOUSE, one of the top-notch anime studios that produced *Prefect Blue* and *Vampire Hunter D: Bloodlust*. *Dirge of Cerberus: Final Fantasy VII* was then released on January 26, 2006 (Square). This is a gun-action game featuring one of the supporting characters in *VII*, who is a gun-wielder. The world depicted is 3 years after *VII* or 1 year after *ADVENT CHILDREN* from the perspective of a sub-character. The last work on Compilation, the PSP action RPG *Crisis Core–Final Fantasy VII* (Square 2007), was released on September 13, 2007. The character featured in this game was the hero's best friend in *VII,* appearing only in a flashback scene. The story period spans 7 years, from just before the main story to just before the *VII* storyline. With *the Compilation*, the *Final Fantasy VII* series evolved into an ensemble drama that transcended traditional hero–villain roles. The remake of *VII* began appearing in sales on April 10, 2020 (Square Enix), making the main story itself a trilogy and expanding the world view. The *FINAL FANTASY VII, EVER CRISIS* project updated the entire *FF VII Compilation* in chapters, including a remake of *FFVII.*

39 Square Enix Annual Report Presentation 2004 ► https://web.archive.org/web/20050306003233/http://ir.square-enix.co.jp/j/pdf/0404-200405201430-01.pdf

4.6 Conclusion

This chapter demonstrates that digital games play distinct roles in media franchises, shaped by varied media mix strategies. It provides an overview of these roles and characteristics, then summarizes key findings and outlines important issues for further research.

4.6.1 Findings of the Chapter

This chapter identifies three media mix strategies for integrating a medium game into the broader media franchise business ecosystem. The key findings for each strategy are briefly explained below.

Game and Business Ecology in the Media Franchise in Japan

In Japan, the media industry, along with toy manufacturers, stationery companies, and others, has established a business ecosystem that enables consumers to access media franchises across multiple touchpoints, thereby aggregating brand equity and potential sales. When video games were introduced to a mass audience, thanks to the success of Nintendo, loose alliances of these companies also began collaborating with digital game publishers and thereby solidifying the system, either having digital games as an important subset of popular IPs or having original game IPs as the central component of this business ecosystem. Major players have changed over the decades, but the system itself has remained largely unchanged since its inception. This multimedia media deployment system is usually called a media mix in Japan. For this chapter, we identified the following media mix strategies: variation media mix (VMM), worldbuilding media mix (WMM), and storybuilding media mix.

Variation Media Mix

VMM is the most prevalent among other media mixes, as demonstrated in this chapter. Rebooting and remaking can also be part of their strategy. With this strategy, there is an "anything goes" approach, as long as fans embrace it. Every other category listed in subsequent sections is typically a subset of this media mix as part of the overall portfolio of the media franchise, as the definition of a variation media mix is most broadly interpreted.

Worldbuilding Media Mix

WMMs are closely linked to role-playing games because they draw heavily on how such games construct worlds. Variations are allowed as long as they follow the established rules of the original source. This approach enables co-creation and collaboration within a set worldview, or *Sekaikan*, making it similar to the "shared world" concept. However, in media franchises, IP holders set the initial rules, which distinguishes WMMs from shared worlds built around public-domain properties and that also include fan fiction. Thus, shared worlds are a concept that encompasses a broader range of related activities, while WMM focuses only on the context of media franchise strategies.

Storybuilding Media Mix

SMM is a media mix strategy most closely aligned with what Jenkins and others refer to as "transmedia storytelling." Narrative deployment across multiple media, with well-calculated consistency, is crucial for enabling players to engage with IPs. IP extending into digital games is uncommon, but those that do tend to tell epic stories that not only cover digital games but also develop franchises with grand narratives spanning multiple game series, as well as manga, 3D CG animated features, and television programs, as demonstrated in this chapter.

4.6.2 Issues to Be Explored in Future Studies

Despite the significant development and diversification of the media mix, research on this topic remains relatively limited. The following section explores the areas in the media mix development that require further investigation.

Media Mix and Fan Psychology

Research on fan psychology related to individual content has made some progress, but the study of fan psychology in relation to media mix development for IP has not advanced sufficiently. Further research is needed to understand how fans develop an attachment to an IP, the types of media mix development they prefer based on IP characteristics, and the overall customer journey within the media mix experience. Such research can improve our understanding of how to effectively manage an entire franchise rather than only individual works.

Media Mix and Media Franchise Management

The strategy modes of media mix in this chapter represent only a small aspect of media franchise management. Further research is needed to determine the most effective ways to create and develop an IP to secure sustainable consumer support.

For example, how should an IP be developed based on the characteristics of each experience or content, such as when created as a standalone character, narrative experience, or game experience? Not every IP will become a global media franchise overnight. However, a better understanding of the process of scaling up IP development will enable sustained success based on objective criteria rather than luck.

Media Mix and the Law

As shown in this chapter, media mix strategies are often implemented through loose collaborations between multiple companies. However, these practices have not been sufficiently examined from a legal perspective. The commercial development of IP and the proliferation of counterfeits and pirated products go hand in hand. Moreover, with the adoption of the first-to-file trademark principle in many countries, IP holders may lose their trademark rights to other companies if not secured early enough. However, the cost-effectiveness of registering an IP trademark acceptable to consumers worldwide is uncertain. Therefore, an urgent need has arisen to study the legal aspects of media mix development, such as the legal measures that should be implemented across different regions to support the creation and development of an IP as a media franchise, the strategic appropriateness of allowing secondary creations, and the ideal clauses to be created for this purpose.

4 Ludo Mix within Media Mix Strategies

Throughout the chapter, we examine various media mix franchises that integrated video games into their portfolios and find that the majority of franchises include video game products across multiple genres and versions. This is not only true of popular nongame IP such as Gundam or Dragon Ball, but also of IP that originated in computer games as the driving content of the media franchise. This is what Hanna et al. refer to as ludomix. The term ludomix was proposed at DiGRA 2019 as a relational concept that "may include several versions of the games or several different games together with other content, thus resulting in novel media ecologies, business models, and development of consumption culture (Wirman 2021)."

This chapter clarifies that, according to this definition, the practice of incorporating multiple game genres as vital components of media franchise portfolios has existed since at least the 1980s. Not only aforementioned Gundam franchise but also Star Wars franchise was one of such media franchise; only one year after the first licensed computer game was released for Atari 2600 in 1982, computer game focused on Jedi training and also Vector based First Person Acton Shooting game was released for Arcade games, already diversifying the game portfolio, perfectly coincide with the release of the final chapter of original trilogy, which was on July 2, 1983. It was also around the same period when IP originating from digital games offered a diversified ludic experience. There have been many sequels or successors to popular arcade games, such as Space Invaders, Defender, and Galaxian. However, Nintendo was likely the first company to offer sequels with completely different game mechanics. In Donkey Kong, players assume the role of Jumpman (who would later have his own spin-off). In contrast, in Donkey Kong Jr., released in 1982, players take on the role of the son of the former villain, Donkey Kong. The game mechanics were also completely different. Its successor, Donkey Kong 3, offered yet another distinct ludic experience compared with its predecessors, creating a diverse ludomix within the franchise.

As with any other media franchise, however, a certain combination of game genres persists over time, as seen in the *Dragon Quest* and *Pokémon* franchises, while others do not. It is crucial to identify the most effective ways to manage a portfolio of diverse game genres within a media franchise. This may be vital for an IP to gain sustainable development over time.

Media Mix Strategies Measurement Scale

Although there are matrices to evaluate individual creative works and business activities, there are no established indicators to evaluate the media mix development of a media franchise. To evaluate multiple works as a cohesive whole, it may be necessary to go beyond simply averaging the individual works. Additionally, the long-term added value of a media franchise cannot be accurately measured solely by sales expansion. In today's age of widespread public access to information, it is essential to consider trends in consumer and fan behavior when evaluating media franchises. Although it would be challenging to integrate all these factors into a single objective index, the creation of such an index would enable effective monitoring of media franchise development processes.

References

Akiyama, Shin, and MYST. 2013. Kidō senshi patoreibā to iu purojekuto: Patoreibā no tanjō = shōhin-ka no haikei [The project Mobile Police Patlabor: birth of Patlabor = background of commercialization]. In *The Mobile Police Patlabor: the 25th anniversary memorial book*. Tokyo: Takarajimasha.

Allison, Anne. 2000. A challenge to Hollywood? Japanese character goods hit the US. *Japanese Studies* 20 (1): 67–88.

Allison, Anne. 2006. *Millennial monsters: Japanese toys and the global imagination*. Vol. 13. Univ. of California Press.

American Broadcasting Company. 1989. The Ice Capades with Jason Bateman and Alyssa Milano. Television special. *American Broadcasting Company*, December 28. https://www.imdb.com/title/tt1716771/

Azuma, Hiroki. 2001. *Dōbutsuka suru posutomodān. Otaku kara mita Nihon shakai* [Japan's database animals: Japanese Society from the Otaku's perspective]. Tōkyō: Kōdansha.

Billboard. 1982. For cross-merchandising, 'Pac Man' made in heaven. *Billboard*, April 24, 6.

Bjarnason, Nökkvi Jarl. 2021. The Ludo mix and the loss of in-game narrative: a case study of the final fantasy XV universe. *Transactions of the Digital Games Research Association* 5 (2): 71–99.

Blom, Joleen. 2021. Characters in fire emblem three houses: a Ludo mix perspective. *Transactions of the Digital Games Research Association* 5 (2): 101–130.

Capcom Resident Evil Portal – Looking back on the Resident Evil universe (n.d.) Resident Evil Portal. Capcom. Available at: https://game.capcom.com/residentevil/en/re-history.html (Accessed: 30 May 2026).

Dengeki Hobby Web. 2018. *Majingā Z Daihyakka zuroku* [Mazinger Z Encyclopedia Catalog]. KADOKAWA Ascii Media Works.

Famikon denshō iinkai. 2016. *Shūkan Shōnenjanpu hiroku! ! Famikonshinken! ! !* [Weekly Shonen Jump Secret!! Famicom Shinken!!!]. Tokyo: Shueisha.

Famitsu.com. 2015. Josei-muke gēmu no kusawake "neoromansu" 20 shūnenkinen erikawakeiko-shi intabyū kotoshijūni "odoroku yōna kikaku" o happyō! ? (1/2). *Famitsu.com*, June 29 [Interview with Keiko Erikawa to Commemorate the 20th anniversary of 'Neo Romance', the pioneer of games for women: announcing a 'surprising project' this year! ? (1/2)]. https://www.famitsu.com/news/201506/29081240.html

FamitsuTUBE. 2023. *Eiga Sūpā Marioshanpurā Rīpōto. Miyamoto Kono sakuhin de Mario ga Nihonjin ni natta eiga e no chōsen o kataru* [YouTube]. 19 April 2023. Available at: https://www.youtube.com/watch?v=5xLZCZImYIg&t=332s (Accessed: 30 May 2026).

Haruhiki, Tsujimoto. 2010. Kabushikigaisha Kapukon [Capcom Co. Ltd.]. In *Gurōbarugēmubijinesu tettei kenkyū*, ed. Akinori Nakamura [In-depth study of the global game business]. Tokyo: KADOKAWA ASCII Research (Digital Book).

Hirayama, Tohru. 2012. *Nakimushi purodūsā no iuigonjō: TV hīrō to ayunda 50-nen* [The testament of a crybaby producer: 50 years walking with TV heroes]. Tokyo: Kōdansha.

Honma, Masayuki. 2001. *Shōnengahō Taizen:20 Seiki Bōkenkatsugeki no Shōnensekai* [Shonen Gaho Taizen: boys' world of 20th century action-paced adventure]. Shōnengahōsha.

Hutchinson, Rachael. 2018. Refracted visions: transmedia storytelling in Japanese. Games. *REPLAYING JAPAN* 00:68–76.

Ishii, Jiro. 2020. *IP no tsukurikata to hirogekata* [How to create and expand intellectual property]. Seikaisha.

Ito, Mizuko. 2001. The media mix: multiple embodiments of Japanimation characters. *Paper presented at the Society for Social Studies of Science Annual Meeting*, Boston, MA, December 1. https://mimiito.com/wp-content/uploads/2020/09/Ito.mediamix.pdf.

Ito, Mizuko. 2005. Technologies of the childhood imagination: Yugioh, media mixes, and everyday cultural production. *Structures of Participation in Digital Culture* 2005:88–111.

Ito, Seinosuke. 2019. Mashirito ga Iku! [Chūhen] 'Kore sa~a, Warui ndakedo, Sutete kureru?':"Janpu" Densetsu no Henshū-chō ga, Sū oku-en o Tsuiyashita "Doragonbōru no Gēmu jigyō" o Yōshanaku "Botsu" ni Shita Shinsō. *ITmedia.co.jp*, Nov 5 [Mashirito Goes! [Part 2] I'm sorry, but can you throw this away?: the truth about the legendary editor-in-chief of "JUMP" mercilessly rejected the "Dragon Ball game business," which had cost several hundred million yen.# SHIFT by IT media Business]. https://www.itmedia.co.jp/business/articles/1912/06/news020.html

Jenkins, Henry. 2003. Transmedia storytelling: moving characters from books to films to video games can make them stronger and more compelling. *MIT Technology Review*, January 15. https://www.technologyreview.com/s/401760/transmedia-storytelling/

Jenkins, Henry. 2006. *Convergence Culture*. New York: New York University Press.

Jenkins, Henry. 2007. Transmedia storytelling 101. *Henry Jenkins Pop Junctions*, March 21. http://henryjenkins.org/blog/2007/03/transmedia_storytelling_101.html

Kenji, Hatakeyama, and Masakazu Kubo. 2000. *Pokemonsutōrī* [Pokémon story]. Tokyo: Nikkei BP.

Kim, Gi-Hyun. 2007. 원소스 멀티유즈 OSMU 콘텐츠에 대한 연구 [A study on OSMU content: focusing on domestic and overseas success cases]. 한국디자인포럼 (*Journal of Korea Design Forum*), 16, 73–82. https://doi.org/10.21326/ksdt.2007..16.007

Kimura, Tomoya. 2020. *Tōei dōga shiron: Keiei to sōzō no teiryū* [A historical study of Toei Animation: The undercurrent of management and creation]. Tokyo: Nihon Hyōronsha.

Masuda, Hiromichi. 2007. *Anime bijinesu wa gokai sarete iru* [Anime business is misunderstood]. Tokyo: Kinema Junpōsha.

Miyahara, Teruo. (2005). *Jissroku! Shōnen magajin meisaku manga henshū fūtōki* [Real record! Shōnen Magazine masterpiece manga editing struggle chronicle]. Tokyo: Kōdansha.

Mizuno, Ryo. 2018. Dai 2-shō sekai-kan to kyarakutā [Chapter 2: The worldview and character]. In *Rōdosu Tosenki to sono jidai: Reimei-ki Kadokawa mediamikkusu shōgen-shū*, eds. Eiji Ōtsuka et al., 67–99 ["Record of Lodoss War" and its era: a collection of testimonies from Kadokawa Media Mix in the early days]. Tokyo: Kadokawa.

Nakamura, Akinori. 2009. Rekijo ttenanda? ! Sengoku akushongēmu o torimaku dōkō o tettei kaimei!:Kīwādo wa 'motenashi' to 'chihō to no koraborēshon'〜) [What's a "Rekijo"? A thorough clarification of the trends surrounding Sengoku Action Games!: the keywords are "hospitality" and "collaboration with local regions"]. *INSIDE*, Jun 17. https://www.inside-games.jp/article/2009/06/17/35859.html

Nakamura, Akinori. 2018a. Comparative case studies on transmedia storytelling practices in Japan. *Journal of College of Image, Arts and Sciences, Ritsumeikan University* 11:7–27. (in Japanese).

Nakamura, Akinori. 2018b. China game industrial history. *KADOKAWA ASCII*.

Nakamura, Akinori. 2021. [Burogu] gēmu o katsuyō shita chiiki kassei-ka o seiri Suru (sono 2) [[Blog] Organizing regional revitalization using games (Part 2)]. *Famitsu.com*, April 21. https://www.famitsu.com/serial/nakamura_game_industry/202012/02210488.html.

Nakamura, Akinori, and Susana Tosca. 2019. The mobile suit Gundam franchise: a case study of transmedia storytelling practices and the role of digital games in Japan. In *Proceedings of the 2019 DiGRA International Conference: game, play and the emerging Ludo-Mix*. http://www.digra.org/wp-content/uploads/digital-library/DiGRA_2019_paper_235.pdf

Nakamura, Akinori, and Susana, Tosca. 2020. The origin of the media mix in Japan in a media ecological perspective: examining the situation from 1917 to 1945. *Journal of College of Image, Arts and Sciences, Ritsumeikan University*, 13 (2020):31–54.
Nakamura, Akinori, and Susana Tosca. 2021. The mobile suit Gundam franchise: a case study of transmedia storytelling practices and Ludo mix in Japan. *Transactions of the Digital Games Research Association* 5 (2).
Nasu, Kinoko. 2019. Special Interview 05 Nasu kino ko-shi ni kiku" FGO" no arikata to mirai [Special Interview 05: interview with Kinoko Nasu about the state and future of "FGO"]. *Shūkan famiutsu* 2019/8/22(29) [Weekly Famitsu 2019/8/22(29)]: 120–125.
Nasu, Kinoko. 2021. Special Interview 05 Nasu kino ko-shi ni kiku" FGO" no arikata to mirai [Interview with Kinoko Nasu and Takashi Takeuchi on the 6th anniversary of "FGO"]. *Shūkan famiutsu* 2021/8/19(26) [Weekly Famitsu 2021/8/19(26)]: 120–125.
Nishimura, Shigeo. 2004. *Saraba, waga seishun no 'Shōnen Janpu'* [Farewell, 'Shōnen Jump' of my youth]. Tokyo: Gentōsha.
Noboru, Tsuburaya. 1972. *Kaijū: Urutoraman ga sodateta Tsuburaya shōhō* [Kaiju: Tsuburaya method raised by Ultraman]. Tokyo: Seikisha Shuppan.
Ōtsuka, Eiji. 1989. *Monogatari shōhi-ron: Bikkuriman no shinwa-gaku* [Narrative consumption theory: Bikkuriman's mythology]. Tokyo: Shinyosha.
Ōtsuka, Eiji. 2014. *Mediamikkusu-ka suru Nihon* [Japan becoming a media mix]. Tokyo: EASTPRESS.
Ōtsuka, Eiji. 2017. Senji-ka no mediamikkusu: Yokusan Ikka to tonari gum [Media mix under the war: the Yokusan Family and Tonari Gumi]. In *Dōin no mediamikkusu: Sō Saku Suru taishū no senji-ka, sengo*, ed. Eiji Ōtsuka, 29–53 [Media mix of mobilization: during and after the war]. Kyoto: Sinbunkaku.
Ōtsuka, Eiji. 2018. *Taisei yokusan-kai no mediamikkusu*. Tokyo: Heibonsha.
Ōtsuka, Eiji. 2020. Gensakusha Atogaki [Original author's postscript.] In *MADARA* (Blue), ed. Yoshiko Hanatsu and Eiji Ōtsuka, Vol. 1. Tokyo: Kadokawa.
Patrickson, Bronwin, and Sherman Young. 2013. The transcultural transmedia media mix. *Journal of American Studies of Turkey* 33:43–64.
Picard, M., and J. Pelletier-Gagnon. 2015. Introduction: Geemu, media mix, and the state of Japanese video game studies. *Kinephanos: Journal of Media Studies and Popular Culture* 5 (1): 1–19. http://www.kinephanos.ca/2015/geemu-media-mix/.
Pratten, Robert. 2011. *Getting started with transmedia storytelling*. London: CreateSpace.
Rikio, Harada, and Tachibana Shiina. 1986. *Adobenchāhīrōbukkusu: Sūpāmarioburazāzu gaiden* [Adventure Hero Books No. 5: Super Mario Bros. Gaiden]. Tokyo: Keibunsha.
Sato, Tatsuo. 2021. *KADOKAWA no mediamikkusu zenshi: Sabukaruchā no sōzō to hatten* [KADOKAWA media mix complete history]. Tokyo: KADOKAWA.
Sakagami, Akinari and TYPE-MOON. 2017. *TYPE-MOON no kiseki* [The trajectory of TYPE-MOON]. Tokyo: Seikaisha.
Shimura, Miyoko, 2013. *Eiga Jin Kikuchi Hiroshi* [Filmmaker Hiroshi Kikuchi]. Tokyo: Fujiwara-Shoten.
Square Enix (Planning & Production), and Studio BentStuff, eds. 2011. *Doragon Kuesuto 25th anibāsarī: Bōken no rekishisho* [Dragon Quest 25th anniversary: adventure history book] (SE-MOOK). Square Enix.
Steinberg, Mark. 2012. *Anime's media mix, franchising toys and characters in Japan*. Minneapolis: University of Minnesota Press.
Steinberg, Mark. 2015a. *Naze Nihon wa "media mikkusu suru kuni" na no ka* [Why is Japan a media mix nation?]. Supervising Ed. E. Ōtsuka, Trans. Y. Nakagawa). Kadokawa.
Steinberg, Mark. 2015b. 8-Bit Manga: Kadokawa's Madara, or, the Gameic media mix. *Kinephanos: Journal of Media Studies and Popular Culture* 5:40–52.
Sugaya, Mitsuru. 2009. Korokoro no Manga-ka-tachi ① [Mangaka of CoroCoro①]. In *Korokoro baku den 1977–2009*, ed. Shibuya Chokkaku, 172–174 [CoroCoro Record 1977–2009]. Tokyo: Asahishinsha.
Sugaya, Mitsuru. 2022. *Komikauraizu damashii: 'Kamen raidā' ni hajimaru jidō manga shi* [Comic-adaptation soul: The history of children's manga starting with 'Kamen Rider']. Tokyo: Kawade Shobō Shinsha.

Tanaka, Ema. 2009. Industrial structure of "Japan Cool" co-existence of media-mix and diversity by product commission systems in Japan. *The Journal of the Japan Association for Social and Economic Systems Studies* 30 (October): 45–53.
Terpstra, Arjan, and Tim Lapetino. 2021. *Pac-Man: birth of an icon*. London: Titan Books.
Tosca, Susana, and Akinori Nakamura. 2025. The Gundam games ecology in a media industry perspective. In *Handbook of Japanese games and gameplay*, 264–280. Routledge.
Tran, Vincent. 2024. *A brief history of the shared universe in popular culture*. PhD thesis, Swinburne University of Technology.
Uemura, Masanori, Koichi Hosoi, and Akinori Nakamura, 2013. *Famikon to sono jidai* [The life and times of the Nintendo Famicom: the birth of TV games]. Tokyo: NTT Publication.
Wang, S. 2021. Platformization, pan-entertainment and piracy: what the fast-changing Chinese mediasphere tells us about technology, policy and the state. *Journal of Digital Media & Policy* 12 (2): 293–309.
Wirman, Hanna. 2021. Introduction to the special issue on DiGRA 2019: game, play and the emerging Ludo mix. *ToDiGRA 5* (2): ix.
Yamaguchi, Katsunori, and Yasushi Watanabe. 1978. *Nihon animēshon eiga-shi* [The history of Japanese animation]. Osaka: Yubun-Printing.
Yamamoto, Naoto. 2011. *Chō jitsuroku urabanashi famimaga: Sōkan 26-nen-me ni akasa reru seisaku hiwa-shū* [Super true story behind the scenes Fami Maga: a collection of untold production stories revealed in the 26th year of its publication]. Tokyo: Tokuma Shoten.

Ludography

Aniplex. 2015. Fate grand order. iOS, Android. Tokyo, Japan.
Aniplex. 2021. Demon Slayer-Kimetsu no Yaiba- The Hinokami Chronicles. PS4, PS5, Xbox One, Xbox Series X/S and Steam. Tokyo, Japan.
Bandai. 1985. Kinnikuman muscle tag team match/tag team match: MUSCLE. Family Computer. Tokyo, Japan.
Bandai. 1989. Famikonjanpu eiyū Retsuden (Famicom Jump: Hero Retsuden). Family Computer. Tokyo, Japan.
Bandai. 2002. .hack//Infection Vol. 1 PlayStation 2. Tokyo, Japan.
Capcom. 1991. Street fighter II: the world warrior. Arcade. Osaka, Japan.
Capcom. 1996. Resident evil. PlayStation. Osaka, Japan.
Capcom. 2004. The nightmare before christmas Oogie's revenge. PlayStation 2. Osaka, Japan.
Capcom. 2005. Sengoku BASARA. PlayStation 2. Osaka, Japan.
Capcom. 2006. Sengoku BASARA 2. PlayStation2. Osaka, Japan.
Capcom. 2009. Sengoku BASARA battle heroes. PlayStation Vita. Osaka, Japan.
Capcom. 2010. Sengoku BASARA 3. PlayStation3. Osaka, Japan.
Capcom. 2011. Sengoku BASARA 3 UTAGE. PlayStation3. Osaka. Japan.
Capcom. 2017. Resident evil 7: biohazard. PlayStation 4, Xbox One. Osaka, Japan.
Capcom. 2021. Resident evil village. PlayStation 4 PlayStation 5 Stadia Windows Xbox One Xbox Series X/S. Osaka, Japan.
DMM.com. 2013. Kantai collection. Browser. Tokyo, Japan.
DMM.com. 2015. Touken Ranbu Online. iOS and Android. Tokyo, Japan.
Enix. 1986. Dragon quest (dragon warrior). Family Computer. Tokyo, Japan.
Enix. 1991. Dragon quest IV: chapters of the chosen. Super Famicom. Tokyo, Japan.
Enix. 1992. Dragon quest V: hand of the heavenly bride. Super Famicom. Tokyo, Japan.
Enix. 1995. Dragon quest VI: realm of revelation. Super Famicom. Tokyo, Japan.
Enix. 2000. Dragon quest VII: warriors of Eden. PlayStation. Tokyo, Japan.
Kadokawa. 1987. Hinotori:hōō-hen: Gaōnobōken (Phoenix chronicles: Gaou's adventure). Family Computer. Tokyo, Japan.
Koei. 1994. Angelique. Super Famicom. Yokohama, Japan.
Marvelous AQL. 2013. Fate/EXTRA CCC. PlayStation Porable. Tokyo, Japan.
Marvelous Entertainment. 2010. Fate/EXTRA. PlayStation Portable. Tokyo, Japan.
Namco. 1980. Pac-Man. Arcade. Tokyo, Japan.

4

Namco. 1984. Pac-Land. Arcade. Tokyo, Japan,
Niantic, Inc. 2016. Pokémon Go. iOS and Android, California, Japan.
Nintendo. 1983a. Popeye. Family Computer. Kyoto, Japan.
Nintendo. 1983b. Popeye's English play. Family Computer. Kyoto, Japan.
Nintendo. 1985. Super Mario Bros. Family Computer. Kyoto, Japan.
Nintendo. 1990. Super Mario World. Super Famicom. Kyoto, Japan.
Nintendo. 1996. Pokémon red, green, and blue. Gameboy. Kyoto, Japan.
Production IG. 2000. Mobile Police Patlabor: Game. Edition. PlayStation. Tokyo, Japan.
Sega. 1996. Sakura wars. Sega Saturn. Tokyo, Japan.
Square. 1997. Final fantasy VII. PlayStation. Tokyo, Japan.
Square Enix. 2002. Kingdom hearts. PlayStation 2. Tokyo, Japan.
Square Enix. 2004. Before crisis-final fantasy VII. I mode FOMA900i. Tokyo, Japan.
Square Enix. 2006. Dage of Cerberus - final fantasy VII. PlayStation 2. Tokyo, Japan.
Square Enix. 2007. Crisis core - final fantasy VII. PlayStation Portable. Tokyo, Japan.
Square Enix. 2020. Final fantasy VII REMAKE. PlayStation4. Tokyo, Japan.
Taito. 1978. Space invader. Arcade. Tokyo, Japan.
The Pokémon Company. 2016. Pokémon detective Pikachu. Nintendo 3DS, Tokyo, Japan.
The Pokémon Company. 2020. Pokémon UNITE. iOS, Android. Tokyo, Japan.
TYPE-MOON. 2004. Fate/stay night. Windows. Tokyo, Japan.
Ubisoft. 2017. Mario + Rabbids Galaxy battle. Nintendo. Switch. Paris, France.

Akinori Nakamura, Ph.D., is a Professor at the College of Image Arts and Sciences, Ritsumeikan University, and a Researcher at the Ritsumeikan Center for Game Studies. For over 20 years, his work has examined the formation and evolution of digital entertainment media in China, the United States, and Japan through the lens of business ecosystem studies. He is the author of "China Game Industrial History" (Kadokawa ASCII, 2018) and "The Chinese Game Business 2005: A Full-Scale Report" (Enterbrain, 2005). Regarding studies about transmedia and media mix, numerous studies on the Gundam franchise and its various extensions have been presented at conferences, such as DiGRA, and published as a chapter in the "Handbook of Japanese Games and Gameplay" (edited by Rachael Hutchinson). He also writes essays on this matter regularly on prominent websites, such as Famitsu.com.

A Study of Japanese Game Centers and Arcade Games

Yasuo Kawasaki

Contents

F. Ikuine et al. (eds.), *Japanese Game Studies*, https://doi.org/10.1007/978-981-95-9857-1_5

5.1 Introduction: Peculiarities of Japanese Game Center Culture

This chapter summarizes research on Japanese game centers and arcade games. In this chapter, "game center" is defined as "Facility that has created a particular cultural and entertainment space by installing coin-operated amusement machines (Arcade Game)".[1] This definition includes not only facilities similar to "Game Arcade" in the United States, but also spaces where game consoles are installed, where the main industry is already located, such as game corners inside and outside coffee shops and children's stores.

Japanese game centers have a unique history compared to similar facilities in other countries. First, as an industry, game centers have been shaped simultaneously by three streams: rooftop amusement parks (created in 1931), A place inspired by US game arcades (which flowed into Japan in the 1950s and 1960s), and small-sized children's game corners (created in various forms after World War II). And as a social background, private gambling has been completely banned since the late nineteenth century. As a result, even entertainment that is ambiguous as to whether it is gambling or not (e.g., pachinko) is strictly regulated.

The above "diverse game center culture that arose concurrently" and "strict regulations against private gambling in Japanese society" have allowed Japanese game centers to create retail space in a wide variety of locations while adhering to a complete lack of connection with gambling. As a result, game centers in the Japanese market to customers of all ages and genders. And as a result of the continuous provision of space to a variety of people, a diverse gameplay culture was also established.

On top of this, Japanese game centers have been influential in the history of video games around the world. For example, game centers were the site of the first nationwide videogame craze in Japan, centered on the *Breakout* (Atari 1976) clone game[2] and *Space Invaders* (Taito 1978).

Even after this craze, many other video game genres were developed in game centers, including "fighting games," such as the *Street Fighter* series (Capcom), which also influenced the home video game culture. Recently, they have created their own unique video game culture, such as with *Fate/Grand Order Arcade* (Sega 2018–), which works in conjunction with smartphone game content to provide a playing experience that cannot be found on other consoles.

As described above, Japanese game centers are peculiar facilities compared to those in other countries. As a result, the facility and the arcade games that exist within it have continued to have no small social impact to the present day. As a result, there are a number of literary sources documenting the achievements of game centers, as well as a small number of previous studies on the peculiar culture and space.

---

1 This definition is based on Mark, J. P. Wolf's definition of game arcades (Wolf 2012, 34), and is a redefinition of Japanese game centers based on the findings of this chapter's author, Kawasaki (2022), as a result of my doctoral research.

2 In Japan, this type of game was called a "Brokku Kuzushi (block breaker)".

5.2 Previous Studies on Japanese Arcade Games/Game Centers

Based on the above, this chapter summarizes previous studies on arcade games and game centers that are mainly referenced in Japan. As mentioned above, arcade games are seen as virtually inseparable from game centers. Therefore, when previous studies mention arcade games and surrounding phenomena, they almost always mention game centers as well. In light of the above, this chapter will also discuss cases in which studies targeting game centers mention arcade games.

Research on game centers and arcade games is divided into three main categories. The three categories of previous studies are: (1) the studies focusing mainly on game centers, (2) the historical narratives by industry persons and journalists involved in game centers, and (3) the descriptions of arcade games in the studies focusing mainly on video games. The following sections are organized in chronological order in which the studies in each category appeared.

5.2.1 The Studies Focusing Mainly on Game Centers

The first studies in which Japanese game centers were mentioned were studies and survey analyses from various fields that focused on the game centers themselves. As noted in ▶ Chap. 1, game centers were the first places in Japan where video games became popular nationwide. Therefore, studies have appeared that focus not only on the entire craze, but also on its main actors, such as *Space Invaders*, (arcade) video games, and game centers.

An early survey and analysis of the *Space Invader* craze is reported by the Society for Changing Customs in Contemporary Japan, to which Sanae Moritsu and others belong.[3] This research report attempts to investigate the "Invader" epidemic shortly after the end of the epidemic. This report begins by explaining the basic operations and characteristics of video games by comparing them to the pastimes of pachinko and television programs. This report then investigates the distribution map and internal conditions of game centers as a survey of the actual situation in Kichijoji, Tokyo, Kawaramachi, Kyoto, and finally, a survey of mass media trends. Although this report is the earliest research analysis of video games, it clarifies one of the aspects that is still often cited as an important characteristic of video games, the pleasure of interaction that allows people to move the TV screen as they wish, as a difference from TV broadcasting. In analyzing the game centers of the time, they also left behind some survey data on the actual conditions of game centers at the time, comparing urban areas with traditional areas.

References to early game centers include an analysis and discussion of early arcade games by Shinichi Nakazawa 1984 = 1988). Nakazawa's analysis focuses on how to enjoy and express the installed game machines in game centers, especially the pinball machine *Shangri-La* (Williams 1967), and the video games *Pong* (ATARI 1971), *Space Invader*, and *XEVIOUS* (Namco 1983), with particular

3 Moritsu et al. (1979).

emphasis on their operability and narrative. Nakazawa's study is important as an analysis of the state of early arcade games. In particular, "XEVIOUS" is often referenced even today because it suggests the emergence of a new community culture not found in existing pastimes, through the discovery of glitches, tricks and game strategies among players.

In addition to this, Geoffrey R. Loftus and Elizabeth F. Loftus' study of psychological analysis of video games (1983) was translated into Japanese in 1985, which includes a chapter that attempts to analyze the social and psychological aspects of Game Arcade in the United States (Nishimoto 1985, 107–144). In this chapter, Loftus used interviews and previous studies to analyze the young people who gather at Game Arcade.

As described above, the discussions that led to the current game center studies were born in the 1970s and early 1980s. On the other hand, this period of research was triggered by the nationwide craze for *Space Invaders*. Therefore, during this period, studying arcade games was practically connected to studying video games. As a result, as the video game market shifted from the introduction of the *Family Computer* (Nintendo 1983) to the home video game market, the number of studies focusing primarily on game centers in Japan declined.

The study of game centers as the main focus of the study again began in the 2000s. As noted earlier, unlike in other countries, Japanese game centers maintained their industry and culture in a wide variety of forms. Also in Japan, game centers have developed a peculiar way of being that is different from other game-playing spaces such as homes.

Among the studies that have emerged are those by Hiroyasu Kato (2011) and Yoshiaki Kijima (2014), who study communication spaces centered on players within game center facilities. Kato (2011) conducted a survey and analysis of the forming of a communication space among young people playing games in game centers from the perspective of communication studies. In particular, Kato focused on the "communication notebooks" in game centers, which are notebooks prepared by the game center for questions and interactions between store employees and players, as well as between players. In his discussion, Kato analyzes game centers as spaces where face-to-face and indirect communication mutually function, where unfocused interactions generated by various tacit understandings are facilitated by diverse gameplay cultures and communication notes.

Kato has also conducted other research and analysis between 2014 and 2019, including a survey analysis of online communities, primarily game centers, targeting high school students who use social networking services (Kato 2014), and communities within game centers that hold live events (Kato 2017), as well as field survey analysis of the game center's core customer base (Kato 2019). Arcade games are not the primary subject of these studies by Kato, but they are treated as a necessary part of the game center space.

Like Kato, Kijima (2014) also analyzes the communication space of game centers. Kijima attempts to analyze fighting game players as a whole, and then discusses the particularities of the communication space through fighting games, focusing on the community of Nakano TRF, a game center located in Nakano Ward, Tokyo. Elsewhere, Jérémie Pelletier-Gagnon (2019) analyzes players' use of communication spaces, including non-gaming use, in small Japanese game center facilities.

Regarding communication through arcade games other than video games, Bottos Benoit (2020) analyzes a group of "crane games[4]"in Japanese game centers, mainly the *UFO Catcher* series (Sega, 1985), which are particularly well developed in Japan. Benoit researches and analyzes Japanese "crane games" for their characteristics and transition, the way they are staffed, and how they communicate with customers. Benoit argues that the success of the "crane game" series is due to the existence of legal restrictions that were intentionally loosened gradually, and that the peculiarity of the "crane game," which differs from other arcade games, creates a unique communication space centering on negotiations between store staff and customers over prizes.

Additionally, Benoit (2025) investigated and analyzed the historical evolution of the crane game within the context of modern Japanese history. Benoit then used a research methodology known as Japanese "Kō-gen gaku" ("Modernology", a research approach combining qualitative data from field surveys with quantitative data obtained through fixed-point observation within those surveys) to clarify the history of crane games in Japan and their social positioning.

Other studies have targeted game centers for their history. For example, Eric Eickhorst (2006) attempts to historically position the factors that have allowed Japanese game centers to remain to the present day from the perspective of other countries.

Eickhorst traced the history of Japanese machine entertainment culture and game center history back to the Edo period (1603–1868) through the 2000s. As a result, Eickhorst considered that the natural adaptation of Japanese adult entertainment culture to mass entertainment, especially otaku culture, has helped game centers survive.

Also, studies to situate Game Arcade historically are underway mainly in Europe and the United States, and some of these have been referenced by Japanese researchers.

For example, Errki Huhtamo (2005) traces the prehistory of video games back to the freak shows of the nineteenth century and earlier, reviewing the prehistory of video games in the social context of the human-machine connection, and then tracing the historical flow of arcade games and customers exposed to video game consoles. Huhtamo's paper successfully places Game Arcade and arcade games in the cultural history of entertainment leading up to the present, arguing that digital games, which have been considered unique and disconnected compared to previous mechanical entertainment, are in fact a continuum from the nineteenth century

4 The "crane game" is a game genre also known as "claw crane" in Europe and the United States. It refers to a type of game in which prizes in a box are lifted by a device such as a key claw and carried to the location where they can be won. In Japan, various means of acquiring prizes other than Claw have been developed. It is also called "prize game" in Japan mainly because it is a game to obtain prizes.

and earlier. This paper has been translated into Japanese for easy reference in Japan (Huhtamo, Translated by Oota 2015).

Carly A. Kocurek (2015) also analyzes the factors that have transformed the US video game culture from one that originally appealed to both genders to one that is now completely male-dominated, with Game Arcade as the primary target of the transformation. Kocurek's analysis reveals the masculinity of Arcade culture in the United States, its focus on teenagers, and the complexity of social control over Game Arcade in the United States. For this reason, Kocurek's analysis has been referred to in previous studies on Game Arcade culture and the social control of Game Arcade in Japanese game center research.

While several people have attempted to socially and historically situate game centers and Game Arcade outside of Japan as described above, there are still only a few in Japan. In this context, Yasuo Kawasaki (2022) attempts a survey and analysis of the social and historical positioning of game centers from the perspective of "the factors and processes that led to the establishment of Japanese game centers in society," something that previous studies have so far failed to address. Kawasaki attributes the fact that Japanese game centers have taken root in society up to the present day to the diverse types of establishments and game-playing culture that emerged while adapting to Japan's unique social environment and culture, including gambling and the protection of youth. The study also clarifies various aspects of the culture that game centers have cultivated throughout their history with the help of previous studies, field research, and various literature sources.

As described above, there are various forms of research being conducted on current Japanese game centers and locations connected to Game Arcade.

To summarize previous studies, research and analysis on game centers has focused on the relationship between the facility itself, the communication space, and the arcade games that connect them. However, only a small number of studies have yet been conducted on game centers, mainly those mentioned above. In the future, it will be important to conduct further research and analysis on, for example, arcade games unique to Japan that exist in game centers, and on the social environment surrounding game centers.

5.2.2 The Historical Narratives by Industry Persons and Journalists Involved in Game Centers

The next research on Japanese arcade games that appeared after studies focusing mainly on game centers was the organization and analysis of game center history by industry persons involved in the game center industry and by journalists. This type of research refers to the documentation of the accumulation of literature materials and interviews by journalists and industry persons interested in the game center industry. Overall, this tends to look at game center history from the perspective of the video game industry in general.

As background for this type of research, Japanese game centers had a major impact on the history of video games in the early days, and the main market was shifting to home use. For this reason, game center histories were beginning to be written, including from the perspective of video game history, with the main goal of preserving the achievements of arcade games and game centers so that players and industry persons would not forget them.

Perhaps because of the above history, there are books on this type of literature that organize game center history for game players first (e.g., Shinseisya 1991). Other examples include an editorial by Suzuki Hisashi (1989), a Sega employee, a book by Katsunori Manabe (1998), the founder of medal games, and the book written by Taito as a company history (Kabushiki Gaisha Taito Syashi Hensyu Iinnkai 1993), which is an attempt to organize the company's history for industry persons and as an internal document.

Others, such as Yasunori Nakafuji (1997), editor-in-chief of "Monthly Amusement Industry" (Amusement Industry Publishing Corp., 1972–), an industry-specific magazine, have organized the history of the amusement industry, centering on amusement machines, and by extension the history of game centers, from his own perspective, and compiled it into research notes.

Of particular importance among the literary materials organized by journalists like Nakafuji is the book by Masumi Akagi, editor-in-chief of "Game Machine," (Amusement Press Inc., 1974–)[5] a magazine dedicated to the game center industry, who organized his own materials, experience, and knowledge into a book (Akagi 2005). To clarify the developments in the game center industry in general, Akagi focuses in particular on the corporate history and the history of copyright-related lawsuits, as well as the history before and after the enactment of the Entertainment Establishment Law, covering not only Japanese but also Western history.

The history of Japanese game centers has been written by journalists and volunteers not only in Japan but also in the West.

For example, Steven L. Kent (2001) uses interviews and various sources to organize the history of video games; in his book, Kent presents some of the history of Japanese game centers in the 1970s. There are various other references, like Kent's, that also describe game center history in the course of organizing video game history. Tristan Donovan (2010), in particular, differentiates himself from Kent, who focuses mainly on US game history, by discussing the history of video games and game centers in European countries and Japan. This makes it easy to refer to when making comparisons of game center histories in different countries.

The above descriptions of game center and arcade game history increased in the 2000s for a variety of reasons. As of 2022, there are books compiling personal memoirs and interviews about game development experiences by publishers,[6] interviews with arcade game developers and game center operators on Internet sites,[7]

5 Currently, "The Game Machine" Magazine is officially electronically archived and can be cited academically. For more information, see the website (▶ https://onitama.tv/gamemachine/archive.html, Last Confirmation Date: 2022.09.25).

6 Examples include Satoshi Tajiri (2002), Moriyuki Shigihara (2007), and Zenji Ishi (2017, 2025).

7 For example, there is "Game Culture Preservation Institute" (▶ https://igcc.jp/, Last Confirmation Date: 2022.09.25) and "Denfaminico Gamer" (▶ https://news.denfaminicogamer.jp/, Last Confirmation Date: 2022.09.25).

and even individually produced doujinshi,[8] especially in Western countries and Japan. There are also movie projects that look back on arcade game series while interviewing developers, players, and other people involved at the time (e.g., Enterbrain 2003a, b).

Some of these are difficult to use due to issues of reliability of the materials and the subjectivity of the authors, which is highly intertwined. However, in general, there are many scattered documents and historical materials organized by developers, experts, and industry professionals based on their own experiences and knowledge of the time. Therefore, it can be said that the basic foundation for research on the history of Japanese game centers is gradually beginning to be solidified.

However, these references should be used with caution when referring to them as research. In particular, Huhtamo (2005) points out that these documents mainly describe important people and important works, and not so much peripheral events, and that even when they do touch on video game "prehistory," it is obligatory and not in the direction of investigating and analyzing connections with the past and other social contexts.

Futamo then analyzes that many of those writing game histories have digital games as their original experience, and thus their desire to compile a history of games that they have had intense experiences with comes first. As a result, they lack a critical and analytical approach to the subject matter they deal with (Huhtamo 2005, 4–5, 2015, 110–114).

To the extent of my knowledge, most of the documents in this case are either statements of fact, or are intended as retrospectives or preservations of one's own memory. Therefore, the accuracy and reliability of the descriptions often depend on the memories and perceptions of the parties involved. Also, when used for research, it should be noted that these references focus on too much praise for the game and the industry, and too much hostility toward social control and what the parties dislike.[9]

---

8 For example, there is the "Ultimate Video Game List" series by the doujinshi circle AMP GROUP. This is a dojinshi that catalogs Japanese arcade video games from the earliest days to the time of publication, including titles that were changed during the development process. Akagi also highly appreciates this coterie magazine, which he reorganized into a book in 2006, using reference materials from Japan and the United States, including this coterie magazine.

9 For example, when the social control over Japanese game centers is dealt with in the literature and previous studies, it mainly describes opinions that defend the game center industry, with only a few exceptions. As for social control itself, the game center industry has mostly written negative comments about control. The content of the denials is also negative in some cases, such as Akagi (2005, 310–328), who writes about the historical process and concludes almost all of it negatively against the methods of public authorities, and in others, such as Ishi (2017, 148–163), who introduces the surrounding social situation but also negatively through his own experiences in game centers, as in many cases, he suggests a negative opinion.

5.2.3 The Descriptions of Arcade Games in the Studies Focusing Mainly on Video Games

In Japanese arcade and game center studies, the last area to emerge is a reference to the achievements and position of game centers from the perspective of video game studies. As mentioned earlier, game centers and arcade games have had a significant impact on the history of video games. Therefore, from the perspective of global video game history, some studies have analyzed Japanese game centers, Game Arcade in the United States, and the arcade game machines installed in those facilities.

Naoki Fujita (1999), for example, reviewed the history of game centers up to around the 1970s, and then described the technological importance of early arcade video game titles in the history of video games. For this perspective on the history of technology, United States and European studies, such as Mark J. P. Wolf (2007), which is mainly an analysis of US game history, have also been referenced in Japan.

Moreover, early game center history is also important in terms of the formation of game culture, and as a result, there are various studies. For example, Shinichi Nakazawa's 1984 survey and analysis described in ► Sect. 5.2.1 of this chapter is considered important as an analysis of video games in the early history of game studies. However, it is mainly an analysis of arcade games and player culture in the early history of game centers. In addition, Masayuki Uemura, Koichi Hosoi, and Akinori Nakamura (2013) analyze only the social and industrial impact of the *Family Computer* mainly. However, as a preliminary step, they suggest that early arcade game consoles centered on *Space Invader* had a significant impact on the formation of video game culture in Japan and the United States.

In addition to game culture, the history of the game center industry is also being analyzed. The gaming industry has become a global industry over the past half-century or so, and each country has its own unique historical flow, each with its own complex history. To reorganize this complex history, there have been attempts to summarize it with a focus on the Japanese industry, as in Yusuke Koyama (2016). There are also attempts to get a rough grasp of the history of the industry worldwide by organizing the history and current status of the industry in each country, as in *Video Games Around the World* (Wolf 2015), compiled by Mark J.P. Wolf. Of these, the game center history is still important. Koyama, for example, has his own chapter analyzing arcade games, and in the chapter organizing Japanese and United States in Video Games Around the World (Wolf 2015), he describes the achievements and current status of game centers.

In this other example, Sayawaka (2012) comprehensively focuses on individual video games and looks at games from a perspective similar to that of art history. In this book, Sayawaka looks at arcade games with a focus on sensory games such as Sega's "Hang On" (Sega, 1985) and fighting games, while providing an overview of game center history from the 1980s to the 1990s. In addition, Nakagawa Daichi (2016) has organized the history of video games mainly from the perspective of the history of contemporary thought and social thought. In this book, Nakagawa provides a bird's-eye view of major arcade game productions from the early days to the 2000s, analyzing them overlaid with their respective social conditions. In an international study, Todd Harper (2013), in his analysis and discussion of "fighting game" culture in video game culture, also includes a chapter on the importance of game centers and game centers, and also mentions Japanese arcade games.

Other oral history-style reports in the Hitotsubashi University Innovation Center's RESEARCH LIBRARY interviewed people involved in the history of the video game industry about their memories of development and management experiences at the time.[10] Many of the developers interviewed in this report are early arcade game developers, and many of their reports are related to the history of the arcade game industry.

Overall, descriptions of arcade games and game center history from the perspective of video game studies focus primarily on industrial history, early game productions, and the importance of specific genres, as described above. On the other hand, since the 2000s, there have been various forms of video games that operate in a different chassis than previous video games, and previous studies have pointed out some of their importance. In the future, it would be important for video game studies to conduct research on the state of these games and other video game consoles and genres other than those currently covered.

5.3 Conclusion: Future Challenges and Prospects for Arcade Games and Game Centers Research

As mentioned above, there have been various forms of research and accumulation through literature sources targeting game centers and arcade games. In this transition, there were also various studies on the relationship with industrial history, player culture, and historical and social positioning.

On the other hand, the number of studies on arcade games and game centers is still small compared to that of home video games, and it is important to continue to promote research in this area. In particular, arcade game research, both in Japan and in the United States, has focused primarily on video games, with little research on other game machines.

Medal game machines, for example, were "gambling games completely devoid of gambling elements" using non-convertible medals, which were born out of Japan's unique social conditions (Manabe 1998). However, the medal game has changed significantly today, incorporating elements of video games as well, except for the lack of gambling, and some games have become a completely different genre of game.

Furthermore, Benoit (2025) conducted research on prize games, and such initiatives require further development. A wide variety of other game machines and devices exist in game centers, many of which have yet to be researched and studied.

10 "RESEARCH LIBRARY", Hitotsubashi University Innovation Center (▸ http://pubs.iir.hit-u.ac.jp/ja/pdfs/index?cid%5b%5d=6&lid%5b%5d=51&lid%5b%5d=52&q=%2318-&s=di&ppc=20, Last Confirmation Date: 2022.09.25).

Other studies of the relationship between game centers and the social conditions surrounding them are also lacking. In particular, social control over game centers has had a major impact on arcade games, and has influenced the current video game culture.

Finally, comparisons between these Japanese game centers and foreign game centers will be necessary in the future. It is important to compare game center-like facilities in other countries with Japanese game centers in terms of their evolution to the present, the influence they have received from the social background, and the major works they have produced, in order to study not only the game center culture but also the video game culture in general. Including these and other factors, it would be beneficial for the future development of game center research if the situation of game centers and similar facilities is grasped on a worldwide basis and discussions are conducted jointly in each country.

References

Akagi, Masumi. 2005. *Sore ha "Ponn" Kara Hajimatta Ākēdo TV-Gēmu no Naritachi* [It began with "Pong" The origins of arcade TV games]. Amusement Press, inc.

Benoit, Bottos. 2020. Kurēn Gēmu ga Nihon no Gēmu Sentā Bunka ni Motarasita Henka -Amūsumento Sangyō Toshiteno Sokumen to Gēmu Sentā Tennin no Yakuwari ni Chakumoku Shite - [The change that crane games have brought to Japanese game center culture -focusing on the aspect as an amusement industry and the role of game center staff]. *Gendai Fūzoku Gaku Kenkyū* [Bulletin of Society for Changing Customs in Contemporary Japan] 20: 3–11.

Benoit, Bottos. 2025. *Kurēn Gēmu Kenkyū: Keihu-gaku, Kōgen-gaku, Media-ron*, [The medium of the crane game: archaelogy, modernology, theory]. Fukumura Shuppan.

Daichi, Nakagawa. 2016. *Gendai Gēmu Zenshi Bunmei no Yūgishi-kan Kara* [A complete history of modern games: from the history of games of civilization]. Hayakawa Shobō.

Donovan, Tristan. 2010. *Replay: the history of video games*. Yellow Ant Media Ltd.

Eickhorst, Eric. 2006. *Game centers: a historical and cultural analysis of japan video amusement establishments*. University of Kansas. M.A. Thesis.

Enterbrain. 2003a. *Famitsū DVD Bideo STREET FIGHTER SAGA Kakutou Bushin Den* [Famitsu DVD video STREET FIGHTER SAGA KAKUTOU BUSHINDEN]. Enterbrain.

Enterbrain. 2003b. *Bācha Faitā 10 Nen no Kiseki* [Virtua Fighter: 10 Years of History]. Enterbrain.

Fujita, Naoki. 1999. "Famikon" Toujou Mae no Nihon Bideo *Gēmu Sangyō* Gendai Bideo *Gēmu Sangyō* no Keiseikatei (2) [The Japanese Video Game Industry before the "Famicom": the formation of the modern video game industry (2)]. *Keizai Rongi* [Economic Series in Kyoto University] 163: 59–76.

Harper, Todd. 2013. *The culture of digital fighting games: performance and practice*. London: Routledge.

Hisashi, Suzuki. 1989. Gēmu Sentā ha Haiteku Entateinnmento wo Mezasu [Game centers aim for high-tech entertainment]. *Nihon Kikai Gakkai Shi* [Journal of the Society of Mechanical Engineers] 92(851): 943–946.

Huhtamo, Erkki. 2005. Slots of fun, slots of trouble: an archaeology of arcade gaming. In *Handbook of computer game studies. Cambridge*, ed. Joost Raessens and Jeffrey Goldstein, 3–21. Massachusetts: The MIT Press.

Huhtamo, Erkki. 2015. Yukai na Surotto, Komatta Surotto- Ākedo Gēmu no Kouko Gaku [Slots of fun, slots of trouble: an archaeology of arcade gaming]. In *Media Kouko Gaku* [Media archaeology]. Trans. Junki Oota, 107–146. NTT Shuppan.

Ishi, Zenji. 2017. *Gēmu Sentā Kuronikuru ~Boku ha Jinsei no Taihan wo Gēmu Sentā de Sugosita~* [Game center chronicles -I lived most of my life in a game center-]. Standards.

Ishi, Zenji. 2025, *Gēmu Sentā wo 10 Bai Omoshiroku Shita Hon!* [The book that makes game centers 10 times more fun!], Standards.

Kabushiki Gaisha Taito Syashi Hensyu Iinnkai [Editorial Committee for Taito Corporation's corporate history]. 1993. *40th history of Taito Corporation: Asobi Dukuri 40 Nen no Ayumi* [40th history of Taito Corporation: about 40 years of creating games]. Taito.

Kato, Hiroyasu. 2011. *Gēmu Sentā Bunkaron Medexia Jidai no Komyunikēsyon* [Game center culture theory: communication in media age]. Shinsen-sha.

Kato, Hiroyasu. 2014. Dai 8 Shou Onrain Jidai no Gēmu Sentā [Chapter 8: Game centers in the online era]. In *Dejitaru no Kiwa* [At the time of digital], ed. Shigeo Kawashima, 267–305. Seigakuin Daigaku Shuppan Kai.

Kato, Hiroyasu. 2017. Dai 4 Shou Gēmu Jikkyou Ibento - Gēmu Sentā ni Okeru Jikkyou no Seiritsu wo Tegakari ni [Chapter 4: Game live events: the establishment of live events in game centers]. In *Gendai Medexia/Ibento Ron Paburikku Byūingu Kara Gēmu Jikkyou Made* [Contemporary media and event theory: from public viewing to live video games], eds. Yutaka Iida and Shoko Tateishi, 109–151. Keisou Shobou.

Kato, Hiroyasu. 2019. Dai 3 Shou Gēmu Sentā Kougen Gaku - Gēmu Sentā ni Okeru Kourei-sha Zouka no Gensetsu wo Megutte [Chapter 3: Game center study of modern social phenomena: the discourse on the increase in the number of elderly people in game centers]. In *Ta-genka Suru Gēmu Bunka to Shakai: Gēmu Bunka, Soshite Gēmu Kenkyū no Genzaikei* [Diversifying game culture and society: present state of game culture and game studies], eds. Hiroshi Matsui, Takanori Igushi, Masumi Ōishi and Mikako Hata, 67–89. New Games Order.

Kawasaki, Yasuo. 2022. *Nihon no "Gēmu Sentā" Shi: Goraku Shisetsu Toshite no Hensen to Syakaiteki Ichiduke* [The history of "Game Centers" in Japan: historical changing and social positioning as entertainment facilities]. Fukumura Shuppan.

Kent, Steven L. 2001. *The ultimate history of video games: the story behind the craze that touched our lives and changed the world.* Roseville, CA: Prima Publishing.

Kijima, Yoshimasa. 2014. Kakutō Gēmu no Otaku Komyunitexi Karera ha Nani wo "Kisotte" Irunoka [The Fighting Game Otaku Community: What Are They "Competing" For?]. In *Otaku-teki Souzou-ryoku no Rimitto* [The limits of the Otaku imagination], eds. Shinji Miyadai, Izumi Tsuji, Daisuke Okabe, and Mizuko Ito, 405–441.

Kocurek, Carly A. 2015. *Coin-operated Americans: rebooting boyhood at the video game arcade.* Minnesota: University of Minnesota Press.

Koyama, Yusuke. 2016. *Nihon Dejitaru Gēmu Sangyō Shi* [History of the Japanese digital game industry]. Jinbun Shoin.

Loftus, Geoffrey R., and Elizabeth F. Loftus. 1985. *Bideo Gēmu no Shinri-gaku Kodomo no Sainō wo Nobasu Sono Himitsu* [The psychology of video games: the secrets of developing children's talent]. Tlans. Takehiko Nishimoto. Companion Shuppan.

Manabe, Katsunori. 1998. *Korekara Masumasu 4-Jigen Gēmu Sangyō ga Omoshiroi* [The four-dimensional game industry will become more and more interesting in the future]. Kanki Shuppan.

Moritsu, Sanae, Michitarou Tada, Hidemitsu Tabuki, Takuji Okuno, Kohei Tsunemi, Shoichi Inoue, and Yasuyuki Kawaura. 1979. Shiryō Hōkoku Inbēdā no Ryūkō [Material report the invader craze]. In *Gendai Fūzoku '79* [Contemporary customs '79], 26–43.

Nakafuji, Yasunori. 1997. Waga Kuni ni Okeru Amūsumento Sangyō no Seiritsu to Hatten: Nokisaki Shōbai kara Gēmu Sentā Soshite Toshi no Naka no Yūenchi he [The expansion of the amusement industry in Japan]. *Shinshu Tanki Daigaku Kenkyū Kiyō* [Shinshu Junior College Research Bulletin] 9(1): 66–76.

Nakazawa, Shinichi. 1988. Gēmu Frīku ha Bagu to Tawamureru [Game freaks playing with bugs]. In *Seppen Kyokusen Ron* [Snow flake threads theory], 174–197. Chuo Kouron-Sha. (First appearance: 1984. *Gendai Shisou*, Seido Sha, 12(6): 190–203.)

Pelletier-Gagnon, Jérémie. 2019. Players, cabinets, and the space in-between: case studies of non-ludic negotiation of video game cabinet spaces in Japanese game centers. *REPLAYING JAPAN* 1: 29–39.

Sayawaka. 2012. *Bokutachi no Gēmu Shi* [The gistory of games for us]. Seikai Sha.

Shigihara, Moriyuki. 2007. Gēmu Shokunin Dai 1 Shou [Game craftsman chapter 1]. Micro Magazine Sha.
Shinsei Sha. 1991. *Gekkan Gēmesto Zoukan Za Besuto Gēmu Shijou Saikyou no Bideo Gēmu Hon!!* [Monthly Gamest extra issue The best game: the strongest video game book ever!]. Shinsei Sha.
Tajiri, Satoshi. 2002. *Pakku Rando de Tsukamaete – Terebi Gēmu no Seishun Monogatari* [Caught in Pac Land - a coming-of-age story of video games]. Enterbrain.
Uemura, Masayuki, Koichi Hosoi, and Akinori Nakamura. 2013. *Famikon to Sono Jidai* [The Famicom and its era]. NTT Shuppan.
Wolf, Mark J. P., ed. 2007. *The video game explosion: a history from PONG to playstation and beyond.* Westport, CT: Greenwood Press.
Wolf, Mark J. P. 2012. Arcade. In *Encyclopedia of video games: the culture, technology, and art of gaming*, ed. Mark J. P. Wolf, vol. 01, 34–37. Westport, CT: Greenwood Press.
Wolf, Mark J. P., ed. 2015. *Video games around the world.* Cambridge, MA: The MIT Press.

Yasuo Kawasaki, He received his Doctor of Philosophy degree in 2020. Currently, he is a Research Fellow at the Kinugasa Research Institute, Ritsumeikan University. His doctoral research examined the historical and sociological aspects of game culture, particularly the process by which Japanese game centers took root in society. He is currently conducting social historical research focusing on the relationship between game culture and society, particularly regional difference. He is the author of Nihon no "Gēmu Sentā" Shi: Goraku Shisetsu Toshite no Hensen to Syakaiteki Ichiduke [The History of "Game Centers" in Japan: Historical Changing and Social Positioning as Entertainment Facilities], 2022, Fukumura Shuppan.

Exploring the History of Independent Digital Games in Japan, with a Focus on "Doujin Games"

Nobushige Kobayashi

Contents

F. Ikuine et al. (eds.), *Japanese Game Studies*, https://doi.org/10.1007/978-981-95-9857-1_6

6.1 Introduction

This paper aims to describe the history of independent[1] or self-made digital games in Japan. More specifically, this study discusses the history of doujin games that have been distributed at doujin events ("Doujinshi Sokubaikai" (同人誌即売会)), doujin shops, and other related venues.

A doujin event is a gathering where people with shared hobbies and interests—referred to in Japanese as "doujin" (同人)—distribute independent works such as manga, novels, games, and music, and interact with each other. While paper publications called "doujinshi" (同人誌) are the main focus at these events, digital games are also distributed. These games are typically called "doujin software" (同人ソフト) or "doujin games" (同人ゲーム).[2]

Independent digital games have existed in Japan since the 1970s, and of these games, doujin games have particularly attracted academic attention. Since the 2000s in particular, original doujin games such as "Tsukihime," "Higurashi When They Cry," "Toho Project," "Corpse Party," "Lucetia," and "The House in Fata Morgana" have become popular. These alternative games, born outside the traditional game industries, have garnered attention not only in Japan but also internationally (◘ Figs. 6.1, 6.2, and 6.3).

◘ **Fig. 6.1** Examples of doujin games on CD-ROM and DVD-ROM

1 In this paper, the term "independent games" refers to games that creators plan and produce independently, outside of large-scale commercial production.

2 Independent digital games distributed at doujin events are generally referred to as "doujin software" within the doujin community. However, since the term "doujin software" can also encompass CG collections and animations, this paper will use "doujin games" to specifically refer to these games. While doujin games can also include analog games such as board games, this paper focuses exclusively on digital doujin games that run on computers.

Fig. 6.2 Doujin game distribution at a doujin event (2010)

Fig. 6.3 Doujin game distribution at a doujin shop (2013)

Game studies have shown that the Western digital game industries were established and developed partly on the basis of self-made games by hobbyists (Levy 1984; King et al. 2003; Tyni and Sotamaa 2014; Mäyrä 2015; Hichibe 2013; Kobayashi 2019; Lehtonen et al. 2019). Similarly, in Japan, doujin games and other independent games have had a significant impact on the establishment and development of the game industries (Hichibe 2013; Kobayashi (Hichibe) and Koyama 2020). Therefore, understanding the history of independent games (doujin games) in Japan is considered crucial for the study of Japanese games and their history.

However, to the best of my knowledge, there are very few studies written in English that focus on the history of Japanese independent games. While several researchers (e.g., Ito 2007; Hichibe 2006, 2009a, 2009b, 2010, 2011; Picard 2013; Hichibe and Tanaka 2016; Vogel 2017; Helland 2018; Imagire 2018; Fiadotau 2019) have attempted to clarify the characteristics of Japanese independent games, especially doujin games, by comparing them with Japanese commercial and overseas independent games, their studies have not focused on their history. In contrast, Hichibe (2013), Miyake (2011), and Kobayashi (2024) have explored the history of doujin games, but their works are written in Japanese. Two works, Kobayashi (Hichibe) and Koyama (2020) and Grau de Pablos (2024), describe this history in English. However, the former focuses on the period from the 1970s to the 1980s when the games first emerged, while the latter concentrates on the late 2000s onwards, when Japanese doujin games began to gain international attention. Koyama (2023), who discusses the history of digital games in Japan, also touches upon doujin games but provides limited information. Thus, this study discusses the history of Japanese independent games, particularly doujin games, from the 1970s to the 2020s, based on the author's research (Hichibe 2013; Kobayashi and Koyama 2020; Kobayashi 2024, etc.). By doing so, this paper aims to fill these research gaps and contribute to the further development of research in this field.

Before proceeding, it is important to note what this paper will not cover. The differences between the content of doujin, indie, and commercial games, as well as the motivations and habits of their creators, are interesting topics, but they will not be addressed in this paper. This is because these topics have already been discussed in detail in English by Hichibe and Tanaka (2016). Those interested in these topics should refer to that publication, or to Kobayashi (2024), although the latter is written in Japanese (an English translation is planned).

6.2 Methods

To address the research questions of this study, data were collected and analyzed through interviews, questionnaire surveys, and document research.

Interviews were conducted mainly between July 2004 and August 2014 with 78 independent game creators (doujin game creators) who distribute their games at doujin events etc., as well as with event staff and doujinshi consignment stores (doujin shops). The long duration of the research was due to the author's involvement in another project.

The interview method was semi-structured, with main questions provided to the interviewees in advance and additional questions asked during and after each interview. Interviews were often conducted by the author alone, but sometimes other researchers and creators were present.

Of the interviewees, 71 were male, seven were female, and 43 were professional game creators. In terms of age, 30 were in their 20s, 36 in their 30s, and nine in their

40s. The ages of five interviewees were unknown because they did not respond to the question, or we neglected to ask.

To clarify recent changes in the creative activities of doujin game creators, this study also utilized presentation materials from five doujin game creators at the workshop "Trends of Doujin Games After 10 Years," held by the author in March 2018 at Digital Hollywood University in Tokyo. Additionally, it incorporated information from interviews conducted in January 2020 with two organizers of the doujin and indie game exhibition and sales event "Digital Game Expo" (デジゲー博).

Furthermore, to supplement the results of the qualitative data analysis, this study utilized quantitative data from the 30th, 35th, and 40th anniversary surveys of "Comic Market (Comiket)" (コミックマーケット [コミケット]), Japan's largest doujin event, as well as a survey conducted at the Digital Game Expo 2020.

The Comiket 30th Anniversary Survey was a comprehensive survey of doujin creators (referred to as "circles"), staff, and general participants of Comiket 66 in August 2004. Similarly, the 35th anniversary survey was conducted at Comiket 78 in August 2010, and the 40th anniversary survey at Comiket 88 in August 2015. These surveys were administered via paper or web-based questionnaires. This study used the results of the 30th anniversary survey published by the Comic Market Committee (2005) and analyzed the raw data from the 35th and 40th anniversary surveys.[3]

In contrast, the Digital Game Expo 2020 survey was a complete survey of all exhibitors and sponsors conducted by the event's committee and the authors on November 29, 2020 (Digital Game Research Group 2020). This was a web-based questionnaire survey using Google Forms. For this research, the data from the exhibitors was used.

6.3 The History of Independent Games in Japan, with a Focus on Doujin Games

Based on the data obtained from the methods described in ► Sect. 6.2, ◘ Table 6.1 summarizes the history of Japanese independent games, particularly doujin games, from the late 1970s to the present, by dividing it into five periods. The characteristics of these periods are discussed below.

6.3.1 Period of Establishment: Late 1970s to 1980s[4]

In August 1976, the popularity of the "TK-80" microcomputer assembly kit from NEC sparked a boom in microcomputers and personal computers (PCs) in Japan.

3 Permission to use the data from the 35th and 40th anniversary surveys was obtained from the respective organizations.
4 For a more detailed discussion of this section's content, please refer to Kobayashi (Hichibe) and Koyama (2020).

Table 6.1 The history of independent games in Japan, with a focus on doujin games

Period	Characteristics
Period of establishment (Late 1970s–1980s)	Through publishing and networking in magazines and doujin events, amateur independent creators developed their skills, gained recognition, built connections, and earned income. The transition of some of these creators into the commercial game industries also had a significant impact on their establishment in Japan.
Period of stagnation (Early 1990s)	While changes in the game production environment caused doujin game production to stagnate, Sony computer entertainment's (SCE) support for entrepreneurs helped some doujin creators move into the console game industry with the launch of the PlayStation. This migration of talent, however, also had a negative impact on the doujin game production field, causing its production to stagnate even further.
Period of revival (Late 1990s)	The number of independent games for windows PCs increased, and popular parody doujin games began to emerge. Free game engines created by doujin creators also became available, though support for production and distribution from the Japanese console game industry remained minimal.
Period of development (2000s)	A domestic doujin distribution system, centered around doujin events and shops, was developed. This led to the emergence of hit original games and creators who could make a living from their independent game sales. Similar to the previous period, there was virtually no support from the Japanese console game industry.
Period of globalization (2010s onwards)	The spread of game engines, the rise of online platforms, and sales and translation support have enabled doujin games to be sold easily and globally on a variety of devices. While the number of events and festivals for independent games has increased, the influence of Comiket has waned, and the number of doujin shops has also declined. Furthermore, face-to-face interaction has largely been replaced by social media, and more creators now identify as "indie" rather than "doujin."

The first Japanese microcomputer magazine, "I/O," was published that November, with "ASCII" and "Micom" following in 1977. This period saw a rapid succession of microcomputers, PCs, and game consoles released by Japanese manufacturers. Notable examples include the MZ-80K (1978), PC-8001 (1979), PC-6001, PC-8801, FM-8 (1981), PC-9801, FM-7 (1982), MSX, and the Family Computer (1983). Distributors and retailers also began to appear, and the personal computer market quickly took shape (Sekiguchi 2000, 180–202).

However, at the time, there was little software available for PCs, especially games that were popular with users. As a result, users had to make their own games. They would read PC manuals or type out game programs published in magazines to play them. Some people also modified commercial game programs or created their own from scratch. PC retailers sometimes bought games from these amateur creators to offer as bonuses with new PCs or sold them on consignment. Other creators simply submitted their games to magazines.

Among the PC magazines of the time, "Micom Basic Magazine" (◘ Fig. 6.4), published by Dempa Shimbun-Sha starting in 1982, was the most popular. It reached a peak circulation of 300,000 copies per month. The magazine gained popularity because it featured more articles on the following topics than its competitors:

1. Many easy-to-enter program listings in various BASIC languages, some of which were submitted by readers.
2. Programs for rare or discontinued hardware that didn't sell well.
3. Articles with game walkthroughs.

Another magazine that influenced Japan's game production culture in the 1980s was "LOGiN," initially launched in 1982 by ASCII Corporation as a separate volume of its more serious computer magazine "ASCII." LOGiN focused more on games and entertainment. The magazine also called for game program submissions and hired the amateur creators as staff for ASCII Corporation's game production division.[5]

Additionally, the LOGiN editorial team spearheaded the production of "The Hokkaido Serial Murder Case: The Okhotsk Disappearance," an adventure game

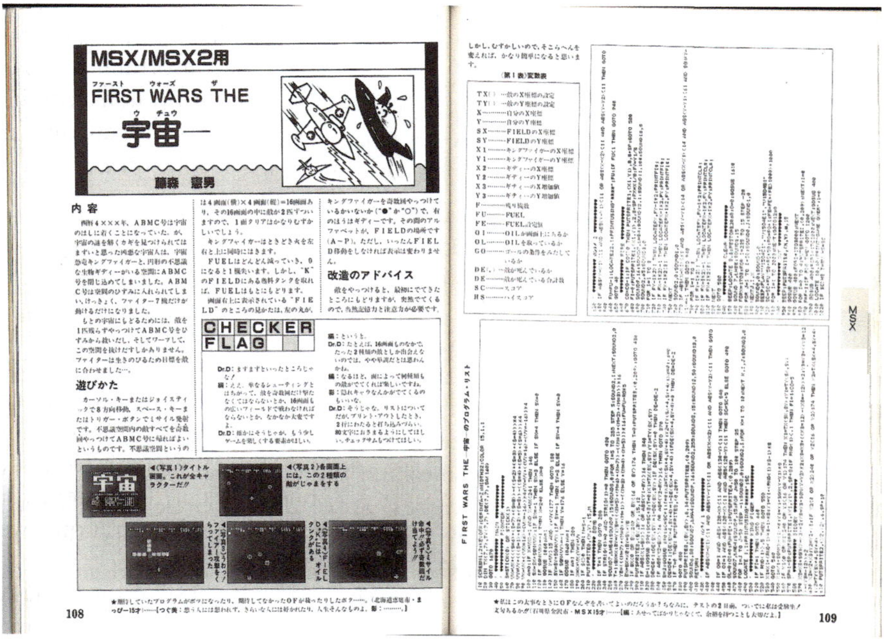

◘ **Fig. 6.4** A sample page from Micom BASIC magazine

5 One such creator was Hiroyuki Sonobe, the future producer of "Best Play Pro Baseball" and "Derby Stallion."

written by freelance writer and manga story writer Yuji Horii. The magazine also published articles about the game's production process in 1984. Horii, who would later become famous for the "Dragon Quest" series, also collaborated with LOGiN editors Gozo Shiozaki and Toshiyuki Ueno to produce the board game "Itadaki Street" in 1991.

Another significant outcome of LOGiN was its role in developing game production software that would later become known as the "Tkool" series. In 1983, LOGiN published the program for "Adventure Tool," a utility for creating text adventures, and continued to feature other game creation tools. By 1987, the magazine had introduced "Adventure Tkool," the first software to bear the "Tkool" name. LOGiN not only published its program but also sold it on floppy disks and tapes via mail order (◘ Fig. 6.5).[6]

LOGiN also hosted contests for games made with the Tkool series and sold some of the best entries. The Tkool series, available for both PCs and game consoles, significantly lowered the barrier to game creation and greatly contributed to the development of Japan's game production culture (Nihei 2006). The most famous title in the series is RPG Tkool (RPG Maker), which allows users to create Dragon Quest-style RPGs.

Those who created and submitted their games to magazines also began participating in doujin events. In 1983, doujin games first appeared at Comiket, an event that has been held since 1975. That year, the "SF-Z Association," a science fiction study group at the University of Electro-Communications, distributed a digital game for the PC-8801 called "Niko-Niko Girls Puzzle." The following year, the doujin circle "Empire Software," composed of former SF-Z Association members, distributed "Mermaid's Tears" for the PC-8801, which they explicitly labeled "Doujin Soft." By 1989, more than 200 circles were participating in Comiket (1989).

Starting in 1988, a doujin event called "Pasoket," which focused exclusively on doujin games, was held monthly across Japan, in addition to Comiket (◘ Fig. 6.6). According to participants we interviewed, creators at Pasoket often distributed upgraded versions of their games and saw sales that were about a third or a quarter of their Comiket levels. The atmosphere at Pasoket was also more intimate than at Comiket, fostering closer interaction between creators and buyers. This environment seemed to lead to discussions on specialized topics, such as machine language, which was not widely documented in books at the time.

Due to the high demand for PC games and the booming "bubble economy," each doujin game sold hundreds of copies. Some doujin circles even traveled nationwide, spending lavishly, thanks to their Pasoket sales. However, since CD and DVD pressing services were expensive at the time, the number of works that could be distributed was limited, making it difficult for creators to earn a living from doujin game sales.

6 The creator of Adventure Tkool was Ueno, who was also responsible for programming the PC version of "The Okhotsk Disappearance." Early stages of that game were included as a sample in Adventure Tkool.

PC-8801シリーズ

アドベンチャーツクール

"オホーツクに消ゆ"のゲエセン上野とログイン編集部が開発した、
世界で一番簡単なアドベンチャーゲーム製作用ツールがここに完成。
「もったいない」との内部の声をふり切って、ここに公開いたします。

世はマルチプレイヤーゲーム時代。孤独にキーボードを叩いて自分だけの世界にひたるなどというスタイルは、もう過去のもの。お友だちとご家族と、はたまた恋人と楽しみを分かち合う、これが最新流行のコンピュータアミューズメントの姿なのであります。

これまで、ひとりで遊ぶものと思われてきたアドベンチャーゲームも、例外ではありません。あなたが書いたアドベンチャーをあなたのお友だちがプレイする。お返しに、お友だち製のアドベンチャーを、今度はあなたがプレイする。これも立派なマルチの哲学。

だけど、どうしたらアドベンチャーゲームが作れるのでしょうか。それなら簡単。この世紀の大発明"アドベンチャー・ツクール"さえあれば、なんと信じ難いことに、かの有名な"オホーツクに消ゆ"とまったく同じメニュー選択方式を採用した、高級テキストアドベンチャーが誰にでもすぐに作れ、しかもその場で遊べてしまうのです。

それもそのはず、"アドベンチャー・ツクール"は、"オホーツクに消ゆ"を製作したログイン編集部が世界に誇る天才プログラマー、ゲエセン上野が、そのノウハウを結集し、インドの山奥にこもること3泊4日、ついに完成させた世界で一番優れた奇跡のアドベンチャーゲーム製作ツールなのであります。

あなたは、日頃慣れ親しんだBASICのREM文で、次にお見せする世界一簡単な使用法にのっとって、頭の中で温めていた血沸き肉躍るシナリオを書いていくだけ。製作途中でも、ボタンひとつでテストプレイができてしまう。表示はひらがな、カタカナ、英数字。その他便利なコマンドを多数盛り込んで、ディスク、テープ両方対応。これだけの機能を備えても、プログラムの大きさは、たったの8キロバイト！　半日でかる～く打ち込める量です。それなのに、作れるアドベンチャーの大きさは、最大32キロバイトまで。これは、大きすぎもせず小さすぎもせず、実に手頃なサイズなのです。

ところでこの"アドベンチャー・ツクール"、今回はPC-8801版のみを発表させていただきますが、後にFM-7版、MSX2版、X1版と続々登場する予定でして、しかも、すべての機種において完全データ互換。つまり、PC-8801で書いたアドベンチャーを、FM-7版ツクールでもプレイ（予定）できるというわけ。

当編集部では、この革命的利点を生かして、アドベンチャーゲーム・コンクールも行ないますので、どうか、ハチハチ以外の機種をご使用の皆様も、今からシナリオを練っておいていただきたいものであります。

では、実践に即した懇切丁寧なる本ツールの使用法説明に続きまして、面白くてタメになるサンプルゲーム2本を紹介させていただきます。世が世なら関係者一同を大金持ちにしたかも知れない世紀のソフト"アドベンチャー・ツクール"で、心ゆくまでお楽しみくださいませ。

●これが"アドベンチャー・ツクール"で作ったゲームの画面だ。"オホーツクに消ゆ"と同等のハイクオリティーが簡単に得られるのだ。

●空前の大ヒット作"オホーツクに消ゆ"から"アドベンチャー・ツクール"は生まれた。

●"オホーツクに消ゆ"を生んだ喜びをみなさんにも、と語るプログラマー、ゲエセン上野。

「アドベンチャー・ツクール」のプログラムリストは、LISTLOG358ページに掲載しました。

214 LOGiN /1987 No.1

Fig. 6.5 A page from LOGiN introducing "Adventure Tkool" (1987)

After observing the growing popularity of doujin games at various events, "Technopolis," a PC magazine launched by Tokuma Shoten in 1982, published a feature on "Doujin(shi) Soft" in 1986. The magazine subsequently began to actively introduce doujin games and provide information on mail-order sales from doujin circles (Fig. 6.7). The magazine's circulation saw a significant increase due to several factors: a scarcity of information about doujin games, the fact that mail-order doujin games were cheaper than their commercial counterparts, and the

■ **Fig. 6.6** A page from a "Pasoket" pamphlet

greater appeal of doujin games with cartoon-style characters compared to the more realistic graphics found in many commercial adult games.

Doujin games were also distributed through vending machines and PC communication services. In April 1986, the manufacturing company Brother Industries launched a vending machine service called "Soft Bender TAKERU" for selling software, particularly games. At its peak, approximately 300 machines were in operation, primarily in PC retail stores nationwide, selling up to 2000 different software titles (Yasutomo 2004).

When a user selected an item and deposited money, the vending machine would write the data, which was distributed from a host computer, to a cartridge, floppy

Fig. 6.7 A special feature on doujin games in "Technopolis"

disk, or CD-ROM. Users would also receive a printed manual and receipt. Around 1990, consignment sales of doujin games began on TAKERU. Creators who contracted with Brother could receive 50% to 60% of the sales and a sales report. At one point, over 300 independent games for all ages were available for sale through the service.

Additionally, after the 1985 privatization of the Nippon Telegraph and Telephone Public Corporation, telephone lines were opened up for more than just telecommunication. This led to the emergence of PC communication services like ASCIInet (1985), PC-VAN (1986), and NIFTY-Serve (1987), as well as grassroots BBSs, all of which began distributing free games. However, due to limited download capacity, games with extensive graphics were still distributed at doujin events rather than online.

Magazines, PC shops, doujin events, vending machines, and PC communication services all played a role in motivating creators to produce, publish, and sell doujin games. These channels also provided access to the knowledge and information needed to create games, as well as connections with fellow enthusiasts, recognition from their peers, and money from sales. However, because it was difficult to earn a living from doujin game sales and the PC and console game industries were just starting to establish themselves, many doujin creators took jobs at game companies and continued making doujin games as a hobby. In other words, the foundation of Japan's game industries was partly built on hobbyist creators who, through independent game production, have accumulated various forms of capital (as defined by Bourdieu), such as knowledge, connections, reputation, and money (Kobayashi (Hichibe) and Koyama 2020).

6.3.2 Period of Stagnation: Early 1990s

The Japanese doujin game production field experienced a temporary period of stagnation in the early 1990s. This was largely due to the widespread adoption of Windows-based PC/AT compatible machines, a trend that accelerated after the release of the Japanese versions of Windows 3.1 (1993) and Windows 95 (1995).

According to interviews with game creators who were active at the time, the important factors that led to this stagnation can be summarized as follows:

1. Mainstream PCs of the past, running operating systems like MS-DOS, were typically bundled with an easy-to-use programming environment (such as BASIC) and a manual. In contrast, Windows machines did not include these tools, making it impossible for new owners to begin game development immediately.
2. The fundamental characteristics of Windows differed from conventional operating systems; it did not allow for direct hardware control via programs and was designed to run multiple applications simultaneously. As a result, creators couldn't use their existing know-how. Although PC performance had increased, the complexity of games they could create decreased, forcing creators to produce only simple games and, in turn, leading to a decrease in their motivation.
3. The early APIs, libraries, and Game SDKs (such as DirectX1 and WinG) provided by Microsoft for Windows were inadequate for game development.
4. The documentation within DirectX was written in English, and there were almost no explanatory Japanese-language materials or information. As a result, it took time for Japanese amateur creators to understand the specifications of Windows and DirectX.
5. Sony Computer Entertainment's (SCE) project to support commercial game production drew many leading amateur creators away from the doujin game field and into the professional console game production.
6. Many young people who had created games as a hobby during their student years left the doujin field after graduating and entering the workforce.

Especially, factors 1 through 4 posed significant barriers to doujin game creation. As a result, while games continued to be made for established platforms like the PC-9800, X68000, FM-TOWNS, and MSX, few people attempted to produce games for Windows machines. Even when Brother Industries held seminars aimed at increasing the number of independent games for Windows sold through its TAKERU distribution system, few doujin creators attended.

When creators were hesitant to produce games for Windows, SCE launched a competitive program. From 1995 to 1999, SCE ran the "Game Yaroze!" initiative six times to increase the number of game titles and development talent for the PlayStation console, which had been released in 1994.

Participants who had their game production plans approved were given a PlayStation development environment. The program also offered opportunities to commercialize their games, get hired by SCE, and receive business startup support. As a result, some creators chose to pursue the PlayStation platform over Windows, thinking, "If we have to learn a new development environment, we'll try PlayStation, not a Windows machine." This led them to shift to the console game industry.[7]

Meanwhile, a number of people began to leave the doujin game production field. At the same time, many computer magazines that published program lists for independent games ceased publication (◘ Table 6.2). Additionally, TAKERU, a service that sold independent games, shut down in 1997.

During this period, doujin creators utilized the superior graphics capabilities of Windows machines to produce full-color CG collections, desktop accessories, and simple puzzle games instead of more complex games.

As a result, some people who were introduced to doujin games after the rise of Windows machines believe that only CG collections, accessories, and simple games existed until the mid-1990s and that complex doujin games first appeared in the late 1990s. In reality, complex games were already being produced and distributed in the doujin game field well before the late 1990s. The mid-1990s can, therefore, be seen as a stagnant period for doujin game production.[8]

◘ Table 6.2 Publication history of computer magazines (launch and suspension years)

	Publisher	Launch year	Suspension year
I/O	Kohgaku-Sha	1976	Still published
Micom	Dempa Shimbun-Sha	1977	1995
ASCII	ASCII Corporation	1977	2010
Technopolis	Tokuma Shoten	1982	1994
Oh!PC	Softbank	1982	2000
Oh!MZ	Softbank	1982	1995
Oh!FM	Softbank	1982	1996
Micom Basic Magazine	Dempa Shimbun-Sha	1982	2003
LOGiN	ASCII Corporation	1982	2008
POPCOM	Shogakukan	1983	1994
MSX Magazine	ASCII Corporation	1983	1992
Comptiq	Kadokawa Shoten	1983	Still published
Beep	Softbank	1984	1989
MSX-FAN	Tokuma Shoten	1987	1995

7 Notable doujin creators who made their commercial debut on PlayStation through this project include Kazunori Nanji, the creator of "Doko Demo Issyo," and Kuniaki Watanabe, the creator of "Panekit."

8 The stagnation during this period is also detailed in Miyake (2011) and Koyama (2023). This research by Miyake and Koyama is based on interviews primarily conducted by the author of this paper (Miyake 2019).

6.3.3 Period of Revival: Late 1990s

In the late 1990s, doujin game production became active again, and the complexity of games began to increase. The key factors behind this revival can be summarized as follows:

1. Microsoft upgraded and provided the necessary APIs for 2D and 3D game development. This was complemented by the publication of instructional books on DirectX in Japanese, as well as the availability of numerous online resources and game program lists.
2. The success of parody doujin games demonstrated that game production on Windows machines was feasible. Also, people who saw the popularity of doujin games began to participate in doujin game production.
3. Game production engines were provided for free on the Internet.

As for action games, in addition to ports of doujin games for the X68000, parody fighting game "Tokimeki Taisen" featuring characters from Konami's commercial romance adventure game "Tokimeki Memorial" (Konami, 1994) were produced for Windows machines in 1997 (the latter was discontinued at Konami's request). In 1998, "The Queen of Heart (QOH)" by the doujin circle Watanabe Seisakusho gained huge popularity. This parody fighting game, which featured characters from the romance visual novel "To Heart" (Leaf, 1996), proved that action games with high-speed graphics could be created even on Windows 95 (◘ Fig. 6.8).

After "QOH," which is said to have sold about 100,000 copies, creators who previously developed games for the X68000 and PC-9800 machines began producing doujin games for Windows 95 one after another. Fighting games, side-scrolling action games, shooting games, RPGs, SLGs, and more were produced for Windows 95. Following the success of "QOH," "Party's Breaker" (Watanabe Seisakusho, 2001), a fighting game featuring characters from the visual novel "Comic Party"

◘ **Fig. 6.8** "The Queen of Heart" (Watanabe Seisakusho) and other doujin games of the time

(Leaf, 1999), and "Eternal Fighter Zero" (Twilight Frontier, 2001), a game based on characters from works by the PC game brand Key, became immensely popular.

The availability of free online software also stimulated doujin game production by making it easier to create games for Windows machines. For example, Hot Soup Processor (HSP) 1.0, a tool for creating a wide variety of games, was released in 1996. In 1999, NScripter and KiriKiri, game engines for creating visual novels, also became available. The availability of instructional books, plug-ins, guides, and materials for these tools further boosted doujin game production.

Furthermore, since NScripter and KiriKiri could be used for commercial projects for a fee, it was technically easy for doujin creators who had mastered these tools to enter the PC game industry. It was also during this period that an increasing number of creators began to move between the doujin game field and the PC game industry, based on the knowledge, connections, reputation, and money they gained through doujin game production.

Meanwhile, in the console game industry, the industry organization CESA held a doujin event for independent games at the first Tokyo Game Show in August 1996. However, as the Tokyo Game Show grew in size, it was moved from Tokyo Big Sight to Makuhari Messe in the fall of 1997, and the doujin event was terminated. The gap between the console game industry and the doujin game field widened once again.

6.3.4 Period of Development: 2000s

During the 2020s, the doujin game production field experienced the following key developments:

1. An increase in original (non-parody) doujin games
2. A rise in both parody works and media mix of doujin games
3. The professionalization of doujin game production
4. An increase in game maturity

First, regarding (1 and 2), while parody doujin games based on commercial works were popular in the late 1990s, original doujin games began to emerge in the 2000s for a variety of reasons. This trend was sparked by the visual novel "Tsukihime" (月姫), which was released by TYPE-MOON in December 2000.

Using NScripter, Tsukihime tells the story of a boy who can see "the death of things." He confronts a series of murders alongside girls burdened with cruel fates. The game received high praise for its shounen manga-like fighting elements, which were largely absent from late-1990s romance visual novels. Its quality and sheer volume, which exceeded that of many commercial games (5000 manuscript pages and 500 pages of CG), earned it strong support from fans. The popularity of Tsukihime was further accelerated by the rapid release of related works, as well as popularity polls and mail-order sales on its official website.

Tsukihime stimulated the creation of original doujin games that were not parodies of commercial content, and gave rise to unprecedented phenomena: The production of parodies of doujin games by other doujin creators and commercial media mixes of doujin games.

As for Tsukihime, fan-made content, including manga, novels, games, music were created, and dedicated doujin events for it were held frequently. Tsukihime also attracted the attention of doujin shops, which saw it as the next major hit after The Queen of Heart and Eternal Fighter Zero, and actively promoted the sales of Tsukihime and its parody works.

Furthermore, Kadokawa Shoten and other companies began commercial media mixes of Tsukihime. In 2002, a commercial parody manga anthology was released, followed by other official manga, animation, novels, music, figures, etc. "MELTY BLOOD," a doujin fighting game co-produced by Type-Moon and Watanabe Seisakusho (the creators of QOH) in 2002, was adapted into a commercial arcade game in 2005 and into a console game in 2006. MELTY BLOOD offered other doujin circles the option of joint production of doujin games, and similar games were later produced.

"Touhou Project" (東方Project) and "Higurashi When They Cry" (ひぐらしのなく頃に) are two of the most successful doujin games, along with Tsukihime. The Touhou Project is a series of bullet hell shooter games. Production for the P-9800 began in 1996, and it moved to Windows in 2002. It has become extremely popular, leading to a huge number of fan-made parodies at doujin events and on streaming websites like Nico Nico Douga and pixiv.

Meanwhile, Higurashi When They Cry, a murder mystery visual novel series first produced for Windows since 2002, was released for game consoles and mobile phones. The franchise expanded into manga, anime, films, pachinko, etc. The series also gained widespread public attention due to media reports speculating on its potential influence on juvenile crime.

In the 2000s, doujin games pioneered a broader trend in Japan where popular, independently produced works gained prominence. This trend included "Koizora," "Hetalia," "Voices of a Distant Star," and songs created using Vocaloid, a voice synthesis technology like Hatsune Miku.

In this period, doujin game production also became more professional. Prior to this, with the exception of the period just before the commercial game market was established in the 1980s, it was difficult to make a living from doujin game sales. Most people who wanted to continue making games ended up working for a game company. However, as the cost of writing data to CDs and DVDs became cheaper, more people were able to make a living by selling their doujin games at events, in doujin shops, or through digital download services, or by doing it as a second job. Additionally, some commercial game creators began producing their own games as a hobby or for stress relief after work.

As it became possible to earn a living from the doujin game sales, some creators chose to continue making them rather than joining the commercial game industries. With the rise of professional doujin creators and more accessible game production software and materials, the quality and complexity of doujin games have increased year by year. Some doujin games now offer tens of hours of gameplay and can compete with commercial titles.

6.3.5 Period of Globalization: 2010s Onwards[9]

Since the 2010s, smartphones, which are mobile phones equipped with an operating system (OS), and high-capacity communications through mobile communication networks (mobile broadband) became widespread. The usage rate of social media such as Twitter (now X) and YouTube also increased significantly. The digitalization and informatization of society advanced during this period. Under these macro-social changes, there have been major changes in the production, distribution, and communication platforms for doujin games, as well as how creators think. Among these changes, the following are some of the most important:

1. Free or inexpensive game production software (game engines) has become widely available.
2. The number of online platforms and devices that support doujin games has increased.
3. Major players in the industries, including console manufacturers, mobile platform operators, and translation and sales agencies, have begun to actively support the production and sale of doujin games.
4. As a result of (1–3), it became much easier for doujin games to be sold globally.
5. The increasing number of PCs without optical drives led to the popularity of download cards.
6. As a result of (4 and 5), the number of doujin shops that handle doujin games has decreased.
7. While the number of doujin game sales events and festivals has increased, the presence and importance of Comiket for doujin game creators has declined.
8. Communication, evaluation, and scouting have become more common on social media than in person.
9. An increasing number of creators now identify as "indie" rather than "doujin."

Here is a detailed explanation of these changes.

The first change is the spread of free or inexpensive digital game production software (game engines). Even before the 2000s, game production software like RPG Tkool (RPG Maker), NScripter, and HSP made it relatively easy to create games. However, the games that could be created with these were mainly 2D games for PCs. Tools for creating 3D games or titles for consoles and smartphones were not widely used within the doujin game production field.

In the 2010s, general-purpose game engines like Unity, Unreal Engine, and DX Library became available for free or at low cost. This allowed creators to develop and sell games of any genre on a wide range of devices, including PCs, consoles, and smartphones. Consequently, even doujin circles that had previously not used game engines or had created their own began to adopt them.

According to a 2017 study by Imagire, Unity was the most-used engine among dōjin games at Comic Market 92, with 22% of identified games using it. This was

9 For more on the changes in the doujin game field since the 2010s, refer to Kobayashi (2024).

followed by Unreal Engine (12%), KiriKiri (10%), and TyranoScript (8%) (Imagire 2018). A separate survey by the author on exhibitors at Digital Game Expo 2020 found an even higher usage rate: 75.0% used Unity, 16.7% used their own engines, and 8.3% used Unreal Engine. Both studies clearly show that game engines have become a widely adopted tool among doujin game creators.

The second change is the increase in online platforms and devices that support doujin games. Traditionally, these games were usually sold at doujin events or doujin shops as physical media, like floppy disks or optical discs. However, since the mid-2000s, the number of platforms and devices for distributing and selling doujin games has rapidly expanded. This includes platforms such as Steam, PlayStation®Store, and Nintendo eShop, along with others like App Store, Google Play, and itch.io.

In addition, the wider use of game engines, doujin circles can now distribute their games on devices other than PCs, and creators are taking advantage of these opportunities. According to the Digital Game Expo 2020 survey, 41.7% of exhibitors sold their games on Steam, followed by Google Play, doujin shops, and Nintendo eShop. The survey also found that 80.6% of exhibitors produced and distributed games for PCs, with smartphones and game consoles as the next most popular platforms.

The third change is sales support from the console industry, mobile platform operators, and translation and distribution agencies. As previously mentioned, it was difficult to sell doujin games on consoles, but in the 2010s, in response to the growing popularity of independent games (Juul 2019), Sony Interactive Entertainment (SIE, formerly SCE) and Nintendo began to actively support Japanese independent games. This led to doujin games being sold on the PlayStation®Store and Nintendo eShop. Additionally, sales of doujin games became more active on the App Store and Google Play (formerly Android Market), which were launched in 2008.

At roughly the same time, translation and distribution agencies began to support the global spread of doujin games. One such company, Carpe Fulgur, translated the doujin circle EasyGameStation's "Lucettia" and sold it on Steam in 2010. This is considered the first Japanese doujin game to be sold on the platform, and it became a hit, selling over 100,000 copies by the end of that year. This success prompted overseas translation and distribution agencies to start actively reaching out to Japanese doujin circles[10] (Murasame 2018).

In parallel with this, the number of Japanese companies translating and selling doujin games for overseas markets also increased. Through these overseas and domestic translation and distribution agencies, Japanese doujin games that had been distributed only locally in Japan began to be distributed in Europe and the United States in the early 2010s, and in China in the late 2010s.

10 From a Western perspective, Consalvo (2016) provides a detailed account of how Japanese doujin games were translated and distributed to English-speaking countries by independent distributors like Carpe Fulgur.

The fourth change is a result of the previous three: Doujin games can now be easily distributed globally.

The fifth change is the increase in the number of PCs without optical drives and the rise of download (DL) cards. In the 2000s, doujin games were distributed on optical discs like CD-ROMs or DVD-ROMs. However, as more users acquired PCs without optical drives and the production of discs and their envelopes ceased, it became difficult for doujin circles to distribute their games this way. As a result, recent years have seen a shift toward distributing DL cards with serial codes and other information (Murasame 2018; Yoko 2018). For example, at the 2020 Digital Game Expo 2020, 55.6% of exhibitors distributed DL cards, while only 36.1% used optical discs.

The sixth change is the decrease in the number of doujin shops that sell doujin games. Sales at these shops have declined due to the rise of online platforms for distributing doujin games and a decrease in the number of players who prefer physical media (such as optical discs). As a result, fewer doujin shops are now stocking many doujin games. For example, the Sangatsu Usagi Sangetto store, which had been a major seller of doujin games in Akihabara, closed in October 2016.

The seventh change is the increase in doujin events and festivals that focus on doujin games, alongside a decline in Comiket's presence. As online platforms have become more widespread, digital games produced by individuals or small groups—known as independent or "indie" games—have gained worldwide popularity (Juul 2019).

Also, in Japan, doujin events such as Digital Game Expo (2013–) and festivals like BitSummit (2013–), the Tokyo Game Show's Indie Game Corner (2013–), TOKYO SANDBOX (2015–), and Zentame (National Entertainment Festival) (2017–) have increased. Before the 2000s, Comiket and a few other events were the only venues where individuals or small groups could exhibit and distribute their independent games, which made Comiket's presence highly significant. However, creators now have more options, which has led to a relative decline in Comiket's influence.

The eighth change is the increase in communication, evaluation, and scouting via social media rather than in person. Social media is a medium designed for interactive communication of information among a large number of people. Doujin circles can now use social media platforms like SNS or video-sharing sites to communicate with fans of their games and get feedback and evaluations from many people—something that was previously only possible face-to-face. Additionally, images and videos uploaded before or during the production of a game often attract a lot of attention on SNS platforms like X (formerly Twitter). It has also become common for game translation and sales agencies to contact creators after their games in development have become popular on social media.

In the past, doujin games often improved and gained popularity through distribution and interaction at doujin events like Comiket. Additionally, sales agents sometimes approached creators based on their popularity at doujin events and shops. However, in recent years, communication, evaluation, and scouting have become more common via social media rather than face-to-face (a trend boosted by the COVID-19 pandemic). As a result, it has become less common for an unknown doujin circle to suddenly become famous at a doujin event.

Finally, the ninth change is the increase in creators who identify themselves as "indie" rather than "doujin." Creators who once relied on the doujin distribution system—consisting of doujin events and shops—to sell their games can now use online platforms and social media. As a result, the number of small-scale game creators who consider or call themselves "indie" rather than "doujin" has increased. The changing social context surrounding game creators in the age of globalization is also affecting their identity.

6.4 Conclusions and Future Issues

This paper has provided an overview of the history of independent games in Japan, particularly digital games known as "doujin games," based on data obtained from various social research. The history of doujin games from the 1970s to the 2020s is divided into five periods: establishment, stagnation, revival, development, and globalization. The characteristics of each period are as follows (see also ◘ Table 6.1).

During the "Period of Establishment" (late 1970s to 1980s), as personal computers became more accessible, a culture of homemade digital games emerged among computer hobbyists. Computer magazines provided game program lists and creation tools, and doujin games began to be distributed at doujin events such as Comiket and Pasoket. Independent games like doujin games were distributed through magazines, sales events, shops, and online computer networks, allowing creators to acquire skills, recognition, connections, and even some money. However, it was still difficult to make a living from doujin games. The transition of skilled hobbyists into the commercial game industries played a significant role in the establishment and growth of Japan's game industries.

During the "Period of Stagnation" (early 1990s), with the introduction of Windows 95, doujin game production temporarily stagnated. This was due to the difficulty of adapting to a new operating system and changes in the game creation environment etc. During this period, CG collections and desktop accessories were produced rather than complex games. In addition, as a result of start-up support from Sony Computer Entertainment (SCE), some famous doujin creators moved to the console game industry.

During the "Period of Revival" (late 1990s), the number of doujin games for Windows increased. This was partially due to Microsoft's DirectX upgrade and the release of many instructional books and online resources. Also, with hit parody games like "The Queen of Heart" and the rise of free game engines, doujin game production became active again, and games became more complex. However, there was almost no support for independent game production or distribution from the Japanese console game industry.

During the "Period of Development" (2000s), the creation of original doujin games increased, and extremely popular original games like Tsukihime were born. Thanks to the domestic doujin distribution system of events and shops, some creators were able to start making a living from their sales.

During the "Period of Globalization" (2010s and onward), the spread of game engines, along with the rise of various online platforms and services for translation and sales, led to the global distribution of doujin games. Thanks to digitalization, creators could now distribute their independent games internationally without depending on local doujin distribution systems, and more people began to identify as "indie" rather than "doujin."

As mentioned in ► Sect. 6.1, independent games and their production have significantly impacted the establishment and development of the game industries in Japan, just as they have in Europe and the United States. Therefore, a historical understanding of Japanese independent games—particularly doujin games, which hold a prominent position—is crucial for studying the history of Japanese games. However, there are very few English-language studies on the history of doujin games. Existing research either doesn't focus on their history, covers only specific periods, or is written in Japanese. This study, by discussing the history of doujin games from the 1970s to the 2020s in English, fills a gap in the research on doujin games and other Japanese independently produced games, and thus holds significant value.

On the other hand, the history of Japanese independent games other than doujin games (particularly from the 1990s onward) needs a more detailed discussion. Additionally, our findings on the changes that have occurred since the 2010s require further qualitative and quantitative data for support. The author intends to explore these issues in the future through interviews, historical document research, and the "Comic Market 50th Anniversary Survey" currently being conducted in 2025.

In closing, in order to further advance research on doujin games and other independent Japanese games, this paper identifies certain issues with previous studies and proposes avenues for future research.

As mentioned in ► Sect. 6.1, there is a growing body of research on the content of Japanese independent games, particularly doujin games, and the motivations and habits of their creators. However, some of these studies seem to have certain difficulties. The primary issue is that the content of Japanese independent games and the motivations and habits of their creators tend to be portrayed quite homogeneously.

While certain trends and patterns are visible, it's crucial to acknowledge that not all games and creators are the same; there is a notable degree of diversity among them. While many doujin games feature deformed characters influenced by Japanese manga and anime, as well as bishojo (美少女, beautiful girl) characters, there are also many others. These include games based on creators' personal experiences, games that use abstract symbols, games focused on realistic expression, romance games featuring bishōnen (美少年, beautiful boy) characters, and boys' love games with themes of male homosexuality (Hichibe 2013, 88–91, Hichibe and Tanaka 2016, 60–63). "The House in Fata Morgana," a popular doujin game from recent years, is a work that truly deviates from the stereotypical view of doujin games.

The same holds true for the motivations and production habits of creators, as well as the history of independent games. In Hichibe and Tanaka (2016), the authors presented an analytical framework of three types of game creators, "hobbyist (crafter)," "indie," "commercial creator," as ideal types as described by Max Weber. It also stated that the production motivations and habits of many Japanese doujin game creators fall into the "hobbyist (crafter)" category, who create games based on noneconomic motivations. However, as the same paper noted, it cannot be argued that all doujin game creators do not seek money, or conversely, that all actual indie creators create games for money.[11] Furthermore, it cannot be said that such tendencies are universally seen among Japanese creators across different eras. As this paper has demonstrated, the platforms for independent game distribution are becoming increasingly online and globalized, and there are signs that the dispositions of many Japanese independent game creators are changing.

Grau de Pablos (2024) also argues that with the spread of digital distribution, independent creators in Japan have been divided into those who rely on traditional domestic distribution (such as doujin events) and those who utilize global digital distribution. While this observation is suggestive, in reality, many creators flexibly use both local and global distribution. There is also active social interaction between those who identify as "doujin" and those who identify as "indie." For example, Digital Game Expo mentioned above, one of Japan's leading independent game events, positions itself as a "Doujin & Indie Game Only Exhibition and Sales Event" and serves as a symbolic venue for such social interaction.

Overemphasizing the homogeneity, static nature, and passivity of Japanese independent games (doujin games) and their creators, especially when comparing them to their overseas (usually Western) counterparts, risks (re)producing stereotypes and orientalism about Japanese games and their creators.

To avoid these pitfalls, researchers of Japanese independent games and their history must move beyond relying solely on English-language research, literature, and online sources. They should not omit on-site research in Japan or focus exclusively on famous games and creators. Instead, it is advisable to thoroughly read research and materials written in Japanese, conduct long-term on-site research in Japan, directly interview numerous Japanese creators and event organizers, and play a wide variety of doujin games.

Through these various and consistent research efforts, researchers can gain a more detailed understanding of the following:

- The diversity, dynamism, and proactivity of Japanese independent games (including doujin games) and their creators
- The diverse "tactics of appropriation"—in the sense of Michel de Certeau's cultural studies—that creators are using to adapt to digitalization and globalization
- The actual state of interaction between Japan and overseas independent game cultures

11 Fiadotau (2019) interprets Hichibe and Tanaka (2016) as claiming that all real indie game creators make games for money, but this is a misreading of our work. This point is discussed in detail in Kobayashi (2024).

It is hoped that these efforts will lead to further developments in research on doujin and other Japanese independent games and their history.

Acknowledgments This research was supported by grants from the Foundation for the Fusion of Science and Technology (FOST) and the Hayao Nakayama Foundation for Science & Technology and Culture. I would like to express my deep gratitude for this support.

References

Comiket. 1989. *Personal computer Doujin soft catalog*. Kubo Shoten. (Japanese).

Consalvo, Mia. 2016. *Atari to Zelda: Japan's videogames in global contexts*. The MIT Press.

Digital Game Research Group. 2020. *The present state of game creation activities: digital game expo 2020 survey report*.

Fiadotau, Mikhail. 2019. Indie and Dojin games: a multilayered cross-cultural comparison. *Gamevironments*. 10:39–83.

Grau de Pablos, Tomás. 2024. Between Indie and Doujin: the creation of the Japanese Indie. *Game Studies* 24 (3). https://gamestudies.org/2403/articles/grau_de_pablos.

Helland, Christopher. 2018. Geemu on! A preliminary study of Indie and Doujin game development in Japan. *Gamevironments* 8:38–48.

Hichibe (Kobayashi), Nobushige. 2006. Amateurs and content creation: cultural sociology of PC game production. *Sociological Papers*. 15:69–76. (Japanese).

Hichibe (Kobayashi), Nobushige. 2009a. "Structures" that enable to develop Doujin and Indie games: a sociological study on the current state and history of Doujin/Indie game production. *Journal of Contents History Studies* 1:35–55. (Japanese).

Hichibe (Kobayashi), Nobushige. 2009b. Possibilities of sustainable small-scale game development: qualitative data analysis of development of Doujin and Indie games. *Journal of Digital Games Research* 3 (2): 171–183. (Japanese).

Hichibe (Kobayashi), Nobushige. 2010. Logics of "Doujin field": interests of agents and conversion of capitals. *Journal of Contents History Studies* 3 (2): 171–183. (Japanese).

Hichibe (Kobayashi), Nobushige. 2011. Why are many original high-quality Doujin games are developed in Japan?: three social conditions giving influences to contents of Doujin games. *Journal of Digital Games Research* 5 (1): 65–78. (Japanese).

Hichibe (Kobayashi), Nobushige. 2013. *Independent game production culture as a key to growth of Japanese game industry*. PhD diss., Tokyo Institute of Technology. (Japanese).

Hichibe (Kobayashi), Nobushige, and Ema Tanaka. 2016. Content production fields and Doujin game developers in Japan: non-economic rewards as drivers of variety in games. In *Transnational contexts of culture, gender, class, and colonialism in play*, ed. Alexis Pulos and S. Austin Lee, 43–80. Palgrave Macmillan.

Imagire, Takashi. 2018. Game engines at Comiket 2017. In *Trends in Doujin games: after 10 years*. http://digrajapan.org/?p=5387. (Japanese).

Ito, Kenji. 2007. Possibilities of non-commercial games: the case of amateur role-playing games designers in Japan. In *Worlds in play: international perspectives on digital games research*, ed. Suzanne De Castell and Jennifer Jenson, 129–142. Peter Lang.

Juul, Jesper. 2019. *Handmade pixels: independent video games and the quest for authenticity*. MIT Press.

King, Brad, John Borland, and Roger Stewart. 2003. *Dungeons and Dreamers: The Rise of Computer Game Culture from Geek to Chic*. Osborne.

Kobayashi (Hichibe), Nobushige. 2019. From protestant ethic to <ludification>: games, players and game studies in Finland. In *New era of game studies*, ed. Shinichi Nakazawa and Daichi Nakagawa, 67–83. NTT Shuppan. (Japanese).

Kobayashi (Hichibe), Nobushige, and Yuhsuke Koyama. 2020. The early history of the hobbyist production field of video games and its impacts on the establishment of Japan's video game industries. *Replaying Japan Journal* 2:73–82.

Kobayashi (Hichibe), Nobushige. 2024. The production motivations of Doujin circles and their changes: focusing on Doujin game creators in the age of digitalization and globalization. In *Sociology of "Doujin culture"*, ed. Hiroaki Tamagawa, 135–201. Shichigatsusha. (Japanese).

Koyama, Yuhsuke. 2023. *History of the Japanese video game industry*. Springer.

Lehtonen, Miikka J., Antti Ainamo, and J. Harviainen. 2019. The four faces of creative industries: visualising the game industry ecosystem in Helsinki and Tokyo. *Industry and Innovation* 27 (9): 1062–1087. https://doi.org/10.1080/13662716.2019.1676704.

Levy, Steven. 1984. *Hackers: heroes of the computer revolution*. Anchor Press/Doubleday.

Mäyrä, Frans. 2015. Finland. In *Video games around the world*, ed. Mark J. P. Wolf, 159–173. MIT Press.

Miyake, Youichirou. 2011. The history of technology in Doujin and Indie game development: reconstruction of the history from interviews with Doujin and Indies game developers. *Journal of Digital Games Research* 5 (1): 57–64. (Japanese).

Miyake, Youichirou. 2019. A history of interview with game developers in DiGRA Japan. In *Proceedings of DiGRA Japan 2023 summer conference*, 11–14. (Japanese).

Murasame. 2018. Single action Doujin game. In *Trends in Doujin games: after 10 years*. http://digrajapan.org/?p=5387. (Japanese).

Nihei, Akira. 2006. Pedigree of Tkool series. In *Reviving PC-8801 legend*, ed. ASCII Books Editorial, 168–173. ASCII. (Japanese).

Picard, Martin. 2013. The foundation of Geemu: a brief history of early Japanese video games. *Game Studies* 13 (2). http://gamestudies.org/1302/articles/picard.

Sekiguchi, Waichi. 2000. *First runners of personal computer revolution*. Nikkei. (Japanese).

Tyni, Heikki, and Olli Sotamaa. 2014. Assembling a game development scene? Uncovering Finland's largest demo party. *G| A| M| E Games as Art, Media, Entertainment* 1 (3):

Vogel, Michael. 2017. *Japanese independent game development*. Georgia Institute of Technology Master Thesis. http://hdl.handle.net/1853/58640.

Yasutomo, Yuichi. 2004. TAKERU's Real Face now revealed. In *Reviving PC-9801 legend*, ed. ASCII Books Editorial, 164–167. ASCII. (Japanese).

Yoko. 2018. RebRank Chronicle: a look back at Doujin game production now that i'm an adult. In *Trends in Doujin games: after 10 years*. http://digrajapan.org/?p=5387. (Japanese).

Nobushige Kobayashi is a Professor in the Department of Data Science at the Faculty of Information Science, Tohoku Gakuin University. He received his Ph.D. from the Tokyo Institute of Technology for his thesis "Independent Game Production Culture as a Key to Growth of Japanese Game Industry," which analyzed the relationship between independent game production and the game industries in Japan from a social science perspective. In June 2020, he edited and published "An Introduction to Digital Games Research" (Minerva Shobo), which is considered Japan's first textbook in this field. His specialties are sociology, cultural studies, and game studies.

Part II

Joining Japanese Game Research

Contents

Access Game Resources with Game Archives

Kazufumi Fukuda

Contents

F. Ikuine et al. (eds.), *Japanese Game Studies*, https://doi.org/10.1007/978-981-95-9857-1_7

7.1 Background

Do we really need to maintain game archives in the world of game studies?[1]

Regarding existing academic resources,[2] such as books and papers, researchers in game studies generally agree on the importance of archiving and accessibility. This is similar to other academic fields, where everyone knows that archived resources shape the study of games. However, within the gaming community, there is no clear consensus on whether we should archive the games themselves, and the slow progress in game archives compared to books and papers indicates a lack of agreement.

Several basic factors contribute to the slow development of game archives. For example, games are a new form of media compared with traditional academic resources; thus, they do not fall within the general scope of conventional archive institutions such as libraries and museums. The cost of obtaining and maintaining the hardware required for gaming is also a barrier to its widespread adoption. Additionally, the limited use of game archives in research compared with traditional media is a significant factor, although this might be because the archives are not well established.

From interviews with academic professionals, Barwick et al. (2009) found that increasing interest in digital games is hindered by a shortage of research collections for historical studies. In other words, game studies thus far have been biased because of the lack of game materials. Creating archives that are comprehensive and easy to access could open up new areas of research and generate more interest.

7.2 Scope

In this section, we explore the world of game archives in Japan and discuss the possibility of using their original materials and data. First, let us understand what archives mean. Recently, the term has broadened to cover places such as libraries to data and content on platforms such as social networking sites (SNS) and YouTube. In this study, we recognize video games as cultural heritage and focus on the institutions that preserve and document them.

Starting with an overview of the game archives situation in Japan, we examined how domestic institutions allow research-oriented access to game resources. We introduce you to each institution and the resources they offer.

1 In this chapter, we define an archive as "a collection of cultural resources that are gathered, preserved, and provided, along with the mechanisms facilitating these processes." While the term "archive" is sometimes broadly used for collections of digital information resources influenced by platforms like SNS and video-sharing services, our focus is on the activities of institutions with the mission outlined in the earlier definition. We specifically target activities conducted by institutions, such as libraries, museums, and organizations dedicated to archive formation and research.

2 Resources refer to identifiable and accessible individual entities. In this chapter, we primarily focus on academic or cultural subjects as a substantial part of these resources.

Next, we discuss the data generated by archives, especially metadata that are openly licensed. Copyright laws significantly affect archival content. Among the contents held by archival institutions, metadata faces relatively fewer copyright challenges. Consequently, the field has seen progress in practices like data creation, publication, and research accumulation. Therefore, metadata is a key theme in this chapter.

We also discuss the services and activities of the Media Arts Database, a hub for data from Japanese game archive institutions. Exploring linked open data and its technical background, we discuss how it can be used, particularly in collaboration with fields such as social research and digital humanities.

This chapter provides a guide for exploring game archives in Japan or online from anywhere in the world, which is perfect for students and researchers interested in Japanese game studies.

7.3 The Situation of Game Archives in Japan

Japanese video games have played a significant role in the formation of global gaming culture and industry (Consalvo 2016), but the development of their archives has been limited. Although it is challenging to specify the reasons, some domestic factors can be considered in addition to the aforementioned ones:

- There are archival functions in the market, and the need for archives by public institutions is weak.
- Game holdings are perceived as unsuitable for traditional archival institutions.

What functions are related to the market archives mentioned above? These include, for example, game shops that buy and sell used items, game centers (arcades) providing nostalgic retro games, and the re-release sales of works such as FAMICOM MINI[3] and Game Archives. Given this market environment, obtaining specific game titles to play is not particularly challenging for game users. However, the re-release market, for instance, is limited to certain titles, and surveys in the United States indicate that it constitutes only 13% of classic video games (Salvador 2023). Nevertheless, considering the strong influence of market functions, the difficulty of nurturing archival culture is highlighted not only in games but also in discourses surrounding archives in Japan (Nemoto 2021).

Regarding the second point about the culture of archival institutions, Japanese libraries do not possess games. Although the National Diet Library, as mentioned later, holds games, its accessibility is limited. However, at the annual Library Comprehensive Exhibition, the "Library and Game Club" events organized by the library gained attention, and the use of board games in library events has become a movement. Consequently, although the collection of board games is slowly

3 "FAMICOM MINI", 2004. Nintendo. Accessed January 1, 2023. 7 https://www.nintendo.co.jp/n08/fmk/

increasing (Inoue et al. 2018), the collection and service provision of video games in libraries have not become active.

Due to these factors, games are likely not included within the scope of traditional archival institutions in Japan. However, as discussed in the past, games are being lost daily due to the deterioration of media and the obsolescence of platforms (Lowood et al. 2009; Gooding and Terras 2008). Numerous games have been created and distributed in Japan, including several works and versions that have not been officially released overseas. In essence, except for a few collectors, Japanese gaming products are not intended to be experienced by overseas users, and opportunities are limited. Games released as "Japanese games" overseas are mostly limited to localized products. Game packages, manuals, and even in-game texts and visual representations may differ. In recent game studies, bibliographical perspectives such as these might not be highly emphasized, perhaps because they seem too obvious to us living in the same era. However, such studies of different versions are crucial, as they provide evidence of a work's existence and demonstrate differences in time, region, authorship, and publishing, offering an essential perspective in game studies. This approach is expected to become more important in the future when users with memories of actual experiences become dust.

However, there are several unique and challenging issues associated with building game archives. These include methods for the long-term physical preservation of media, creating catalogs for accessible resources, digitizing packages and manuals, copying game content for preservation, setting up environments to play games on obsolete game consoles and platforms, and developing methods to preserve the vast number of online resources of video games. Moreover, the accumulation of these methodologies, training archivists, establishing sustainable systems for archives, and more collectively pose significant challenges. These challenges can only be addressed through diligent daily practices and research on archival institutions.

In this context, game research has been developing in Japan since the late 1990s, and institutions specializing in game education have been established since the 2000s. Details of these developments are discussed in a separate section. However, with the institutionalization of activities related to game research and education and the clarification of societal needs, there is an increasing need to gradually consider archives.

7.4 Game Archives in Japan

As discussed thus far, game archives are still being developed; however, several noteworthy initiatives are underway. Considering that the readers of this book are mainly researchers investigating Japanese games from abroad, with a focus on supporting research activities during limited stays in Japan, I introduce three Japanese archive institutions. These institutions provide online catalogs that are accessible overseas, thus allowing limited access to the materials. Subsequently, I briefly introduce other video game holding institutions in Japan. It is important to note that the web services operated by these institutions are primarily in Japanese, and even if there is English information, it is often supplementary. Therefore, overseas users may need to be Japanese language learners or use translation services to access them. However, contact with individual institutions is likely to be possible in English.

7.4.1 National Diet Library (NDL)

Tokyo Main Library: 1-10-1 Nagatacho, Chiyoda-ku, Tokyo, 100-8924, Japan.

► https://www.ndl.go.jp/

The National Diet Library (NDL) is the parliamentary library that supports legislative research by Japanese parliamentarians and is the only library in Japan that collects materials through the legal deposit system.

The NDL holds the largest collection in the country, including video games as part of the legal deposit (National Diet Library 2022). These video games are searchable through an online public catalog called NDL Online (National Diet Library 2018).

To retrieve information on their holdings, a service called Japan Search, which targets regional portal services, such as Europeana and DPLA, was used. A search was conducted using specific call numbers (YH219, YH239, YH259, YH279, YH519) for video games, and as of the writing of this article (2023-01-02), there are 5965 holdings.[4] These include home consoles, portable games, and PC games, with a breakdown by era, as shown in ◘ Table 7.1.

Since the legal deposit system began in the 2000s, the collections at the National Diet Library (NDL) have primarily focused on video games. Initially, the legal deposit rate was not high (Saito 2012), but it has been on the rise, partly because of increased awareness among game publishers. For research purposes, the NDL provides limited accessibility, allowing the play and handling of some games as long as they own the gaming console for which the game is intended. Although accessibil-

◘ **Table 7.1** Number of video games held by year (National Diet Library)

Period	Number of held
1980s	5
1990s	251
2000s	2796
2010s	2550
2020s	362

4 Snorql for Japan Search. Accessed January 3, 2023.

ity is limited, the recent addition of gameplay is indicative of ongoing efforts to enhance services.

Additionally, for game researchers, it is crucial to not overlook nongame resources related to gaming when considering the NDL, particularly magazines and books. The role of media has been extensively discussed in the context of the rise and cultural establishment of Japan's video game industry.

The resources available, such as magazines and books, are far more extensive than the limited game collections. For researchers focusing on these resources, there is significant value in accessing them.

Moreover, the NDL offers access to a portion of its holdings through the "NDL Digital Collection" service (National Diet Library 2011). This service provides access to digitized content for materials that are challenging to obtain in the market for reasons such as being out-of-print and still under copyright or rights confirmation.[5] Full-text content is searchable through OCR, and the user interface was updated at the end of 2022, receiving high usability ratings. The digitized materials include 1.28 million books, 1.35 million magazines, and more.[6] Game magazines, such as the industry paper "Amusement Industry," fall under this category. Users with borrowing rights residing in Japan can freely access digitized materials anywhere through the personal delivery service.[7] However, for users residing outside Japan, a visit to the National Diet Library or its partner libraries is necessary for access.[8]

7.4.2 NPO Game Preservation Society (GPS)

Tokyo Head Office: 8-19-1 Todoroki, Setagaya-ku, Tokyo, Japan.

► https://www.gamepres.org/

The NPO Game Preservation Society, established in 2011, is a nonprofit organization (NPO) to preserve and research games, related equipment, and materials, as well as promote culture.[9]

They house a collection of over 15,000 game titles[10] with a primary focus on PC games. Their collection of retro PC games distributed in Japan since the 1980s is unparalleled, particularly in comparison to other domains. Despite the lower inter-

5 National Diet Library. n.d. "About". NDL Digital Collection. Accessed January 2, 2023. 7 https://dl.ndl.go.jp/en/intro.

6 Ibid.

7 National Diet Library. n.d. "User Registration". National Diet Library. Accessed January 5, 2023. 7 https://ndl.go.jp/en/registration/.

8 National Diet Library. n.d. "List of the "Digitized Contents Transmission Service for Libraries" partner libraries". NDL Digital Collection. Accessed January 5, 2023. 7 https://dl.ndl.go.jp/en/soshin_librarylist.

9 Game Preservation Society. n.d. "Organization Overview". Accessed January 3, 2023. 7 https://www.gamepres.org/overview/.

10 Game Preservation Society. n.d. "Business Report for Fiscal Year 2021". Accessed January 3, 2023. 7 https://www.gamepres.org/public/2021%E5%B9%B4%E5%BA%A6_%E4%BA%8B%E6%A5%AD%E5%A0%B1%E5%91%8A%E6%9B%B8.pdf.

national recognition of Japanese PC games compared with competitive home and arcade games, these PC games represent a significant genre that predates or runs parallel to the widely played home console games.

On their web page, the Game Preservation Society offers a game catalog for the PC-8001 and PC8801 game packages,[11] allowing users to search for a subset of titles in their main collection list.[12] Given the vulnerability of media types, such as magnetic disks and cassette tapes, commonly used in PC games of that era, society places significant emphasis on constructing a preservation environment, including temperature and humidity control, as well as material-specific categorization and management.

They also possess extensive knowledge about preservation techniques related to retro PC games and are actively involved in various research and development projects.

In addition to games, they maintain a vast collection of over 2200 magazines, including Monthly Micro Computer Magazine, Maycom Basic Magazine, I/O, and PiO, as related materials.[13,14]

While they provide archive access as a service, many of their preserved materials are inherently fragile because of the nature of the media. Consequently, there are usage restrictions, requiring users to apply through the Archive Usage Request Form[15] and explicitly state the purpose of access. Additionally, they recommend supporter registration for those who intend to use their services.

7.4.3 Ritsumeikan Center for Game Studies, Ritsumeikan University (RCGS)

56-1 Toji-in Kitamachi, Kita-ku, Kyoto (Kinugasa Campus, Ritsumeikan University)

► https://www.rcgs.jp/

Established in 2011, the Ritsumeikan Center for Game Studies (Ritsumeikan University) is an academic institution specializing in game research. Serving as a prominent academic hub in Japan, it encompasses a wide range of research projects, including Game Studies, societal applications of games, serious games, gamification, industrial research, and legal studies, such as copyright. The center hosted

11 Game Preservation Society. n.d. "Game Catalog". Accessed January 3, 2023. 7 https://www.gamepres.org/dbsearch/.
12 Game Preservation Society. n.d. "Archive List". Accessed January 3, 2023. 7 https://www.gamepres.org/overview/archive-list/.
13 Game Preservation Society. n.d. "Notice of Opening of Headquarters Reference Room". Accessed January 3, 2023. 7 https://www.gamepres.org/2015/05/02/library/.
14 Game Preservation Society. n.d. "Reference Room List". Accessed January 3, 2023. 7 https://www.gamepres.org/overview/booklist/.
15 Game Preservation Society. n.d. "Request Form for Archive Use (Guest)". Accessed January 3, 2023. 7 https://www.gamepres.org/contact-visitor/archive-visitor/.

DiGRA 2019,[16] which was held in Japan, and has a track record of hosting numerous international researchers.

Their involvement in operating the "Replaying Japan" conference,[17] an international conference focusing on Japanese games, aligns with the concept of this book. They excel at networking with international entities. Although it's a slight deviation, the content presented at the Replaying Japan conference and the "Replaying Japan Journal," the conference's magazine, may align with the interests of this book's readers. I recommend exploring the bibliographic information, DOI, and the list of open-access PDF links to papers on their website.[18]

The establishment of game archives as cultural resources is one of the most crucial projects of the center. This project traces its roots back to the "Game Archive Project"[19] initiated at Ritsumeikan University in 1998, operating since the dawn of Japanese game research.

Bibliographic data regarding their collection is available on the online catalog service "RCGS Collection" (Ritsumeikan Center for Game Studies 2017), as shown in ◘ Figs. 7.1 and 7.2. This service, the result of research focusing on video

◘ **Fig. 7.1** RCGS collection top page

16 "DiGRA 2019 KYOTO JAPAN Aug. 6-10, 2019 - Game, Play and the Emerging Ludo Mix". DiGRA 2019. Accessed January 3, 2023. 7 https://www.digra2019.org/.

17 Replaying Japan. Accessed January 3, 2023. 7 http://replaying.jp/.

18 "Journal Replaying Japan". Ritsumeikan Center for Game Studies. Accessed January 3, 2023. 7 https://www.rcgs.jp/?page_id=200.

19 GAPweb: GameArchiveProject. Accessed January 3, 2023. 7 http://www.gamearchive.jp/.

Fig. 7.2 Resource detail for “The Legend of Zelda: Breath of the Wild”—RCGS collection [English translation]

Table 7.2 Top 10 numbers of titles by platform on RCGS collection

Platform	Number
PlayStation	2231
PlayStation 2	1325
Microsoft Windows	791
Super Famicom	643
PlayStation portable	513
PC engine	499
Family computer	445
Nintendo DS	389
Dreamcast	382
Sega Saturn	380

game cataloging, was built using the open-source digital curation application Omeka S,[20] which provides Linked Open Data.[21]

According to the service, their collection comprises 9541 game packages and 7492 game-related materials, including books, game magazines, pamphlets, and flyers. Considering the multiple copies, the item count reached 20,123 as of November 2023.[22] The collection predominantly centers on home video games, mainly from the 1990s onward. Table 7.2 lists the title counts by platform. These include a significant number of PC games and an extensive collection of game magazines published since the 1980s. Information about the table of contents and articles can be found; for more details, a dashboard presenting data summaries is available for reference.[23]

Unfortunately, as of 2022, they do not provide public access to their materials. However, many international researchers have utilized these resources. If you are considering conducting research involving their archives, please check the contact information available on their website.[24] In addition, they are actively developing services, including hosting archive access days within the institution, and there are

20 Omeka S. Accessed January 3, 2023. 7 https://omeka.org/s/.
21 Ritsumeikan Center for Game Studies. n.d. "About this site". RCGS Collection. Accessed January 3, 2023. 7 https://collection.rcgs.jp/doc/about.
22 The number is counted by RCGS SPARQL.
Ritsumeikan Center for Game Studies. 2017. "RCGS SPARQL". RCGS Collection. Accessed November 3, 2023.
23 Ritsumeikan Center for Game Studies. n.d. "Data Overview | RCGS Collection." RCGS Collection. Accessed November 3, 2023. 7 https://collection.rcgs.jp/page/dashboard.
24 Ritsumeikan Center for Game Studies. n.d. "Contact". Ritsumeikan Center for Game Studies. Accessed January 3, 2023. 7 https://www.rcgs.jp/?page_id=275.

expectations for the future expansion of services to the general public (Mohri et al. 2023). Given that it is an institution affiliated with numerous researchers, it provides opportunities for discussions related to game research and archives.

7.4.4 Other Archives in Japan

In addition to the mentioned institutions, there are several game-related archive organizations in Japan. We briefly introduce the following:

- Analog Game Museum. ► http://analoggamemuseum.org/.
- BANDAI Musuem (Tochigi). ► https://www.bandai-museum.jp/.
- Japan Game Museum (Gihu). ► http://japangamemuseum.com/ (Currently closed).
- Natsuge Museum (Shinjuku-ku, Tokyo). ► http://www.t-tax.net/natuge/.
- Nintendo Museum (Kyoto). ► https://museum.nintendo.com.

The Analog Game Museum is an archive institution that focuses on tabletop games such as board games, card games, tabletop role-playing games, and traditional games. It was established in 2021. It houses samples from Game Market, Japan's largest analog game expo, showcasing a variety of major and indie tabletop games. The museum provides an online catalog[25] and datasets.[26]

The BANDAI Museum, located in the Tochigi Prefecture, specializes in toys produced by companies such as BANDAI and Poppy. The museum exhibits a collection of toys from Japan and around the world, including Gundam, video games, and penny arcades.

The Japan Game Museum, based in Aichi Prefecture, preserves a large-scale arcade archive focusing on interactive games. Despite a temporary closure in 2016, the museum plans to reopen and boasts expertise in maintaining retro arcade games like Ere-meka, pinball, and table games.

The Natsuge Museum, a game center-themed museum in Shinjuku-ku, Tokyo, offers convenience to visitors. It houses a substantial collection of arcade games from the 1980s to the 1990s, actively participating in arcade game exhibition events organized by institutions without game collections (Ritsumeikan Center for Game Studies 2016, 17–21).

The Nintendo Museum, established in 2024 in Uji City, Kyoto Prefecture, showcases a vast array of products previously released by Nintendo. In addition to the exhibits, the museum features hands-on gaming zones and various workshops. As of 2026, entry operates on a prior-booking system requiring reservations three months ahead.

In relation to this, the Research Project for Collaboration of Game Archive Institutions, led by Ritsumeikan University, investigates and promotes the collabora-

25 AGM Search. Accessed January 4, 2023. 7 https://id.analoggamemuseum.org/.
26 "GitHub—agmsearch". Github. Accessed January 4, 2023. 7 https://github.com/fukudakz/agmsearch.

tion of game archive institutions globally. This is described in Japanese, and referring to their report provides further insight.[27] Additionally, the Consortium for Game Archives Promotion,[28] a consortium involving many archive institutions, conducts seminars on game archive topics several times a year. Researchers who conduct surveys at multiple archive institutions can use this council as a valuable contact resource.

7.5 Media Arts Database: The Aggregator

7.5.1 Overview

The Media Arts Database, as introduced in the previous section, is a service that aggregates bibliographic data published by Japanese game archive institutions. Operated by the National Center for Art Research (NCAR), this service underwent significant improvements by Agency for Cultural Affairs in 2019 after its initial release in 2015, transitioning into a beta version, and operations were transferred to the National Center for Art Research in 2023.

The term "Media Arts" (Media Geijutsu) is defined in Article 9 of the Basic Act for Culture and the Arts and refers to artistic endeavors involving movies, manga, animation, and art utilizing computers and other electronic devices.[29] Computer-based art includes video games and media art. Although the terminology and structure may seem unconventional, they align with the definitions used in administrative and private initiatives. For a more detailed history of the development of media arts policies, please refer to Mihara (2022).

Currently, the Media Arts Database functions as an aggregator for archives in four fields: manga, animation, games, and media art. An aggregator collects reliable data through the collaboration of archive institutions within a specific domain and promotes data standardization. This concept was inspired by Europeana, a portal service for cultural heritage data in the European region (Liaison and Working-Level Consultative Meeting of Relevant Ministries and Agencies on Collaboration of Digital Archive 2017; Europeana n.d.). Positioned as an aggregator in the field of media arts, the Media Arts Database also serves as a hub for Japan's cultural heritage portal service Japan Search. ◘ Figure 7.3 illustrates the aggregation of archive institutions and metadata.

Through such data aggregation, the Media Arts Database contains metadata based on an extensive collection of information.

In the Media Arts Database, the primary unit of identification and description is termed as an "item." Given that media arts focus on art involving media and are

27 "Media Arts Related Projects". Ritsumeikan Center for Game Studies. Accessed January 3, 2023. 7 https://www.rcgs.jp/?page_id=1316.

28 Consortium for Game Archives Promotion. Accessed November 22, 2023. 7 https://consortiumforgamearchive.blogspot.com/.

29 "Basic Act for the Culture and the Arts". e-Gov Law Search. Accessed January 3, 2023. 7 https://elaws.e-gov.go.jp/document?lawid=413AC1000000148.

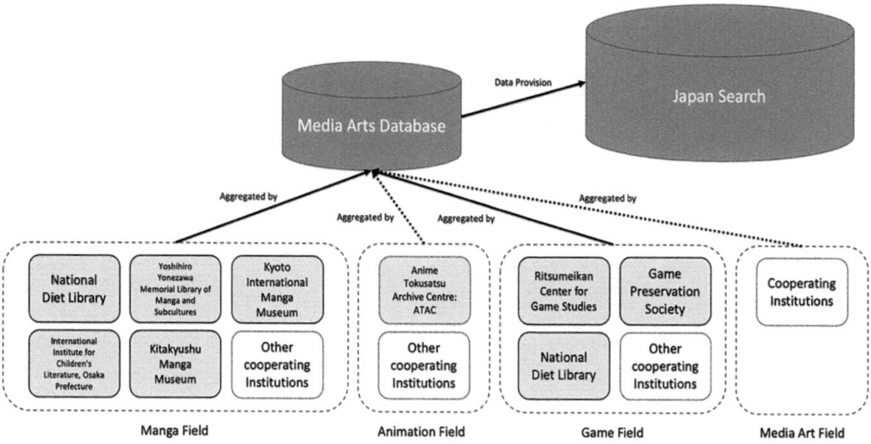

Fig. 7.3 Data aggregation by media arts database

often characterized by their replicable nature, they share similarities with library materials. Therefore, the Media Arts Database adopts models, such as FRBR (IFLA Study Group on the Functional Requirements for Bibliographic Records 2009), IFLA LRM (Riva et al. 2017), and BIBFRAME (The Library of Congress n.d.), the latter being a redefined model by the Library of Congress for Linked Open Data. For instance, BIBFRAME describes entities equivalent to items in the Media Arts Database, referred to as instances, as follows:

> Instance. A Work may have one or more individual, material embodiments, for example, a particular published form. These are Instances of the Work. An Instance reflects information such as its publisher, place and date of publication, and format. (The Library of Congress 2016)

In the context of media arts, a work is realized in specific formats, and these manifestations are referred to as "Item." In the case of manga, they exist as manga magazines or bound volumes; for animation, as television programs or DVDs; and for games, as physical products or online resources in the form of product packages. Media art, however, is an exception within media arts, as its materials are less often replicated. In this field, exhibitions and performances define the concept of items in which the realization of media art occurs through displays or performances in specific museums or galleries.

The term "Work" here refers to created content, which can be equated to game titles in the gaming domain. Examples include titles such as "The Legend of Zelda," "Final Fantasy VII," "Bayonetta," and "Cave Story." While these may seem abstract compared with tangible materials and products, people routinely identify games on a work-by-work basis. In fact, knowledge databases on the Internet, such as Wikipedia (n.d.) and its knowledge base, Wikidata (n.d.), along with MobyGames (1999), IGDB (Twitch n.d.), and BoardGameGeek (2000), often record resources at the level of "Work."

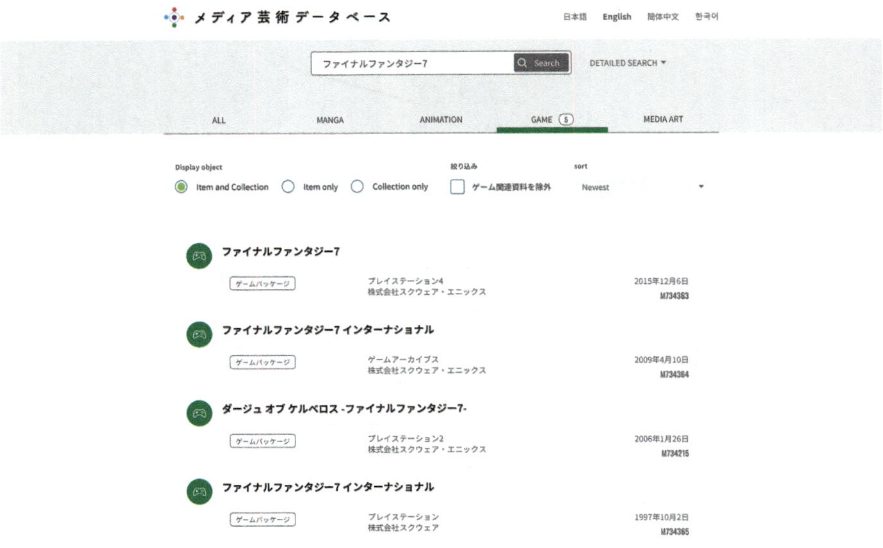

Fig. 7.4 Search results for "Final Fantasy 7"—Media Arts Database

To better understand the distinction between items and works, consider the following question: How many times has "Final Fantasy VII" been packaged? Initially, there were releases in various regions, including special edition packages. Economy versions of the package, such as the PS One Books edition in Japan, may also have been released. Originally on the PlayStation platform, the game was ported to other platforms, such as Windows. Additionally, there is an enhanced edition known as the Final Fantasy VII International version, which potentially doubles the number of versions. In 2020, a remake version titled Final Fantasy VII Remake was released, adding complexity as it is part of a series, with only the first installment available at the time of writing.

The logical and practical descriptions of complex resources and the relationships between resources for such cases have been addressed by various researchers (McDonough et al. 2010; Fukuda and Mihara 2018; Hoffmann 2019; Lee et al. 2020). Building on this research, the Media Arts Database defines the information format for each field while considering commonalities. Details are outlined in the metadata schema of the Media Arts Database (Fukuda et al. 2022).

Following the defined information format (metadata schema), the data were registered and integrated into the Media Arts Database. Figure 7.4 illustrates the search results for "Final Fantasy 7" in the Media Arts Database. The total count was 44 items, comprising 36 manga, 8 games, and 2 compilations. The manga resources include magazine articles related to strategy and release information. The eight game items all represent the physical manifestations of "Final Fantasy 7" and its related works as product packages. Collections are entities defined separately from items and used to group items. Collection subtypes include game works and game software versions (Game Variation), as well as individuals or organizations.

Table 7.3 Number of resources in media arts database

Type	Number of resources
Manga—Item	522,426
Animation—Item	136,768
Game—Item	49,684
Media art—Item	14,335
Collection	271,178

The two collection resources in this case are both game works, namely, "Final Fantasy VII"[30] and "Final Fantasy 7 Crisis Core."[31]

The overall status of resource registrations in this database is outlined in Table 7.3 as of the writing of this article (Agency for Cultural Affairs 2019).

Although the coverage of resources in the gaming domain is not yet comprehensive, registrations are extensive, particularly for home consoles and arcade games. Furthermore, with the inclusion of data from the Game Preservation Society, there is an anticipated increase in registrations in the PC gaming domain. When an archive institution holds a specific game package, the collection information is strategically designed to be displayed on the lower section of the item details page, guiding users to access the materials.

7.6 Archival Data Utilization: Linked Open Data

The Media Arts Database offers access to numerous archival collections through a web-based user interface (Web UI), as introduced earlier. This enhances accessibility to primary materials, such as games, books, magazines, flyers, and other gaming-related documents, providing opportunities for broader and deeper research in areas such as game history, game design theory, and even game archeology.Another significant feature of the Media Arts Database is its functionality in Linked Open Data (LOD). This involves the mechanized readability of data, connecting with external datasets, and aiming to facilitate the private use of data, as well as its application in research. This serves as an accessible service and dataset for readers without the need for on-site visits. This section discusses its overview.

30 Agency for Cultural Affairs. 2019. "Final Fantasy VII". Media Arts Database. Accessed January 4, 2023. https://mediaarts-db.artmuseums.go.jp/id/C32402

31 Agency for Cultural Affairs. 2019. "Final Fantasy VII Crisis Core". Media Arts Database. Accessed January 4, 2023. https://mediaarts-db.artmuseums.go.jp/id/C31565

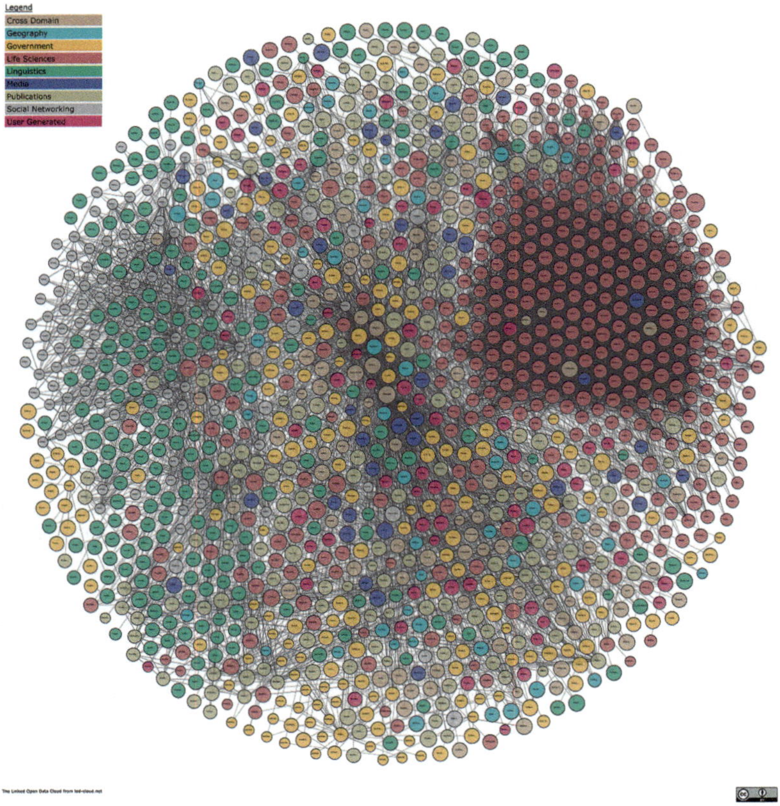

Fig. 7.5 Linking among LOD datasets on the Internet (The Linked Open Data Cloud n.d.)

Linked Open Data refers to the foundational technology of the Semantic Web for publishing and exchanging data on the Internet, simultaneously acting as a type of social movement. This technology allows the connection of multiple publicly available datasets. Figure 7.5 illustrates the connectivity of the Linked Open Data datasets on the web. Datasets using this technology are continually increasing, with various systems and applications actively utilizing it. Linked Open Data has become a standard for data publication by various archive institutions and aggregators collecting data from these institutions, considering it a superior form of open data.

Linked Open Data utilizes URI-based global resource IDs through the Resource Description Framework (RDF), describing data models that can be represented as directed graphs (networks) (RDF Working Group 2014). RDF datasets are compatible with data queries using a language called SPARQL (SPARQL Protocol and RDF Query Language; The W3C SPARQL Working Group 2013). Both RDF and SPARQL are technologies aligned with web standards promoted by the World Wide Web Consortium (W3C). Using these, multiple datasets can be queried as if they were a single dataset. Moreover, specific patterns and filtering can be specified, allowing the selection and extraction of various resources in almost any form as long as they are connected.

The update to the beta version of the Media Arts Database in 2019, because of renovations, aimed to publish data as Linked Open Data. Since then, all metadata registered in the service has been converted into Linked Open Data and made publicly available. The features related to Linked Open Data in the Media Arts Database were consolidated in the MADB Lab (Agency for Cultural Affairs 2021) service, where users can download Linked Open Data dumps. In addition, a dynamic access provision in the form of a SPARQL endpoint, a Linked Open Data API, is available. The SPARQL endpoint is a web interface that allows users and other devices to query and retrieve specific data dynamically.

Now, let's briefly consider the scholarly use of this dataset.

As a premise, there has been a considerable accumulation of scholarly use of Linked Open Data. For example, in the areas of artificial intelligence, social surveys, genetic research, and data visualization. However, practices exist in cultural studies, particularly in the digital humanities, but the field of humanities as a whole is not very active (Middle 2022; Hawkins 2022). Research in the field of video game culture has been limited. As previously mentioned, the shortage of archives and datasets is presumed to be a significant cause.

In this context, there are actively progressing initiatives such as the diggr project[32] and the Japanese Visual Media Graph (JVMG).[33] These projects, conducted in Germany, aim to construct research datasets for video games and Japanese visual media by collecting, connecting, and standardizing datasets and archival data from various fan community web services for cultural research purposes.

We introduce some of the research outcomes briefly.

Mühleder et al. (2020) interpreted and linked multiple datasets related to video game research using a conceptual model to construct a massive research dataset. This paper explains the process along with the aforementioned technical challenges. The geographical distribution of game development companies in the early stages and in recent years is illustrated to demonstrate their practicality. The construction of research datasets is highly valued in the digital humanities field.

Kacsuk (2021) used the dataset constructed by JVMG to verify one of the claims in Azuma's "Animalizing Postmodern Otaku: Japan's Database Animals". The concept of "database consumption" is well-known in the book, where characters in Japanese anime can be broken down into more elements, and new characters are created from these elements. This study attempted to verify database consumption using large-scale datasets. The results from analyzing datasets of characters in Japanese anime and visual novel games did not provide strong evidence to support the hypothesis that the production of new characters relies increasingly on popular templates. It was suggested that the trend observed during Azuma's analysis might have been a boom concentrated during that period or a fundamental tendency based on the technology represented by Japanese animation. This chapter includes a long manuscript that literature survey on multiple data-driven game expression

---

32 diggr. Accessed December 31, 2023. 7 https://diggr.link/

33 Japanese Visual Media Graph. Accessed December 31, 2023. 7 https://jvmg.iuk.hdm-stuttgart.de/

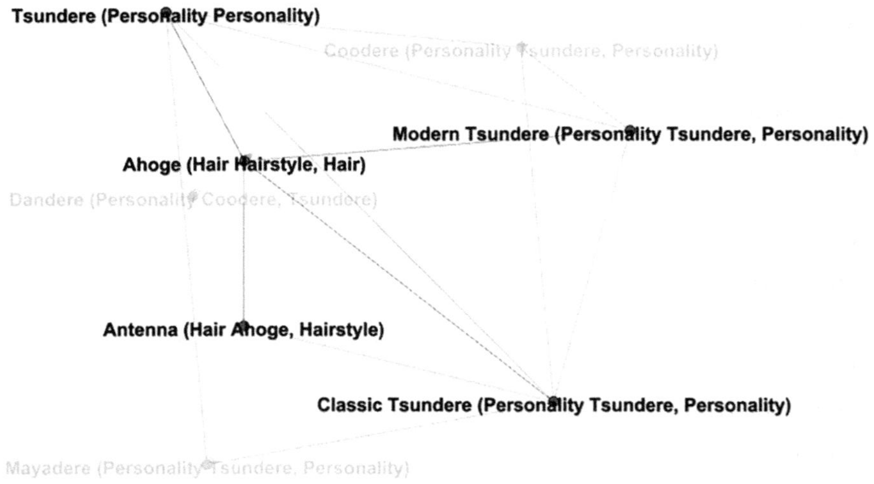

Fig. 7.6 A limited selection of the graph from the visual novel database (Bruno 2021, 164)

studies and research using fan community datasets, making it highly useful. Additionally, Bruno's article in the same book (Bruno 2021) used JVMG's visual novel dataset to analyze the characteristics of characters. Figure 7.6 shows a limited selection of the graph from the visual novel database (Bruno 2021, 164), illustrating the relevance of the features that constitute characters. This indicates a strong correlation between the term "Ahoge" and the personality archetype "Tsundere" is suggested. In the conclusion of this article, he points out the limitations of Azuma's discourse (Azuma et al. 2009), similar to those of Kacsuk (2021). This suggests that rather than being purely database-centric, it is deeply intertextual. This concept aligns closely with Santos's (2020) discourse based on BL culture analysis. This highlights the idea that fans intricately layer and transform meanings, underscoring the significance of paying attention to this process (Fig. 7.6).

These studies, which rely heavily on datasets generated by fan communities, including archival data and using Linked Open Data technology, have advanced their methodology and conclusions. They provided many implications for the purpose of this section.

7.7 Subjects and Future Perspectives

As discussed thus far, game archives have the potential to significantly transform game studies. With accessible game collections emerging worldwide, how might game research evolve? In fields such as game history and design, researchers can anticipate the expansion of macroscopic and empirical studies based on individual perspectives.

Linked Open Data followed a similar trajectory. While some argue that searching for game data on Wikipedia alone is sufficient, this perspective should recognize that it stems from discourse based on dataset inadequacies. Academic inquiries require more nuanced and detailed data environments, enabling integrated analysis. Explicitly stating the existence of various instantiated items and variations between them, coupled with accessibility, offers considerable room for the advancement or expansion of game research.

However, clear challenges remain in this regard. The underdevelopment of an ecosystem for utilizing digital data in research, represented by Linked Data, is a significant hurdle. Having accessible resources such as datasets or endpoints alone may be challenging for students and researchers who are unfamiliar with these technologies. Tools and the development of new methodologies and perspectives are required to facilitate this. The Digital Humanities (DH) field, which applies computer technology to humanities research, offers insights in this regard. For instance, the concept of "The Methodological Commons" is emphasized in DH, described as "an abstract area for the computational methods that the various disciplines of application share."[34] In other words, it is an approach that shares computational methods and breaks down the black boxes in data usage and analysis. Concerning archival data usage in game studies, there is a high need to consciously develop shared spaces and communities for openness, including not only data but also tools.

Moreover, for game researchers, discussions with technicians are crucial to obtain data that meet the requirements aligned with better ontologies (forms of information) and research objectives. Technicians alone cannot determine the information requirements of game researchers who are domain experts. As mentioned below, collaboration with archivists is indispensable when utilizing archival data.

Archival scholars and practitioners bring their own set of professional concerns and priorities to the Linked Data environment, ranging from rights management and documentation of provenance(s) and other necessary contextual and administrative data to issues regarding the decolonization of archival description and descriptive practices and the long-term preservation of Archival Linked Data (Hawkins 2022).

Additionally, Oldman makes the following observation: "can be explained, in part, by the lack of engagement or involvement of domain experts themselves in the digital representation of their data, and their lack of knowledge about the possibilities of Semantic technologies, ultimately resulting in the dominance of the technologist at the so-called intersection of digital humanities (Oldman et al. 2016)." Therefore, the collaboration between game researchers and technicians is crucial. The risk of not fostering collaboration is the potential strengthening of the political dominance of technicians, leading to the mass production of low-value data. It is essential to emphasize collaboration to mitigate this risk and ensure the creation of valuable and meaningful data in the field of game studies.

---

34 "Methodologies | EADH—The European Association for Digital Humanities", 7 https://eadh.org/methodologies. (Accessed 2023-09-19)

7.8 Conclusion

In this study, we focused on discussing video game archives, particularly emphasizing well-established linked data. However, when considering digital archives and digital humanities, there is an even broader and more substantial research focus on the construction and research utilization of game content archives, including images, videos, and audio. As mentioned earlier, because these are copyrighted works, it is generally not possible to publicly release them owing to copyright restrictions, except for a few public-domain works in which copyrights have expired or been waived. Nevertheless, it is likely that many institutions hold this content data for research purposes. Various research opportunities are expanding in this domain, including quantitative content analysis using techniques such as character recognition and image analysis.

Although the field of game archives remains underdeveloped, it is currently in its early stages, and numerous researchers are beginning to recognize and participate in the vast research opportunities it presents. We look forward to advances in this field of research.

References

National Center for Art Research. 2019. Media Arts Database. https://mediaarts-db.bunka.go.jp. Accessed April 24, 2026.

Agency for Cultural Affairs. 2021. MADB Lab. https://mediag.bunka.go.jp/. Accessed April 24, 2026.

Azuma, Hiroki, Jonathan E. Abel, and Shion Kohno. 2009. *Otaku: Japan's Database Animals*. Minneapolis: University of Minnesota Press. 東浩紀. 2001. 動物化するポストモダン オタクから見た日本社会. 講談社.

Barwick, Joanna, Adrienne Muir, and James Dearnley. 2009. Where Have All the Games Gone? Explorations on the Cultural Significance of Digital Games and Preservation. In *Proceedings of the 2009 DiGRA International Conference: Breaking New Ground: Innovation in Games, Play, Practice and Theory*. London: Brunel University. http://www.digra.org/wp-content/uploads/digital-library/09287.27184.pdf.

BoardGameGeek. 2000. BoardGameGeek | Gaming Unplugged Since 2000. https://boardgamegeek.com/. Accessed April 24, 2026.

Bruno, Luca. 2021. A Glimpse of the Imaginative Environment: Exploring the Potential of Data-Driven Examinations of Visual Novel Characters. In *Japan's Contemporary Media Culture Between Local and Global: Content, Practice and Theory*, 143–170. Heidelberg, Berlin: CrossAsia-eBooks. https://doi.org/10.11588/xabooks.971.

Consalvo, Mia. 2016. Atari to Zelda: Japan's Videogames in Global Contexts. MIT Press.

Europeana. n.d. Europeana Aggregators Forum. Europeana Pro. https://pro.europeana.eu/page/aggregators. Accessed April 24, 2026.

Fukuda, Kazufumi, and Tetsuya Mihara. 2018. A Development of the Metadata Model for Video Game Cataloging: For the Implementation of Media-Arts Database. In *IFLA WLIC 2018—Kuala Lumpur, Malaysia—Transform Libraries, Transform Societies in Session 75—Audiovisual and Multimedia with Information Technology*, 11. http://library.ifla.org/2132/. Accessed April 24, 2026.

Fukuda, Kazufumi, Ikki Omukai, Tetsuya Mihara, Hideyuki Otsubo, Tetsuro Kamura, Shohei Toyota, and Dai Nippon Printing. 2022. Media Arts Database Metadata Schema Ver. 1.1. Agency for Cultural Affairs. https://github.com/mediaarts-db/dataset/blob/main/doc/MADB%E

3%83%A1%E3%82%BF%E3%83%87%E3%83%BC%E3%82%BF%E3%82%B9%E3%82%AD%E3%83%BC%E3%83%9E%E4%BB%95%E6%A7%98%E6%9B%B8.pdf. Accessed April 24, 2026.

Gooding, P., and M. Terras. 2008. Grand Theft Archive': A Quantitative Analysis of the Current State of Computer Game Preservation. *The International Journal of Digital Curation* 2 (3): https://doi.org/10.2218/ijdc.v3i2.56.

Hawkins, Ashleigh. 2022. Archives, Linked Data and the Digital Humanities: Increasing Access to Digitised and Born-Digital Archives Via the Semantic Web. *Archival Science* 22 (3): 319–344. https://doi.org/10.1007/s10502-021-09381-0.

Hoffmann, Tracy. 2019. Developing a Mediated Vocabulary for Video Game Research. In *Proceedings of the Doctoral Symposium on Research on Online Databases in History 2019*, 11p. http://ceur-ws.org/Vol-2532/paper8.pdf. Accessed January 4, 2023.

IFLA Study Group on the Functional Requirements for Bibliographic Records. 2009. *Functional Requirements for Bibliographic Records: Final Report*. The Hague: International Federation of Library Associations. http://www.ifla.org/files/assets/cataloguing/frbr/frbr_2008.pdf. Accessed January 4, 2023.

Inoue, Nachi, Takakura Akihiro, and Yoshikazu Hinata. 2018. *Library and Game: From Event to Collection*. Nihon Library Association. ISBN: 9784820418115 井上奈智，高倉暁大 & 日向良和. 2018. 図書館とゲーム：イベントから収集へ. 日本図書館協会.

Kacsuk, Zoltan. 2021. Using Fan-Compiled Metadata for Anime, Manga and Video Game Research: Revisiting Azuma's 'Otaku: Japan's Database Animals' Twenty Years On. In *Japan's Contemporary Media Culture Between Local and Global*, 117–142. CrossAsia. https://doi.org/10.11588/xabooks.971.

Lee, Jin Ha, Andrew Perti, Rachel Ivy Clarke, Travis W. Windleharth, and Marc Schmalz. 2020. *Video Game Metadata Schema Version 4.1*. UW/SIMM. http://gamer.ischool.uw.edu/official_release/. Accessed April 24, 2026.

Liaison and Working-Level Consultative Meeting of Relevant Ministries and Agencies on Collaboration of Digital Archive. 2017. *Direction of Digital Archive Promotion in Japan*. Cabinet Office. https://www.kantei.go.jp/jp/singi/titeki2/digitalarchive_kyougikai/houkokusho.pdf. Accessed January 3, 2023. デジタルアーカイブの連携に関する関係省庁等連絡会•実務者協議会. 2017. 我が国におけるデジタルアーカイブ推進の方向性. 内閣府.

Lowood, H., D. Monnens, Z. Vowell, J. Ruggill, K. McAllister, and A. Armstrong. 2009. Before It's Too Late: A Digital Game Preservation White Pape. *American Journal of Play* 2 (2): 139–166.

McDonough, Jerome, Matthew Kirschenbaum, Doug Reside, Neil Fraistat, and Dennis Jerz. 2010. Twisty Little Passages Almost All Alike: Applying the FRBR Model to a Classic Computer Game. *Digital Humanities Quarterly* 4 (2). http://www.digitalhumanities.org/dhq/vol/4/2/000089/000089.html. Accessed April 24, 2026.

Middle, Sarah. 2022. *Investigating Linked Data Usability for Ancient World Research*. Milton Keynes: The Open University. http://oro.open.ac.uk/84767/.

Mihara, Tetsuya. 2022. Administrative Measures for Media Arts and Its Relation to Digital Archives. *Journal of the Japan Society for Digital Archive* 6 (1): 15–19. https://doi.org/10.24506/jsda.6.1_15. 三原鉄也. 2022. 「メディア芸術に関する行政施策の展開とデジタルアーカイブ」. デジタルアーカイブ学会誌 6 (1): 15–19.

MobyGames. 1999. Video Games Database. Credits, Trivia, Reviews, Box Covers, Screenshots—MobyGames. https://www.mobygames.com/. Accessed April 24, 2026.

Mohri, Hitomi, Kazufumi Fukuda, and Shin Juhyung. 2023. [A12] Analysis of User's Requirements for Video Game Resources and Information: From the Practice of Archive Access Day. *Dejitaru Akaibu Gakkaishi* 7 (s2): s43–s46. 毛利仁美，福田一史，and シンジュヒョン. 2023. "[A12] ビデオゲーム資料提供サービス利用者の資料要求•情報要求の分析：アーカイブアクセスデーの実践から." デジタルアーカイブ学会誌 7 (s2): s43–46. https://doi.org/10.24506/jsda.7.s2_s43

Mühleder, Peter, Martin Roth, Tracy Arndt, and Florian Rämisch. 2020. Duct-Taping Databases, or How to Use Fragmentary Online Data for Researching 'Japanese' Videogames. *Journal of the Japanese Association for Digital Humanities* 5 (1): 61–83. https://doi.org/10.17928/jjadh.5.1_61.

National Diet Library. 2011. NDL Digital Collection. https://dl.ndl.go.jp/. Accessed April 24, 2026.

National Diet Library. 2018. NDL ONLINE. https://ndlonline.ndl.go.jp/. Accessed April 24, 2026.

National Diet Library. 2022. *Request for Deposit*. National Diet Library. https://www.ndl.go.jp/jp/collect/deposit/pdf/deposit_request_pvt.pdf. Accessed January 2, 2023. 国立国会図書館. 2022. 納本のお願い. 国立国会図書館.

Nemoto, Akira. 2021. *The Idea of the Archive: A Mechanism for Transforming Words into Knowledge*. Misuzu Shobō. 根本彰. 2021. アーカイブの思想: 言葉を知に変える仕組み. みすず書房.

Oldman, D., M. Doerr, and S. Gradmann. 2016. Zen and the Art of Linked Data: New Strategies for a Semantic Web of Humanist Knowledge. In *A New Companion to Digital Humanities*, ed. S. Schreibman, R. Siemens, and J. Unsworth, 2nd ed., 251–273. New Jersey: Wiley Blackwell.

RDF Working Group. 2014. RDF—Semantic Web Standards. https://www.w3.org/RDF/. Accessed April 24, 2026.

Ritsumeikan Center for Game Studies. 2016. Report of Research Project for Collaboration of Game Archive Institutions. https://mediag.bunka.go.jp/projects/project/rits-gamearchive.pdf. Accessed January 4, 2023.

Ritsumeikan Center for Game Studies. 2017. RCGS Collection. https://collection.rcgs.jp. Accessed April 24, 2026.

Riva, Pat, Patrick Le Boeuf, and Maja Žumer. 2017. *IFLA Library Reference Model: A Conceptual Model for Bibliographic Information*. The Hague: International Federation of Library Associations. https://www.ifla.org/files/assets/cataloguing/frbr-lrm/ifla-lrm-august-2017_rev201712.pdf. Accessed January 4, 2023.

7

Saito, T. 2012. Collection and Preservation of Video Game Softwares in the National Diet Library: Necessity for Establishment of the National Cooperation Framework. *Journal of Digital Games Research* 6 (1): 37 - 41. 齋藤朋子. 2012. 「国立国会図書館におけるゲームソフトの収集と保存: ナショナルな協力体制確立の必要性」. デジタルゲーム学研究 6 (1): 37–41.

Salvador, Phil. 2023. Survey of the Video Game Reissue Market in the United States. Zenodo. https://doi.org/10.5281/zenodo.8161056.

Santos, Kristine Michelle L. 2020. The Bitches of Boys Love Comics: The Pornographic Response of Japan's Rotten Women. *Porn Studies* 7 (3): 1–12.

The Library of Congress. 2016. *Overview of the BIBFRAME 2.0 Model*. Washington, DC: Library of Congress. https://www.loc.gov/bibframe/docs/bibframe2-model.html. Accessed April 24, 2026.

The Library of Congress. n.d. *BIBFRAME—Bibliographic Framework Initiative*. Washington, DC: Library of Congress. https://www.loc.gov/bibframe/. Accessed April 24, 2026.

The Linked Open Data Cloud. n.d. The Linked Open Data Cloud. https://lod-cloud.net/. Accessed April 24, 2026.

The W3C SPARQL Working Group. 2013. SPARQL 1.1 Overview. https://www.w3.org/TR/sparql11-overview/. Accessed April 24, 2026.

Twitch. n.d. IGDB.com. https://www.igdb.com/. Accessed April 24, 2026.

Wikidata. n.d. Wikidata. https://www.wikidata.org/. Accessed April 24, 2026.

Wikipedia. n.d. Wikipedia, the free encyclopedia. https://en.wikipedia.org/. Accessed April 24, 2026.

Differences in Research Environments by Domain in Japan

Akito Inoue and Kazufumi Fukuda

Contents

F. Ikuine et al. (eds.), *Japanese Game Studies*, https://doi.org/10.1007/978-981-95-9857-1_8

8.1 Introduction

In this chapter, we aim to quantitatively visualize the trends in Japanese game research based on bibliographic data and other sources. This methodology can be positioned from a bibliometric perspective.

Regarding trends in English-speaking game research, literature employing such an approach includes Martin's (2018) analysis of 24,128 documents, as well as analyses by Engström (2019), Frome & Martin (2019), Coavoux et al. (2017), and Melcer et al. (2015). These studies have identified major domains, important authors, and other aspects of game research based on publication counts, citation numbers, and so on.

However, the aforementioned studies are primarily from the English-speaking world, and such bibliometric research is not very common in Japan. Despite this situation, Fukuda (2022) created a dataset from domestic literature databases and attempted a quantitative analysis. ▶ Chapter 2 provides an overview of organizations and communities in domestic game research, and the first chapter of this book also outlines the history of game research in Japan.

Therefore, this chapter constructs datasets of bibliographic data related to Japanese video games and projects funded by Kakenhi, Japan's primary competitive research funding, based on the dataset created by Fukuda (2022), and visualize these trends.

Furthermore, by comparing these with the characteristics of English-speaking game research revealed by Martin (2018), Coavoux et al. (2017), and others, we will visualize the distinctive features of Japanese game research.

It should be noted that the data presented in this chapter is not intended to unconditionally affirm the current situation indicated by the data. There are various issues in the current state of Japanese game research, and this data is presented as foundational material for examining these current problems, including critical perspectives.

8.2 Dataset

Integrated Dataset (n = 9202): This is an integration of the following three datasets. The combined total of the three datasets below is 10,945, but after removing duplicates, the final count is 9,202.

- **Dataset 1: Bibliography Data (a) CiNii, J-Stage, NDL Search (n = 6583)**
  - (a) Characteristic: Bibliographic data related to Japanese game research. This is the data used in Fukuda's (2022) presentation (Fukuda (n.d.)), and it is a dataset with a few missing values for each item.
  - (b) Search Database: CiNii, J-Stage, and NDL Search.
  - (c) Search Method
  - (c1) Free keyword search:

Theory/discourse on video games or board "games", "game design", "game development", "game history", "games in society", "game industry", "social application of games (serious games/gamification)", "eSports".
(c2) Specification of academic journals specializing in game research:
Japan Association of Simulation & Gaming, Information Processing Society of Japan, The Institute of Image Information and Television Engineers, Digital Games Research Association JAPAN, The Institute of Electronics, Information and Communication Engineers, Amusement Industry Research Institute of Osaka University of Commerce, The Institute of Image Electronics Engineers of Japan, Kaneko Shobo, Nikkei Business Publications, Inc., Japan Society for Contents History.
The lists obtained under these conditions were processed for duplicates, resulting in 6583 URIs. Bibliographic information was then obtained using web scraping with this list.
(d) Data Fields: Attributes include resource type, Japanese title, English title, author, publication date, journal name, publisher, volume, issue, start page, end page, language, external ID, external link, keywords, and abstract.
(e) Data Validity Check: 50 articles were randomly extracted from the dataset and visually inspected to determine if they were appropriate for game research. Eight borderline cases, primarily focusing on simulation or game theory, and one inappropriate case (a table of contents article) were identified. It was confirmed that over 80% of the data was appropriate.
(f) Problem: Since most of the data consists of papers, the coverage of important books and other materials is low. Additionally, it was found that materials substantively related to games but lacking game-related vocabulary in their titles or keywords were not well covered.

- **Dataset 2: Bibliography Data (b) Google Scholar (n = 4277)**

(a) Characteristic: Data created for the purpose of knowing the citation count of literature.
(b) Search Database: Google Scholar (October 2022).
(c) Search Method:
Free keyword search: "Game", "Gaming", "Game Industry", "Gamification", "Serious Game", "Digital Game", "TV-Game", "Video Game".
Except Word: "Game Theory".
(d) Data Fields:
Author, Published year, Paper Title, Publisher or Journal, Number of Citations, Number of Google Scholar search hits, Number of Authors, Description.
(e) Data Validity Check:
Among the 5774 acquired items and 85 books, many were deemed unlikely to be video game research literature. Therefore, items that did not meet multiple of the following conditions were considered research outside of game studies and excluded.
Exclusion criteria: The title contains "game", "gamification", "gaming", "sport","play", The description contains "game", "gamification", "gam-

ing", "play", "sport" multiple times. The publication medium name contains words like "game", "gamification" or "information".

As a result, a total of 4277 items were acquired.

It was recognized that excessively long title strings (exceeding 50 characters) were not accurately acquired.

Citation counts tend to be relatively accurate for literature in fields like computer science. However, for humanities books, the reference list section is often not well incorporated into Google Scholar's citation count. Therefore, for books presumed to have a significant influence (citation count of 30 or more), the total number of hits on Google Scholar was recorded for each item individually.

(f) Problem:

Due to the variety of data source styles, there is considerable variation in data format. In particular, many missing values were observed in the Publisher field.

- **Dataset 3: Important Book List Up to 2016 (n = 85)**

(a) Characteristic:

To select important literature in game research, Shinji Matsunaga took the lead, and with Inoue and Fukuda, they listed important literature and carefully selected those on which they could agree were particularly important (Matsunaga & Fukuda 2018; Matsunaga et al. 2019).

(b) Search Database:

To prevent overlooking particularly important literature, 70 books, 14 doctoral dissertations, and 1 web document selected in the "*Heisei 27 (2015) Fiscal Year Media Arts Collaboration Promotion Project Research Mapping Implementation Report*" were added.

(c) Data Attribution:

Author, Published year, Paper Title, Publisher or Journal.

(d) Data Validity Check:

In addition to visual checks by three researchers in the field (Inoue, Matsunaga, Fukuda), a poster presentation was made at DiGRA Japan to obtain feedback from academic society members.

8.3 Data Overview

8.3.1 Literature Trends

Trends in the Number of Publications Related to Video Games

First, we will examine the chronological trends of the entire dataset.

From ◘ Fig. 8.1, it can be confirmed that research related to video games has been on an increasing trend since the 1990s. The decrease in the number of publications in 2022 is due to the time lag until online publication, given the data collection period.

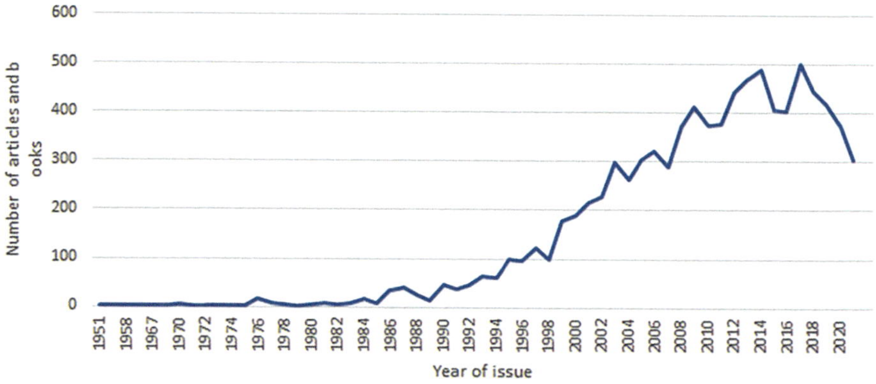

Fig. 8.1 Number of publications presumed to be related to video games by year (n = 9202) (Literature on game theory, etc., was excluded, but some literature related to sports and children's play not related to games is included)

Chronological Changes in Vocabulary Found in Publication Titles

Going beyond simple chronological trends, an analysis was conducted on the collected publication titles using the text mining tool KH Coder. First, to show what kind of topics form clusters overall, the co-occurrence relationships of vocabulary found in publication titles are shown in Fig. 8.2.

From this data, the existence of the following literature clusters can be discerned:

1. A cluster of literature related to game informatics, such as Shogi AI.
2. A cluster of literature related to user-to-user communication, such as in online games.
3. A cluster of literature related to educational applications, such as gamification and education/classes.
4. A cluster of literature comprising survey research on children's culture and life.
5. A cluster of literature on game industry research.
6. A cluster of literature related to simulation & gaming.
7. A cluster of literature on game development technology, such as CG and AI-based automatic generation.

So, during which periods did each domain garner attention? To examine this point, publication titles were subjected to morphological analysis, and data were created showing the frequency of word appearances, with the publication period divided into 10-year intervals (Table 8.1).

Note: Literature from before the 1960s was excluded here because the sample size was too small.

In the 1980s, a large number of publications belonging to cluster (4), survey research on children's culture and life, can be observed. Home computers began to be played with in the early 1980s, followed by a major Famicom (NES) boom in Japan around 1985–86. This was a period when "video games" (テレビゲーム)

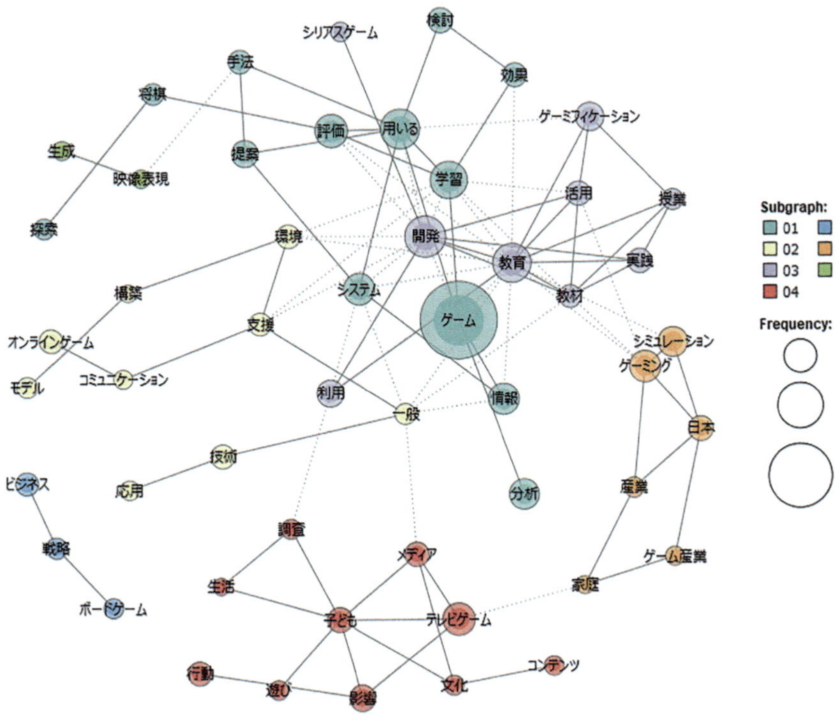

Fig. 8.2 Co-occurrence network of terms in publication titles

became an object of consideration in the context of child life surveys, as an important aspect of children's culture at the time.

This trend continued after 1990, but from the 1990s, many publications related to (6) simulation & gaming began to appear, suggesting that the Japan Association of Simulation & Gaming was actively conducting research.

Entering the 2000s, the number of publications increased significantly. Beginning with cluster (2), literature related to user-to-user communication in online games, research on serious games, e-Learning, VR, etc., also became active.

After the 2010s, vocabulary such as "utilize (用いる)", "education (教育)", "evaluation (評価)", "proposal (提案)", "system (システム)" and "development (開発)" began to be used in publication titles. This suggests an increase in the number of practical reports, including literature related to (1) game informatics, such as Shogi AI, and (7) game development technology such as CG and AI-based automatic generation. Furthermore, the term "gamification (ゲーミフィケーション)" appeared in the top ranks, and literature related to (3) educational applications, such as gamification and education/classes, increased significantly from this period, a trend that has become even more pronounced since 2020.

Also, although it is difficult to confirm from the top 10 keywords alone, the number of publications in cluster (5), game industry research, has increased since the 2010s.

Table 8.1 Frequency of vocabulary found in publication titles (relative frequency)

1970–79 (n = 47)		1980–89 (n = 163)		1990–99 (n = 851)	
Explore (探る)	0.192	Famicom (ファミコン)	0.192	TV game (テレビゲーム)	0.101
LSI	0.100	Play (遊び)	0.065	Game Software (ゲームソフト)	0.065
Dedicated (専用)	0.074	PC (パソコン)	0.061	Simulation (シミュレーション)	0.063
Gravure (グラビア)	0.064	Boom (ブーム)	0.054	Video Game (ビデオゲーム)	0.061
List (一覧)	0.061	Children (子ども)	0.049	Gaming (ゲーミング)	0.047
Color (カラー)	0.057	Modern kids (現代っ子)	0.049	Computer (コンピュータ)	0.042
Possible (可能)	0.056	TV game (テレビゲーム)	0.041	Media (メディア)	0.038
Video Game (ビデオゲーム)	0.053	Consider (考える)	0.040	Children (子ども)	0.037
EVR (EVR)	0.042	Computer (コンピュータ)	0.036	Computer Game (コンピュータゲーム)	0.036
Kit (キット)	0.039	TV (テレビ)	0.033	Analysis (分析)	0.036
2000–09 (n = 2893)		**2010–19 (n = 4332)**		**2020–22 (n = 759)**	
Game (ゲーム)	0.188	Utilize (用いる)	0.098	Utilize (用いる)	0.056
TV Game (テレビゲーム)	0.072	Development (開発)	0.093	Development (開発)	0.055
Gaming (ゲーミング)	0.052	Education (教育)	0.074	Gamification (ゲーミフィケーション)	0.048
Simulation (シミュレーション)	0.050	Learning (学習)	0.071	Education (教育)	0.046
Game Software (ゲームソフト)	0.046	Gamification (ゲーミフィケーション)	0.067	Learning (学習)	0.045
Society (社会)	0.035	System (システム)	0.056	Evaluation (評価)	0.040
Children (子ども)	0.033	Evaluation (評価)	0.055	System (システム)	0.038
Online Game (オンラインゲーム)	0.033	Proposal (提案)	0.052	Method (手法)	0.035
Japan (日本)	0.032	Information (情報)	0.052	Examination (検討)	0.034
Consideration (考察)	0.032	Analysis (分析)	0.045	Utilization (活用)	0.034

Publishers of Game Research

◘ Table 8.2 shows the top 25 publishers with a large number of game research publications. The Japan Association of Simulation & Gaming has the highest number, with 859 publications. However, as Fukuda (2022) also pointed out, this association focuses on simulation and gaming, and it is assumed to include not only direct game research but also many borderline cases.

The Information Processing Society of Japan focuses on game development including AI, the Institute of Image Information and Television Engineers and the Institute of Image Electronics Engineers of Japan focus on video and image technology, the Amusement Industry Research Institute at Osaka University of Commerce focuses on the history of amusement, and Kaneko Shobo publishes "*Jido Shinri (Child Psychology)*" and is dominated by articles on child psychology and health.

The Digital Games Research Association JAPAN and the Ritsumeikan Center for Game Studies, which are thought to have many papers solely on digital games, have relatively fewer publications, partly because they have not been publishing for as long.

Seidosha's contribution is likely due to the frequent special features related to games in its magazine "*Eureka*".

Active Authors

◘ Table 8.3 lists the authors with a particularly large number of publications as the first author.

Overall, the rate of co-authorship is somewhat high, and it can be observed that there are not many authors from the humanities field. Takeshi Ito, who is in first place, is a researcher in the Game AI field; Arata Ichikawa is in gaming & simulation; and Akira Sakamoto is a social psychologist.

Similar to publication trends, this data indicates an accumulation of academic research in fields such as information engineering, gaming simulation, and social psychology.

8.3.2 Trends in Cited Literature

Ranking by Google Scholar System Judgment

Next, to ascertain which publications are actually widely read, we will sort the literature believed to have particularly high citation counts in descending order, using data extracted from Google Scholar citation numbers (see ◘ Table 8.4).

A trend almost similar to that based on the number of publications is that literature related to gamification, serious games, gaming simulation, game informatics, etc., occupies the top positions. Kikkawa (2009) is a book about "*Crossroads*", a serious board game dealing with the Great Hanshin-Awaji Earthquake. Tadahiro Taniguchi's (2013) "*BiblioBattle*" is also a book related to the practice of gamification of reading.

Table 8.2 Top 25 publishers with a large number of game research publications

Publisher name	Number of publications	Percentage of total (%)
Japan Association of Simulation & Gaming	859	9.3
Information Processing Society of Japan	641	7.0
The Institute of Image Information and Television Engineers	313	3.4
The Institute of Electronics, Information and Communication Engineers	285	3.1
Digital Games Research Association JAPAN	240	2.6
Amusement Industry Research Institute of Osaka University of Commerce	201	2.2
The Institute of Image Electronics Engineers of Japan	125	1.4
The Japanese Society for Artificial Intelligence	124	1.3
Kaneko Shobo	116	1.3
Nikkei Business Publications, Inc.	100	1.1
Japan Society for Contents History	90	1.0
Seidosha	89	1.0
The Society for Information on Educational Systems	88	1.0
Japan Society for Educational Technology	73	0.8
Ritsumeikan Center for Game Studies	64	0.7
The Human Ergology Society	63	0.7
Yugishi Gakkai Jimukyoku (Secretariat of the Association for the Study of Play History)	57	0.6
Japanese Society for the Science of Design	53	0.6
Japan Society for Fuzzy Theory and Intelligent Informatics	44	0.5
The Japanese Psychological Association	42	0.5
Human Interface Society	41	0.4
Japan Society for Science Education	37	0.4
The Japanese Association of Educational Psychology	37	0.4
Japan Society for Management Information	34	0.4
Amusement Sangyo Shuppan	31	0.3

Table 8.3 Top 20 authors with a high number of publications related to game research as the first author

	Author name	The earliest article issued	Number of first author articles	Percent age of co-authored publications (%)
1	Takeshi Ito	1999	38	50
2	Arata Ichikawa	1993	33	0
3	Akira Sakamoto	1992	30	53
4	Masayuki Naka-jima	1993	30	21
5	Toshiki Matsuda	2002	29	22
6	Toshiko Kikkawa	1995	24	23
7	Yoichiro Miyake	2008	24	23
8	Takenobu Takizawa	2002	22	0
9	Junkichi Sugiura	1997	20	26
10	Toshiyuki Kaneda	1994	20	20
11	Akito Inoue	2006	20	23
12	Toshiyuki Yamashita	1998	19	34
13	Rei Shiratori	1994	18	0
14	Yuhsuke Koyama	2003	17	15
15	Yasuhira Komago	2010	16	0
16	Nobushige Kobayashi (Hichibe)	2007	16	20
17	Shigeru Aono	2005	16	0
18	Susumu Ohnuma	2001	15	32
19	Kimio Masuda	1987	15	21
20	Hironori Takahashi	2006	15	0

Table 8.4 Highly cited Japanese literature on game research (Google Scholar citation count)

Number of citations in Google Scholar	Author	Issued year	Title
157	Hiroki Azuma	2001	Otaku: Japan's database animals
112	Akito Inoue	2012	Gamification: Games change business
88	Toru Fujimoto	2007	Serious games: Digital games for education and society
85	Roger Caillois	1990	Man, play, and games
70	Akira Nakagawa	1984	Some basic concepts for the study of situational judgment in ball games
61	Kiyoshi Arai et al.	1998	Gaming simulation
51	Akio Mori	2002	Fear of the game brain
48	R Paharia	2013	Loyalty 3.0
47	Hiroki Azuma	2007	The birth of game realism: Animalizing Postmodernity 2
41	Toshiko Kikkawa et al.	2009	Crossroads next
39	Koya Suzuki and Naohiko Nishijima	2002	Causal structure of the attacking skill in soccer games
36	Akira Ito, Mitsuru Kanabuchi	2001	Speeding up multi-agent reinforcement learning by coarse-graining of perception. Hunter game as an example
35	Junjirō Shintaku et al.	2003	Game industry economic analysis
34	Satoshi Okadas et al.	2005	Effect of social skills training including rehearsal of game activities: Comparison of children with LD, ADHD, and Asperger Syndrome
34	Tadahiro Taniguchi	2013	BiblioBattle book review game: Knowing books and knowing people
34	Yoko Onizawa et al.	2007	Improvements in understanding of the knowledge on decision-making in basketball games with numerically uneven sides in upper elementary grades PE classes
33	Atsuko Tominaga and Chiharu Kogo	2014	Developments and issues in practical studies of e-learning

On the other hand, a major difference from the trend based on the number of publications is that humanities books by authors like Hiroki Azuma and Roger Caillois are highly cited. The literature citing these is not necessarily related to games; texts by Azuma and Caillois tend to be widely referenced in the context of contemporary thought. Also, sports research literature ranks high.

As an exception, Akio Mori (2002) is regarded by many researchers as a book that disseminated crude arguments about the negative effects of video games and is often cited in a critical context.

Number of Search Results in Google Scholar

Perhaps due to technical limitations in Google Scholar's citation judgment system, citation counts for Japanese humanities texts are often not accurately read. For example, Huizinga (1938) is an important classic globally, but the Japanese translation by Hideo Takahashi in 1973 is counted as having only five references on Google Scholar.

However, this count is clearly a system issue; in reality, Huizinga (1973 = 1938) is referenced in many Japanese publications. And as mentioned earlier, searching Google Scholar with an exact-title query (e.g., "<book title>") yields a different number than the system's citation count. ◘ Figures 8.3 and 8.4 illustrate this discrepancy.

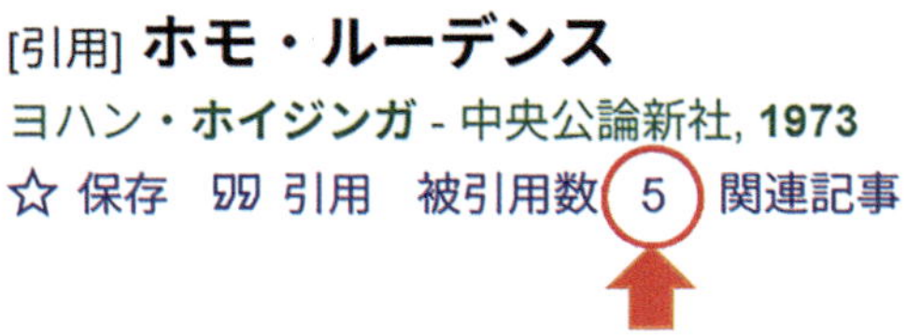

◘ **Fig. 8.3** Johan Huizinga (trans Hideo Takahashi), "*Homo Ludens*" (1973 = 1938), official number of citations in Google Scholar

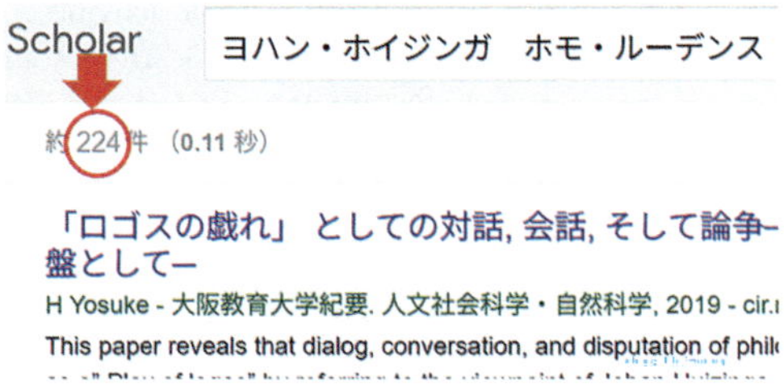

◘ **Fig. 8.4** Johan Huizinga (trans Hideo Takahashi), "*Homo Ludens*" (1973 = 1938), number of search results in Google Scholar

This citation count gap is not an issue in fields like computer science, but it is large for citations of books in the humanities. It is presumed that, as of 2022, Google Scholar's system has issues in its inability to cope with the unique notation practices in the Japanese humanities domain.

In other words, the citation counts from Google Scholar's system should be treated with caution when measuring impact in fields close to the Japanese humanities.

To address this issue, data was created by separately conducting searches for each item and confirming the "Number of search results in Google Scholar" for lists thought to contain particularly important humanities books (► Dataset 3) and for books with over 30 Google Scholar citations (n = 93).

Adopting this method, the literature with the highest citation counts is summarized in ◘ Table 8.5.

◘ Table 8.5 Highly cited Japanese literature on game research (Google Scholar search hit count)

Number of search results in Google Scholar	Number of citations in Google Scholar	Author	Issued year	Title
345	7	A.H. Maslow	1987 (1954)	Motivation and personality
288	157	Hiroki Azuma	2001	Otaku: Japan's database animals
285	85	Roger Caillois	1990	Man, play, and games
224	5	Johan Huizinga	1973 (1938)	Homo Ludens
187	112	Akito Inoue	2012	Gamification: Games change business
174	88	Toru Fujimoto	2007	Serious games: Digital games for education and society
158	61	Kiyoshi Arai et al.	1998	Gaming simulation
155	48	R Paharia	2013	Loyalty 3.0
139	5	Mihaly Csikszent-mihalyi	2000 (1975)	Beyond boredom and anxiety: Experiencing flow in work and play
83	51	Akio Mori	2002	Fear of the game brain
60	35	Junjirō Shintaku et al.	2003	Economic analysis of the game industry: Structure and strategy of content industry development

(continued)

Table 8.5 (continued)

Number of search results in Google Scholar	Number of citations in Google Scholar	Author	Issued year	Title
59	0	Jane McGonigal	2011	Reality is broken
47	70	Akira Nakagawa	1984	Some basic concepts for the study on situational judgment in ball games
39	9	Akira Sakamoto et al.	2003	Media and human development: Psychological Influences of Television, Video Games, Internet, and
38	47	Hiroki Azuma	2007	The birth of game realism: Animalizing Postmodernity 2
37	34	Tadahiro Taniguchi	2013	BiblioBattle Book Review Game: Knowing books and knowing people
35	41	Toshiko Kikkawa et al.	2009	Crossroads Next
34	20	Nobuko Kawashima	2009	Contents industry: Economics, Law and Management of Cultural Creation
31	39	Koya Suzuki and Naohiko Nishijima	2002	Causal structure of the attacking skill in soccer games

By applying this data correction, it becomes clear that citation counts are even more skewed toward certain humanities literature.

First, publications that are frequently mentioned in general books rather than academic papers show a significant increase in reference frequency. First, for example, Japanese translations of Maslow (1987) [1954], Mihaly Csikszentmihalyi (2000) [1975], and Paharia 2013, show a large increase in mentions. These studies are well-known in the Japanese-speaking world but tend to be cited more in the context of casual psychology rather than academic contexts. Second, Jane McGonigal 2011, is often casually mentioned in the context of gamification. Third, Akira Sakamoto et al. (2003), a psychology book on games written as a general book but co-authored by researchers, is also frequently mentioned.

Next, it is clear that literature related to the humanities and thought is also heavily referenced. Johan Huizinga (1973)[1938], Hiroki Azuma (2001), and Roger Caillois (1990), clearly demonstrate this trend.

And books related to the game industry, such as Junjirō Shintaku et al. (2003), and Nobuko Kawashima (2009).

Consistent with other data, areas related to the social application of games, such as gamification, serious games, and gaming simulation, are prominent. Akito Inoue (2012), Toru Fujimoto (2007), and Kiyoshi Arai et al. (1998), can all be seen as reflecting this trend. On the other hand, for areas where texts other than academic papers, such as computer science, are less likely to be written, the change in the method of counting mentions has had little effect.

To summarize the above, a characteristic of humanities in Japan, based on data as of 2022, is that paper-based discussions are still in their infancy, and the academic community is still developing. On the other hand, there is a certain accumulation of discussions through media such as books and magazines.

8.4 The State of Humanities and Sociology

The above has outlined the points seen from basic bibliographic data, but there are some points that are difficult to see from the top-sorted results of the bibliographic data. In particular, I would like to state my impressions of the current state in Japan of humanities and sociology, which are major fields in Western game research.

8.4.1 Philosophy (Aesthetics and Ethics) and Media Theory

As already mentioned, humanistic research on games has historically had a deeper connection with the publishing culture that handles criticism, rather than being conducted through academic journals.

In recent years, a more academic context has been established. (1) An increase in the publication of Japanese game research in the humanities in *Replaying Japan*. (2) The publication of full-fledged video game research by Japanese authors, such as Matsunaga (2018) and Yoshida (2023), who are also contributors to this book. (3) Progress in the translation of important English-language books. Due to these factors, it is gradually being established as an academic research field in Japan as well.

To elaborate on the translation situation, there is a tendency in Japanese humanities in all fields to vigorously promote the Japanese translation of major literature. Influential books in English-language game studies, such as Juul's (2005) "*Half-Real*" and Salen & Zimmerman (2003) "*Rules of Play*", have been translated to some extent. However, due to the limited number of researchers who can be involved in translation, many frequently referenced works have not been translated. For example, translations of B. Sutton Smith (1997) or "*Persuasive Games*" (Bogost 2007) are not available.

8.4.2 Historical Research

Historical research on Japanese games is likely a field where access to Japanese research materials is highly significant. Including research projects that are not strictly academic, a considerable number of projects have been implemented.

In particular, the RCGS, to which the authors belong, is also carrying out projects on resources such as publications of oral histories, statistical materials, and physical materials.

Regarding comprehensive industrial history, there are Koyama (2020) and Nakagawa (2016), and particularly concerning the history of arcade games, there are Akagi (2005) and Kawasaki (2022).

8.4.3 Sociology

While sociological research, similar to humanities, has not become a major trend, various sociologists are discussing video games. A series of Dojin culture studies by Kobayashi (Hichibe), one of the editors (Kobayashi and Koyama 2020; Kobayashi and Tanaka 2016), and Kato's (2011) fieldwork on game centers delve deeply into the unique situation of Japanese game culture and should be referenced by English-speaking researchers as well. Furthermore, a collection of sociological essays on video games by Matsui et al. (2019) has also been published.

While this is the current situation, I would like to mention the status of (1) gender studies and (2) cultural studies, where differences from the research scene in the West can be observed.

First, it can be said that gender studies are relatively scarce compared to overseas. However, this does not mean they are completely non-existent. Regarding the pop culture domain as a whole, there are Saito's (2011) discussion on "*Fighting bishojo (beautiful fighting girls)*" and Saito's (1998) critical discussion. In the field of manga research, gender studies are being conducted, and there is research such as Hata's (2019), primarily in the manga research field, which deals with representation in video games. Works by game researchers such as Shibuya et al. (2022) are beginning to emerge, and texts of feminist game criticism by authors like Kondo (2024) are also appearing, gradually enriching the discussion. Furthermore, there is controversy from various standpoints within Japan regarding gender-related expressions in the game industry. In particular, the placement of images like those in "bishojo games" (beautiful girl games) in public spaces has been a subject of active discussion on SNS daily, even before the research context, and has remained a hot topic on Japan's public agenda for the past decade.

Second, it must be said that the research context of English-language cultural studies—for example, Hardt & Negri's theory of Empire, and the body of research that applied it to the study of game culture, such as Dyer-Witheford and De Peuter (2009)—has a weak presence in the Japanese game research context. In Japanese cultural studies as a whole, discussions related to Hardt & Negri's Empire and idea of multitude are well known and often cited. There are researchers in fields other than game studies who conduct cultural research. However, there are almost no Japanese game researchers committed to this context. Therefore, even if cultural research on Japanese games is conscious of the Hardt & Negri context that exists, most of it is not written by Japanese researchers.

8.4.4 Other Critical Studies of Video Games

Also, distinct from the context of sociology, the existence of critical debates regarding video games in the fields of psychology and psychiatric medicine is almost similar to the international situation. While there is work by Susumu Higuchi (2017, etc.), a Japanese psychiatrist who played a role in advocating for Gaming Disorder to the WHO, there are also many critics of Gaming Disorder. For example, Sohei Ide (2020, etc.) is one of the representative critics. The debate surrounding game disorder remains a controversial topic.

8.5 Conclusion

Research on gamification, serious games, education, and engineering is abundant and often conducted within universities. In terms of the number of publications, presentations, and citations, it can be said that it is gradually being recognized as a research area.

On the other hand, while the institutional foundation for research in social sciences and humanities is gradually being established, there is a need to build more research environments in the future. Humanities may seem accepted when looking only at highly cited works, but there are difficulties in terms of the number of publications, presentations at domestic academic societies, and frameworks for budget acquisition.

In social sciences, Business Administration has a certain number of budget acquisitions, but other fields face challenges similar to those in humanities (it is also possible to interpret that people in management and economics are less language-dependent than in humanities and write English papers, resulting in less Japanese research).

Furthermore, this research primarily acquires data from online sources, focusing on literature where terms like "game" or "play" are directly included in titles or abstracts. However, it cannot be said that literature where such terms are not directly described is sufficiently covered. For example, Satoshi Yamada (1996), who has been researching play for many years, has listed nearly 6000 Japanese play-related documents published since the latter half of the nineteenth century. This is a valuable resource, but this paper aims to collect a list of literature centered on game research as much as possible, rather than play research in general or sports research. Therefore, it should be stated that this is not an integrated account encompassing trends in Japanese play research or sports research as a whole.

Acknowledgments This work was supported by JSPS KAKENHI Grant Number JP25 K03667, 25K03667.

References

Akagi, Masumi. 2005. *Sore wa pon kara hajimatta: ākēdo TV gēmu no naritachi [In the Beginning, There was Pong: The Origins of Arcade TV Games]*. Nishinomiya: Amusement Press.

Arai, Kiyoshi, et al. 1998. *Gēmingu shimyurēshon [Gaming simulation]*. Tokyo: Nikka Giren Shuppansha.

Azuma, Hiroki. 2001. *Dōbutsuka suru posutomodan: Otaku kara mita Nihon shakai [Otaku: Japan's database animals]*. Tokyo: Kodansha.

Bogost, Ian. 2007. *Persuasive Games: The Expressive Power of Videogames*. Cambridge, MA: MIT Press.

Caillois, Roger. 1990. *Asobi to ningen [Man, play, and games]*. Translated by Michitaro Tada and Susumu Tsukazaki. Tokyo: Kodansha.

CiNii Research. n.d.. https://ci.nii.ac.jp/. Accessed September 18, 2022.

Coavoux, Samuel, Manuel Boutet, and Vinciane Zabban. 2017. What We Know About Games: A Scientometric Approach to Game Studies in the 2000s. *Games and Culture* 12 (6): 563–584.

Csikszentmihalyi, Mihaly. 2000. *Beyond Boredom and Anxiety: Experiencing Flow in Work and Play*. 25th Anniversary ed. San Francisco: Jossey-Bass (Published in 1975).

Fujimoto, Toru. 2007. *Shiriasu gēmu: Kyōiku/shakai ni yakudatsu dejitaru gēmu [Serious games: Digital games for education and society]*. Tokyo: Tokyo Denki Daigaku Shuppankyoku.

8

Dyer-Witheford, Nick, and Greig De Peuter. 2009. *Games of Empire: Global Capitalism and Video Games*. Minneapolis: University of Minnesota Press.

Engström, Henrik. 2019. GDC vs. DiGRA: Gaps in Game Production Research. In *The Proceedings of DiGRA 2019: The 12th Digital Games Research Association Conference*.

Frome, Jonathan, and Martin, Paul. 2019. Describing the Game Studies Canon: A Game Citation Analysis. In *The Proceedings of DiGRA 2019: The 12th Digital Games Research Association Conference*.

Fukuda, Kazufumi. 2022. Trends in Game Research in Japan: A Quantitative Analysis with Bibliographic Data. In *The Proceedings of the 12th Annual Conference of DiGRA Japan*.

Fukuda, Kazufumi. n.d. researchopendata. GitHub. https://github.com/fukudakz/researchopendata. Accessed September 18, 2022.

Hata, Mikako. 2019. Pureiyā kyarakutā o jendā no shizen kara miru: 'Doragon Kuesuto' to 'Fainaru Fantajī' no jirei kara [Viewing Player Characters from a Gender Perspective: Cases from Dragon Quest and Final Fantasy]. In *Tagenka suru gēmu bunka to shakai [Diversifying Game Culture and Society]*, ed. Hiroshi Matsui, Takanori Iguchi, Masumi Ōishi, and Mikako Hata, 189–206. Kyoto: Koyo Shobo.

Higuchi, Susumu. 2017. *Sumaho gēmu isonshō [Smartphone Game Addiction]*. Tokyo: Naigai Publishing.

Huizinga, Johan. 1973. *Homo rūdensu [Homo ludens]*. Translated by Hideo Takahashi. Tokyo: Chuo Koronsha. (Original work published 1938).

Ide, Sōhei. 2020. Kagawa-ken netto gēmu kisei jōrei no konkyo o kentō suru [Examining the Basis of the Kagawa Prefecture Internet and Game Addiction Ordinance]. *Kyōiku* 897:72–79.

Inoue, Akito. 2012. *Gēmifikēshon: Gēmu ga bijinesu o kaeru [Gamification: Games change business]*. Tokyo: NHK Shuppan.

J-STAGE. n.d.. https://www.jstage.jst.go.jp/. Accessed September 18, 2022.

Juul, Jesper. 2005. *Half-Real: Video Games Between Real Rules and Fictional Worlds*. Cambridge, MA: MIT Press. Japanese edition: Hāfuriaru. Translated by Matsunaga Shinji. Tokyo: New Games Order, 2016.

Katō, Hiroyasu. 2011. *Gēmusentā bunka-ron: media shakai no komyunikēshon [Arcade Gaming Culture: Mediated Social Communication]*. Tokyo: Shinsensha.

Kawashima, Nobuko. 2009. *Kontentsu sangyōron: Bunka sōzō no keizai, hō, manejimento [Contents industry: Economics, Law and Management of Cultural Creation]*. Kyoto: Minerva Shobo.

Kawasaki, Yasuo. 2022. *Nihon no gēmusentā-shi: goraku shisetsu toshite no hensen to shakaiteki ichizuke [The History of Japanese Game Arcades: Their Changes as Entertainment Facility and Their Position in Society]*. Tokyo: Fukumura Shuppan.

Kikkawa, Toshiko, Katsuya Yamori, and Junkichi Sugiura. 2009. *Kurosurōdo Next: Zoku, gēmu de manabu risuku komyunikēshon [Crossroads next]*. Kyoto: Nakanishiya Shuppan.
Kobayashi(Hichibe), Nobushige and Tanaka, Ema. 2016 Content Production Fields and Doujin Game Developers in Japan: Non-economic Rewards as Drivers of Variety in Games. In *Transnational Contexts of Culture, Gender, Class, and Colonialism in Play: Video Games in East Asia*, 43–80.
Kobayashi, Nobushige, and Yūsuke Koyama. 2020. The Early History of the Hobbyist Production Field of Video Games and Its Impacts on the Establishment of Japan's Video Game Industries. *Replaying Japan 2*:73–82.
Kondo, Ginga. 2024. *Feminisuto, gēmu yatteru [Feminists Are Playing Games]*. Tokyo: Shobunsha.
Koyama, Yūsuke. 2020. *Nihon dejitaru gēmu sangyō-shi: zōho kaitei-ban [A History of the Japanese Digital Game Industry: Expanded and Revised Edition]*. Kyoto: Jimbun Shoin.
Martin, Paul. 2018. The Intellectual Structure of Game Research. *Game Studies 18* (*1*). http://gamestudies.org/1801/articles/paul_martin. Accessed January 9, 2025.
Maslow, Abraham H. 1987. *Motivation and Personality. 3rd ed. New York: Harper & Row. Japanese edition: Ningen-sei no shinrigaku: mochibēshon to pāsonariti*. Translated by Oguchi Tadahiko. Tokyo: Sannō Institute of Management. (Published in 1954)
Matsui, Hiroshi, Takanori Iguchi, Masumi Ōishi, and Mikako Hata, eds. 2019. *Tagenka suru gēmu bunka to shakai [Diversifying Game Culture and Society]*. Kyoto: Koyo Shobo.
Matsunaga, Shinji. 2018. *Bideo gēmu no bigaku [The Aesthetics of Video Games]*. Tokyo: Keio University Press.
Matsunaga, Shinji, and Kazufumi Fukuda. 2018. *Heisei 29-nendo media geijutsu mapping (gēmu ryōiki) sagyō hōkokusho [2017 Media Arts Mapping (Game Field) Work Report]*. Tokyo: Agency for Cultural Affairs. https://mediag.bunka.go.jp/article/article-14419/. Accessed September 18, 2022.
Matsunaga, Shinji, Kazufumi Fukuda, and Muneyuki Takahashi. 2019. *Heisei 30-nendo media geijutsu mapping (gēmu bunya) sagyō hōkokusho [2018 Media Arts Mapping (Game Field) Work Report]*. Tokyo: Agency for Cultural Affairs.
McGonigal, Jane. 2011 *Reality Is Broken: Why Games Make Us Better and How They Can Change the World.* New York: Penguin Books. Japanese edition: Shiawasena mirai wa "gēmu" ga tsukuru. Translated by Fujimoto Tōru and Fujii Kiyomi, ed. Senoo Ken'ichirō. Tokyo: Hayakawa Publishing, 2011.
Melcer, Edward, Zhengzheng Chen, Truong-Huy Nguyen, and Katherine Isbister. 2015. Game Research Today: Analyzing the Academic Landscape 2000–2014. In *The Proceedings of the 10th International Conference on the Foundations of Digital Games* (FDG 2015).
Mori, Akio. 2002. *Gēmu-nō no kyōfu [Fear of the game brain]*. Tokyo: Nippon Hoso Shuppan Kyokai.
Nakagawa, Daichi. 2016. *Gendai gēmu zenshi: bunmei no yūgishikan kara [A Complete History of Modern Games: From a Civilizational Perspective on Play]*. Tokyo: Hayakawa Publishing.
NDL Search. n.d.. https://iss.ndl.go.jp/. Accessed September 18, 2022.
Paharia, Rajat. 2013. *Loyalty 3.0: How to Revolutionize Customer and Employee Engagement with Big Data and Gamification.* New York: McGraw-Hill. Japanese edition: Paharia, Rajat. Biggu dēta jidai shūrai: Kokyaku roiyaruti senryaku wa kō kawaru. Translated by Inagaki Midori. Tokyo: Alphapolis/Seiunsha, 2014.
Saito, Minako. 1998. *Kōitten-ron: anime, tokusatsu, denki no hiroin-zō [The Theory of the "Only Girl": Heroine Images in Anime, Special Effects, and Biographies]*. Tokyo: Village Center.
Saitō, Tamaki. 2011. *Beautiful Fighting Girl.* Translated by J. Keith Vincent and Dawn Lawson. Minneapolis: University of Minnesota Press.
Sakamoto, Akira, ed. 2003. Media to ningen no hattatsu: Terebi, terebi gēmu, intānetto, soshite robotto no shinriteki eikyō [Media and human development: *Psychological Influences of Television, Video Games, Internet, and Robots]*. Tokyo: Gakubunsha.
Salen, Katie, and Eric Zimmerman. 2003. *Rules of Play: Game Design Fundamentals.* Cambridge, MA: MIT Press. Japanese edition: Rules of Play. Translated by Yamamoto Takamitsu. Tokyo: Softbank Creative, 2011.

Shibuya, Akiko, Hibiki Okura, Akiyo Shoun, Naoko Asoh, and Hiroko Otsubo. 2022. Nihon ni okeru gēmu kyarakutā no tayōsei: ninki dejitaru gēmu no naiyō bunseki [Diversity of Game Characters in Japan: A Content Analysis of Popular Digital Games]. In *The Proceedings of the 12th Annual Conference of DiGRA Japan*, 63–66.

Shintaku, Junjirō, Tatsuo Tanaka, and Noriyuki Yanagawa, eds. 2003. *Gēmu sangyō no keizai bunseki: Kontentsu sangyō hatten no kōzō to senryaku [Economic analysis of the game industry: Structure and strategy of content industry development]*. Tokyo: Toyo Keizai Shinposha.

Sutton-Smith, Brian. 1997. *The Ambiguity of Play*. Cambridge, MA: Harvard University Press.

Taniguchi, Tadahiro. 2013. *Biburiobatoru: Hon o shiri hito o shiru shohyō gēmu [BiblioBattle book review game: Knowing books and knowing people]*. Tokyo: Bungeishunju.

Yamada, Satoshi. 1996. *Asobi kenkyū bunken mokuroku [A Bibliography of Play Research]*. Tokyo: Kazama Shobo.

Yoshida, Hiroshi. 2023. *Dejitaru gēmu kenkyū [Digital Game Studies]*. Tokyo: University of Tokyo Press.

8

Field Research in the Japanese Game Industry: Developing an In-Depth Understanding from the Inside Out

Wei Huang

Contents

F. Ikuine et al. (eds.), *Japanese Game Studies*, https://doi.org/10.1007/978-981-95-9857-1_9

9.1 The Current State of International Research on the Japanese Game Industry

Since the advent of the game industry, entertainment products have been offered to the public by combining art and technology, virtual and reality. Currently, the game industry is one of the most important parts of the global entertainment market and playing games has become a part of the daily lives of millions of gamers worldwide. Over the past few decades, the game industry has received considerable attention from researchers and has been analyzed in a variety of fields, including management, economics, and culture. In addition to providing a deeper understanding of the game industry, the results of these studies have been used to address the issues faced by companies and to further the development of the industry itself.

When examining the history of the game industry or examining its current state, Japan is a country that cannot be ignored. What makes the Japanese game industry so important? The reason for this is that Japanese game companies not only laid the foundation for the global game industry's development, but these companies, which have been in operation since the 1980s, continue to lead the direction of innovation in the industry (Consalvo 2009). As for the hardware side, the ecosystem constructed by Sony and Nintendo has contributed to the development of the division of labor and standardization within the industry (Inoue and Tsujimoto 2018). Even if game development technology and game products are updated and iterated, they always retain their competitive advantage in the international market (Ikuine 2015). As for the software side, game publishers such as Bandai Namco Entertainment, Capcom, Square Enix, and game studios founded by famous producers are constantly advancing product innovation through their long-term technical accumulation and rich player experience, while bringing to players around the world new game experiences.

As the world's leading game producer and consumer market, Japan plays an important role in the global game industry (Picard 2013). It should be noted, however, that academic research on the Japanese game industry is very limited. Although the video game industry has received a lot of attention from researchers in recent years, most of these studies have focused on the European and American game industries, with little attention being given to the Japanese game industry. The author conducted a topic search (including title, abstract, author keywords, and Keywords Plus) within the Web of Science Core Collection database using the keywords Japanese game industry, Japanese gaming industry, gaming industry in Japan, and game industry in Japan. After removing several papers that were not related to the game industry, the authors found that only 44 papers were included in the database that dealt with the Japanese game industry.[1]

As shown in ◘ Fig. 9.1, the number of papers on the game industry in Japan is very limited in the fields of economics and management, and there is still a great deal of research to be conducted in other fields. Since the formation of the game

1 The search included papers, conference proceedings and e-publications registered with the databases up to August 31, 2022 (see Appendix for more information on the literature data).

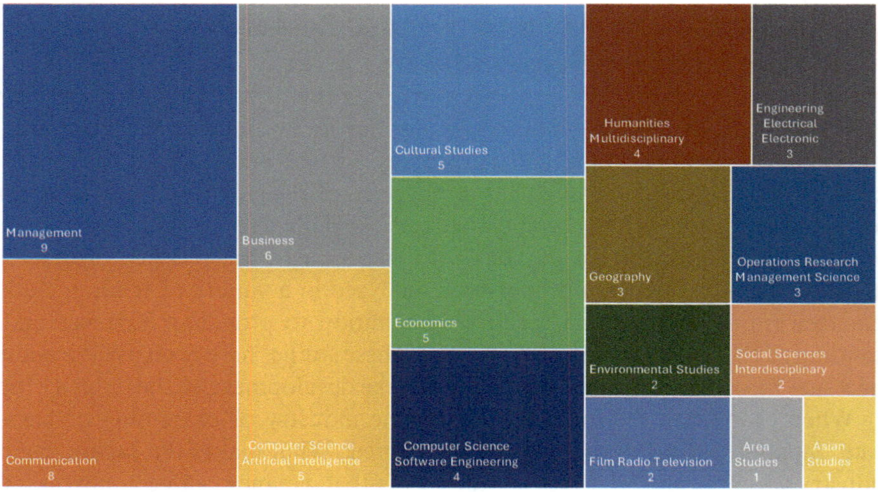

Fig. 9.1 Fields of international research on the Japanese game industry

industry, the Japanese game industry has been at the forefront of the development of the global game market. With the popularity of the Nintendo Family Computer in the 1980s, it accumulated a large and diverse group of players. This long-term interaction between gamers and game companies has created a unique game culture in Japan. There has also been a lack of attention paid to this area of research.

Overall, it appears that the research value of the Japanese game industry has not been sufficiently explored and the relevant data has not been fully examined. With regard to the global game market's diversity, it is difficult for readers to gain an objective understanding of the overall situation of the industry by focusing on studies in Europe and America. Due to this, it is necessary for us to reevaluate the possibility and research prospects of Japanese game industry.

9.2 What Makes It Necessary for International Researchers to Conduct Field Research in Japan?

In the previous section, the authors described the current state of Japanese game industry research. While the Japanese game industry occupies an important position in the global game industry, it has not received much attention from academics, and there are still many gaps in related fields. A major reason for this is that relevant research data have not been fully explored. Both primary and secondary data available to international researchers on the Japanese game industry are extremely limited. Research on the Japanese game industry by international researchers has been significantly impacted by this.

In terms of the primary data, while English is popular in Japan, it is challenging to conduct interviews in English throughout the entire process. The majority of interviewees preferred to communicate in Japanese, even though they were familiar with basic English conversation skills. As a result, the researcher experienced some difficulties when collecting data in Japanese using English. In spite of the fact that the researcher could have studied Japanese to some extent beforehand, the cost of learning Japanese for the purpose of studying the Japanese game industry outside of the context of research and teaching is prohibitively high. In light of this, the Japanese game industry is not an easy subject to investigate from the perspective of the researchers. Primary data collection and research on the Japanese game industry remain stagnant.

Secondary data about the Japanese game industry can be accessed in English on the Internet through sources such as the industry survey reports prepared by the Ministry of Economy, Trade, and Industry (METI) and analysis organizations in Japan. Nevertheless, the number of these materials is extremely limited, and their content is mostly general and lacking in specificity. In the Japanese game industry, the majority of information is not available online but is instead published in physical Japanese books. Due to the fact that these surveys are only published for the Japanese domestic market, they are only available in Japanese. Even though these data are extremely valuable for research, international researchers still have difficulty accessing and utilizing them. Therefore, when international researchers examine the Japanese game industry, they struggle to find macroscopic survey data they can use immediately, and it is difficult to carry out in-depth research.

In summary, international researchers have difficulty collecting primary and secondary data on Japanese game industry, which leads to poorly collected data and insufficient research. It is possible to improve this problem to some extent by ensuring the acquisition of the data directly from the source.

9.3 Conducting Field Research on Japanese Game Industry

What can be done to obtain new primary and secondary data in an efficient and effective manner? The best way for international researchers to gather the necessary data is to conduct field research in Japan. Despite the language barriers and cultural differences, once a researcher has arrived in Japan, he or she will still be able to make new discoveries as they learn and practice. The researcher may also gain a deeper understanding of the Japanese game industry by visiting Japan and observing the industry from the inside out, in addition to understanding it through the information obtained overseas.

In this section, the authors will briefly describe several possible areas for field research in the Japanese game industry.

9.3.1 Surveys of Japanese Game Companies

The steady growth of the Japanese game industry is dependent on the long-term product development activities of game companies (Kohashi and Kurokawa 2005; Storz 2008; Ikuine 2022). Through field research on these companies, we are able to visualize the current state of the Japanese game industry, which is difficult to understand only through quantitative data, as well as understand and analyze the actual situation of the game development sites. The Japanese game industry is divided into three different categories: platformers, publishers, and developers, which form a unique ecosystem. It is noteworthy that most of the well-known game companies are geographically concentrated in major cities such as Tokyo, Osaka, and Fukuoka. Upon selecting the game companies for survey according to research objectives, the researcher can contact the companies' headquarters by email or telephone to inquire about the possibility of conducting a survey. In general, listed game companies have websites in English. Their public contact information can be accessed in English. Alternatively, you may contact the local branch or office of the game company by email or telephone and use this as a means of contacting the company's headquarters. Most small and medium-sized game development companies, however, maintain only Japanese websites since they do not have any overseas business. When investigating such a company, it is advisable to hire a translator for communication and coordination.

Japanese companies are very conscious of their information management. When you visit a game company, you will generally be asked to conceal the name of the target product, and when you describe the details of the development project, you will be asked to leave some details as vague as possible. Because game players are more sensitive to the products than other consumers. Consequently, game companies are very careful in disclosing information about their products. Most game development projects do not disclose development details to the general public. Since mobile games have evolved into very popular products, the interaction and communication between game companies and players has increased. Players' opinions influence the content of games in various ways, which is why game companies seek to keep a certain distance from them in order to control the impact of their opinions. Therefore, when investigating game companies, special attention must be paid to how the data are handled.

During the interview survey, the researcher should pay close attention to the confidentiality of the interview content. Upon requesting an interview with an interviewee, the researcher should inform the interviewee that "the content of the survey will not be disclosed without permission". It may also be necessary to sign a nondisclosure agreement (NDA) if the interviewees request it. Additionally, before releasing the results of the survey, the researcher should send a statement describing the survey results to the interviewees and request their permission to release the content.

9.3.2 Surveys of Japanese Game Players

Japanese game industry prosperity cannot be separated from the rapid growth of the domestic market. During the development of the Japanese game industry, the Japanese game-related market has gathered a large number of players. Japanese game players differ significantly from those in Europe and America in terms of their player characteristics, consumption behavior, and product preferences. Among Japanese gamers, RPG games are more popular than FPS games, which are more popular among Europeans and Americans. Hence, conducting field research with Japanese gamers as the target allows us to examine these potential differences in depth and develop a more comprehensive understanding of the global game market.

As for the implementation, if the researcher does not have many connections in Japan, the easiest way to collect data is through web surveys conducted by Japanese research companies. The research companies have extensive survey experience and online panel participants, and they offer services such as survey design, pre-survey, survey data collection, and data analysis. Their research services are also used by some Japanese researchers to collect data. As soon as the researcher has designed their own survey questionnaire, they can contact the survey company to inquire about the required sample size and the cost of the survey. For example, when doing an international comparison of player groups, the same questionnaire content can be translated into Japanese and then commissioned to a survey company for collection and analysis.

9.3.3 On-Site Surveys of Game Culture Spots

Games play a major role in Japanese pop culture along with anime, manga, and music. In addition to profoundly changing Japanese entertainment, games have also become an integral part of people's daily lives (Aoyama and Izushi 2003; Harada 2007). Unlike the progressively younger player base in Europe and America, Japanese gamers have a long game lifespan, with a wide range of ages among game players. Even after working for a period of time, many Japanese game players remain passionate about games. Due to the coexistence of multi-age gamers and Japan's unique historical and cultural background, there has been a unique game culture in Japan (Kerr 2006). As part of studying game culture, in addition to consulting secondary sources, it is possible to visit the game places where the majority of Japanese gamers gather and observe firsthand how games affect the lives of the players. Game centers and retro game stores are considered to be the two most representative places of Japanese game culture.

Although amusement arcades have passed their prime in Europe and America, they are ubiquitous throughout Japan, whether they are located in busy downtown high-rises or in suburban neighborhoods. In Japan, amusement arcades are commonly referred to as game centers. Office workers in suits and high school students in uniforms can be seen sitting side by side in game centers, enjoying various games together. Despite the popularity of mobile games and video games at home, the physical gaming experience still plays a significant role in electronic amusement parks, where new game machines are regularly introduced.

The game industry has cultivated a large player base since the rise of console games in the 1980s. In spite of the constant evolution of consoles and game software, the entertainment experience that games provide has not changed over the years. It is important to note that the majority of Japanese gamers are between the ages of 40 and 60. They have enjoyed playing games since they were children and have not given up their interest after they began working. This long-term emotional investment also contributes to the continuous demand for retro games. Retro games refer to "old games" as opposed to the current and newest games. Retro game stores can be found in major cities such as Tokyo, Osaka, and Kobe, including chain stores like Super Potato and Surugaya, as well as smaller independent stores. Even though these shops are small in size, they collect game consoles, game software, and game peripherals from various periods, and customers may find the selection process enjoyable. Moreover, the quality of the goods and the variety of goods are both excellent, thus making it an excellent choice for players to collect. Considering the history of games, these are valuable primary sources. Field research can be organized for researchers to visit these stores and interview store owners or customers about retro games. This is an excellent opportunity for researchers to gain a first-hand understanding of Japanese game culture.

9.3.4 Collection of Secondary Data in Japanese

In terms of secondary data on the game industry, the researcher has limited access to data outside of Japan through the Internet alone. Furthermore, most of the data is not available in English. It is therefore necessary for the researcher to conduct field research in order to gather and translate the relevant data when performing a macro analysis of the game industry. The most effective method is to visit the National Diet Library in Japan.

The National Diet Library is the only legal library in Japan that collects and preserves all publications published in Japan. The National Diet Library offers easy access to materials. Bring your passport to the library and get a library card, and then you can start checking out the materials you need. Researchers can order copies of materials from the National Diet Library once they have identified the materials they require. It is possible to pick up copies on the day of application or to have them mailed at a later time. As soon as the data collection has been completed, the researcher can sort the data according to the language and then commission the translation of the Japanese version of the data. Secondary information about the game industry can be obtained from two sources: government survey reports and statistical yearbooks, as well as surveys conducted by private research organizations.

On a policy level, the game industry in Japan is classified as a sub-industry of the content industry, along with the animation industry and the music industry (Holroyd 2019). Surveys are usually conducted by the Creative Industries Division and the Media and Content Industry Division of METI, which is responsible for formulating and implementing Japan's economic and industrial policies. Macro-industry surveys and statistical yearbooks are regularly published by these organizations. There are some of these materials available on METI's website in both English and Japanese.

Aside from government agencies, private research organizations also publish reports on the game industry. The reports provide a macro analysis as well as more in-depth analyses of the game industry's subsectors. These reports are available on the market, but most of them are expensive. Therefore, it would be preferable to collect the desired information from the library.

The most representative industry research reports are the Famitsu game hakusyo and the Japan Online Game Association (JOGA) Online Game Market Research Report. Since its publication in 2005, Famitsu game hakusyo has been analyzing domestic game market trends (hardware market, software market, and detailed data by platform and genre) and player marketing (current game market structure, player data by platform, and market overview). JOGA's online game market research report categorizes the devices on which online games can be played (PCs, smartphones, and tablets) and conducts research on each device. JOGA has made an effort to gather information on the market trends of each device to provide a relative picture of the overall online game business.

9.4 Advice for International Researchers Planning to Conduct Game Research in Japan

In today's increasingly globalized world, international researchers who are determined to conduct field research in Japan still face many challenges. It is extremely important to establish relationships with respondents in order to conduct successful field research, and effective communication with respondents in Japan remains a challenge to overcome (Bestor et al. 2003). The language barrier is a significant challenge for foreign researchers conducting field research in Japan for the first time, particularly if they do not speak Japanese (Norton and Shibusawa 2001). A researcher's time and resources are too limited to devote to learning a new language in addition to his or her research and teaching duties. Furthermore, even if one devotes time and effort to learning Japanese to the level of searching Japanese research literature, it is impossible to achieve this in a short period of time. Consequently, in order to make the most of the limited time available for field research, it is important to collaborate with a local researcher who is familiar with the situation as well as to prepare well in advance (Kottmann and Reiher 2020). Especially when it comes to corporate visits or interviews, the chances of success are not very high without establishing a prior relationship. Getting closer to a research subject through the introduction of a Japanese researcher is the easiest way to proceed.

A good place to start is to search the database of papers and contact Japanese researchers who have published papers on Japanese game industry in international academic journals. These researchers not only possess solid data on Japanese game industry, but they also have a high level of research results that have been published in international journals. Cooperation with them will make conducting joint research easier. If you have a certain level of Japanese, you can also investigate Japanese researchers with the same research direction as yourself by using Japanese-related keywords on Google Scholar or the Japanese research database CiNii Research. In addition to the database of English papers, you can identify potential research partners and contact them by email with the intention of collaborating.

During the COVID-19 pandemic, video conferencing tools, such as Zoom, have become widely used for a variety of purposes, including telecommuting and remote teaching. Researchers can communicate regularly using such tools as long as the time difference problem can be overcome. Once contact is established, researchers can discuss the direction of joint research based on the strengths of both parties.

Additionally, if your research budget is sufficient, you may be able to hire an interpreter. There are many translation companies in Japan that provide interpreter dispatching services. Interpretation support can be customized to the researcher's preferred plan. The possibility of communicating with local people will be greatly improved when you have a Japanese interpreter accompanying you during your field research.

Conducting field research abroad is difficult without sufficient funding. In addition to the research grants available from their home countries, researchers may be eligible to apply for research grants from the Japan Society for the Promotion of Science (JSPS). JSPS is an independent administrative institution, established by way of a national law for the purpose of contributing to the advancement of science in all fields of the natural and social sciences and the humanities.[2] The JSPS is responsible for the administration of many of Japan's scientific and academic programs. JSPS offers a variety of programs that enable international researchers who have demonstrated excellence in their research to conduct collaborative research, discussions, and exchanges of opinions with Japanese researchers.[3] The most representative program is "JSPS International Fellowships for Research in Japan".

In this program, two types of fellowships are available: Postdoctoral Fellowships in Research in Japan for early career researchers, and Invitational Fellowships in Research in Japan for mid-career and senior researchers. Researchers are highly encouraged to apply to these JSPS programs because they provide sufficient funding to support basic research in Japan.

9.5 Advice for International Students Planning to Study Game in Japan

International students planning to study game-related knowledge and work in related research or companies should consider studying in Japan. There can be no continuous growth of the game industry in Japan without the continuous supply of excellent developers from domestic game-related educational institutions. Unlike game education in America, game education in Japan places a high priority on On-the-Job Training (OJT), in which many courses are taught by teachers with extensive experience in game development, providing a series of systematic courses from the development site. The education in the games field in Japan is based on a close collaboration between industry and academia and is considered to be world-leading. In this section, the author briefly discusses the preparation needed prior to studying abroad as well as selecting a school.

There is less demand for English courses in game-related fields, so many schools only offer Japanese courses. Therefore, it is highly recommended that international

2 ► https://www.jsps.go.jp/english/
3 ► https://www.jsps.go.jp/english/e-inv_researchers/index.html

students study Japanese in advance and reach a certain level before taking the entrance examination. There are two ways to learn Japanese. One is to attend a Japanese language institute in your home country before coming to Japan, and the other is to enroll at a Japanese language school once you have arrived in Japan. In Japan, a Japanese language school is a collective term referring to a number of language schools that provide instruction in Japanese to non-Japanese students. As opposed to schools within the general formal education system, Japanese language schools only offer language training courses and do not award degrees upon completion of the program. Japanese language schools are popular among students planning to study abroad in Japan as a means of learning Japanese and preparing for the entrance examination. In Japan, there are over 600 Japanese language schools, with approximately 60,000 students studying the language.

In general, Japanese language schools require applications 6 months to a year in advance and offer four entry dates: January, April, July, and October. Besides short-term Japanese language instruction, these schools offer long-term courses for university admissions, such as University Preparatory Courses.

The Japanese-Language Proficiency Test (JLPT) is held in Japan and abroad to evaluate and certify the Japanese-language proficiency of non-native speakers. Upon completing a sufficient amount of study, you may challenge yourself to take the test. JLPT centers are located throughout the world. Further information is available on the official JLPT website.

In terms of scholarship programs, a wide range of scholarships are available for students who wish to study in Japan. Since the selection process is highly competitive, it is recommended that students secure adequate financial resources prior to enrolling. For more information about studying in Japan, please refer to the "Study in Japan" website.[4] It is a government-approved information site for studying in Japan. It is operated by the Japan Student Services Organization (JASSO). Before planning to study in Japan, it is recommended that you check the contents of interest.

Nowadays, many universities offer degree programs in game studies relating to computer technology, information media, and media arts. Furthermore, several technical colleges offer courses in game development technology that provide students with skills in programming, planning, designing, and sound that can be used immediately by game development companies.

9.5.1 Looking for a Job in the Game Industry

You can choose a school that offers courses related to game development if you are interested in working in a game company in the future. There is great potential in the game industry as a part of Japan's competitive power. There have been many educational institutions that have opened up game-related courses in order to focus on human resource development in the game industry. In most cases, these schools

4 ► https://www.studyinjapan.go.jp/en/

work with Japanese game companies, and the courses they offer tend to be more practical, emphasizing the development of human resources who possess systematic game development knowledge. It is an excellent choice for those who wish to enter the game industry and work at the front lines of the industry. There are numerous colleges and universities in Japan that offer related courses, so you can review their official websites before choosing a school.[5]

9.5.2 Researching Game-Related Topics

You can be more flexible in your choice of school and major if you wish to study the game industry systematically. If you only have a vague understanding of the Japanese game industry prior to studying in Japan, you should take care to choose your major in accordance with your interests and knowledge base. Specifically, when it comes to researching game-related topics, the game industry is only the subject of research, and how to analyze it requires a profound understanding of professional knowledge and research methods.

If you wish to study the corporate activities in the game industry, you may choose management or economics; if you wish to study the game itself or its impact on society, you may choose culture or information science. The list compiled by Professor Nobushige Kobayashi may be helpful in selecting a school.[6] This list provides a detailed listing of universities and graduate schools where game studies can be pursued in Japan. Despite the fact that the subject of study pertains to the game industry, the approach for research will vary depending on the major. It is possible for students to select their own majors based on their interests and aptitudes in the field of game research.

9.6 Conclusion

While the Japanese game industry occupies an important position in the global game industry, it has not received much attention from academics, and there are still many gaps in related fields. The purpose of this chapter is to provide some practical suggestions on the issues related to conducting field research on the game industry in Japan. For international researchers, conducting field research allows them to find potential primary and secondary data regarding the Japanese video game industry while filling in research gaps and gaining a deeper understanding of how games are developed in different regions of the world and the effect these developments have on these regions. For international students, Japan is an excellent choice for both working and doing research in game industry due to its close collaboration between industry, academia, and research. The contents of this

5 ► https://ja.wikipedia.org/wiki/%E3%82%B2%E3%83%BC%E3%83%A0%E5%AD%A6%E7%A7%91

6 ► https://sociology-of-games.blogspot.com/2020/02/list-of-universities-where-you-can.html

chapter are expected to facilitate the expansion of the Japanese game industry research team and increase the number of research on game.

Acknowledgments This work was supported by JSPS KAKENHI Grant Number JP23 K12555.

Appendix

See ◘ Table 9.1.

◘ **Table 9.1** Literature data of international research on the Japanese game industry

	Title	Journal	Publication years	Cites
1	Hardware gimmick or cultural innovation? Technological, cultural, and social foundations of the Japanese video game industry	RESEARCH POLICY	2003	111
2	Console video games and global corporations: Creating a hybrid culture	NEW MEDIA & SOCIETY	2006	77
3	Industry evolution and cross-sectoral skill transfers: A comparative analysis of the video game industry in Japan, the United States, and the United Kingdom	ENVIRONMENT AND PLANNING A-ECONOMY AND SPACE	2006	49
4	A cross-national market segmentation of online game industry using SOM	EXPERT SYSTEMS WITH APPLICATIONS	2004	43
5	Dynamics in innovation systems: Evidence from Japan's game software industry	RESEARCH POLICY	2008	40
6	New market development of platform ecosystems: A case study of the Nintendo Wii	TECHNOLOGICAL FORECASTING AND SOCIAL CHANGE	2018	28
7	Mobility and innovation: A cross-country comparison in the video games industry	RESEARCH POLICY	2015	26

(continued)

Table 9.1 (continued)

	Title	Journal	Publication years	Cites
8	Exploring experiential value in online mobile gaming adoption	CYBERPSYCHOLOGY & BEHAVIOR	2008	26
9	From aggressively formalized to intensely in/formalized: Accounting for a wider range of videogame development practices	CREATIVE INDUSTRIES JOURNAL	2019	15
10	Women's games in Japan gendered identity and narrative construction	THEORY CULTURE & SOCIETY	2009	15
11	Winner-takes-all or co-evolution among platform ecosystems: A look at the competitive and symbiotic actions of complementors	SUSTAINABILITY	2019	14
12	Genres of complementary products in platform-based markets: Changes in evolutionary mechanisms by platform diffusion strategies	INTERNATIONAL JOURNAL OF INNOVATION MANAGEMENT	2018	10
13	Japanese console games popularization in China: Governance, copycats, and gamers	GAMES AND CULTURE	2016	10
14	Global youth and mobile games: Applying the extended technology acceptance model in the United States, Japan, Spain, and the Czech Republic	CROSS-CULTURAL BUYER BEHAVIOR	2007	10
15	The four faces of creative industries: Visualizing the game industry ecosystem in Helsinki and Tokyo	INDUSTRY AND INNOVATION	2020	8
16	Video game demand in Japan: A household data analysis	APPLIED ECONOMICS	2007	6
17	Found in translation: Evolving approaches for the localization of Japanese video games	ARTS	2021	5
18	Bounded careers in creative industries: Surprising patterns in video games	INDUSTRY AND INNOVATION	2017	5

(continued)

9

Table 9.1 (continued)

	Title	Journal	Publication years	Cites
19	A model for collective behavior propagation: A case study of the video game industry	NEURAL COMPUTING & APPLICATIONS	2020	4
20	Differentiation in digital creative industry cluster dynamics: The growth and decline of the Japanese video game software industry	GEOGRAFISKA ANNALER SERIES B-HUMAN GEOGRAPHY	2018	4
21	Construction trial of a practical education curriculum for game development by industry–university collaboration in Japan	COMPUTERS & GRAPHICS-UK	2010	4
22	Digital content promotion in Japan and South Korea: Government strategies for an emerging economic sector	ASIA & THE PACIFIC POLICY STUDIES	2019	3
23	Comparative cultural economy and game industries in Asia	MEDIA INTERNATIONAL AUSTRALIA	2016	3
24	Platform selection by software developers: Theory and evidence	JOURNAL OF THE JAPANESE AND INTERNATIONAL ECONOMIES	2015	3
25	New product development and creativity management in Japanese video gaming software firms	INTERNATIONAL JOURNAL OF TECHNOLOGY MANAGEMENT	2005	3
26	Emergent affect in final fantasy VII and Japanese role-playing games	JOURNAL OF GAMING AND VIRTUAL WORLDS	2018	2
27	The substitution effect of mobile games on console games: An empirical analysis of the Japanese video game industry	REVIEW OF SOCIONETWORK STRATEGIES	2017	2

(continued)

Table 9.1 (continued)

	Title	Journal	Publication years	Cites
28	The role of dual institutional- and technological entrepreneurship in the formation of the Japanese social-game industry	GLOBAL GAME INDUSTRIES AND CULTURAL POLICY	2016	2
29	Complementary products providers' technological adoption and evolution of the business ecosystem: The case study of Nintendo's Wii in Japanese video game sector	PICMET'15 PORTLAND INTERNATIONAL CENTER FOR MANAGEMENT OF ENGINEERING AND TECHNOLOGY	2015	2
30	Co-opting the nation brand: The politics of cross-cultural co-production	INTERNATIONAL JOURNAL OF CULTURAL STUDIES	2020	1
31	Japanese video game industry: History of its growth and current state	TRANSNATIONAL CONTEXTS OF DEVELOPMENT HISTORY, SOCIALITY, AND SOCIETY OF PLAY: VIDEO GAMES IN EAST ASIA	2016	1
32	Career development among Japanese female game developers: Perspective from life stories of creative professionals	GENDER CONSIDERATIONS AND INFLUENCE IN THE DIGITAL MEDIA AND GAMING INDUSTRY	2014	1

(continued)

Table 9.1 (continued)

	Title	Journal	Publication years	Cites
33	A four-stage gate-keeper model of social service engineering: Lessons from golden rules of mobile social game design	2012 9TH INTERNATIONAL CONFERENCE ON UBIQUITOUS INTELLIGENCE & COMPUTING AND 9TH INTERNATIONAL CONFERENCE ON AUTONOMIC & TRUSTED COMPUTING (UIC/ATC)	2012	1
34	The influence of the sexist representation of dark souls and the male gaze in video games that are inspired by it	AREA ABIERTA	2022	0
35	Video games development in the periphery: Cultural dependency?	GEOGRAFISKA ANNALER SERIES B-HUMAN GEOGRAPHY	2021	0
36	Investigating the elusive role of level design	2020 IEEE CONFERENCE ON GAMES (IEEE COG 2020)	2020	0
37	An education model for game development by a Swedish-Japanese industry-academia Alliance	2020 IEEE CONFERENCE ON GAMES (IEEE COG 2020)	2020	0
38	"Cosmopolitanism", "Japaneseness", and video game studies: A review of Mia Consalvo's Atari to Zelda: Japan's videogames in global Contexts	DIGITAL HUMANITIES QUARTERLY	2019	0

(continued)

Table 9.1 (continued)

	Title	Journal	Publication years	Cites
39	Features of the formation and development of the video game industry in Japan in the last quarter of the XX–XXI centuries	NAUCHNYI DIALOG	2019	0
40	Narrative configuration in the crossmedia franchise of berserk	CON A DE ANIMACION	2019	0
41	Are heavy pirates also heavy buyers?: A case of the video game industry in Japan	ASIAN JOURNAL OF LAW AND ECONOMICS	2018	0
42	The Japanese console game industry: Capcom and level-5	ATARI TO ZELDA: JAPAN'S VIDEOGAMES IN GLOBAL CONTEXTS	2016	0
43	Construction and analysis of the purchase factor model by using creativity method	PROCEEDINGS OF THE SIXTEENTH INTERNATIONAL SYMPOSIUM ON ARTIFICIAL LIFE AND ROBOTICS (AROB 16TH'11)	2011	0
44	Examination into the firm without fundamental technology: A case study of Nintendo	PROCEEDINGS OF THE 6TH EUROPEAN CONFERENCE ON INNOVATION AND ENTREPRENEURSHIP, VOL 1 AND 2	2011	0

9

References

Aoyama, Yuko, and Hiro Izushi. 2003. Hardware Gimmick or Cultural Innovation? Technological, Cultural, and Social Foundations of the Japanese Video Game Industry. *Research Policy* 32 (3): 423–444. https://doi.org/10.1016/S0048-7333(02)00016-1.

Bestor, Theodore C., Patricia G. Steinhoff, and Victoria Lyon-Bestor. 2003. *Doing Fieldwork in Japan*. Honolulu: University of Hawaii Press.

Consalvo, Mia. 2009. Convergence and Globalization in the Japanese Videogame Industry. *Cinema Journal* 48 (3): 135–141. https://doi.org/10.1353/cj.0.0122.

Harada, Nobuyuki. 2007. Video Game Demand in Japan: A Household Data Analysis. *Applied Economics* 39 (13): 1705–1710. https://doi.org/10.1080/00036840600660713.

Holroyd, Carin. 2019. Digital Content Promotion in Japan and South Korea: Government Strategies for an Emerging Economic Sector. *Asia & the Pacific Policy Studies* 6 (3): 290–307. https://doi.org/10.1002/app5.277.

Ikuine, Fumihiko. 2015. The Evolution of the Home Video Game Software Industry in Japan: An Empirical Study on Factors in the Industry's Evolution. *Evolutionary and Institutional Economics Review* 9 (1): 37–50. https://doi.org/10.14441/eier.A2012003.

Ikuine, Fumihiko. 2022. *The Efficiency and Creativity of Product Development: Lessons from the Game Software Industry in Japan*. Singapore: Springer.

Inoue, Yuki, and Masaharu Tsujimoto. 2018. New Market Development of Platform Ecosystems: A Case Study of the Nintendo Wii. *Technological Forecasting & Social Change* 136:235–253. https://doi.org/10.1016/j.techfore.2017.01.017.

Kerr, Aphra. 2006. *The Business and Culture of Digital Games: Gamework/Gameplay*. London: SAGE.

Kohashi, R., and S. Kurokawa. 2005. New Product Development and Creativity Management in Japanese Video Gaming Software Firms. *International Journal of Technology Management* 30 (3–4): 365–388. https://doi.org/10.1504/IJTM.2005.006712.

Kottmann, Nora, and Cornelia Reiher. 2020. *Studying Japan: Handbook of Research Designs, Fieldwork and Methods*. Baden-Baden: Nomos Verlagsgesellschaft.

Norton, Joy, and Tazuko Shibusawa. 2001. *Living in Japan: A Guide to Living, Working, and Traveling in Japan*. New York: Tuttle Publishing.

Picard, Martin. 2013. The Foundation of Geemu: A Brief History of Early Japanese Video Games. *Game Studies* 13 (2). http://gamestudies.org/1302/articles/picard.

Storz, Cornelia. 2008. Dynamics in Innovation Systems: Evidence from Japan's Game Software Industry. *Research Policy* 37 (9): 1480–1491. https://doi.org/10.1016/j.respol.2008.05.007.

Part III

Accelerating Game Research in Japan

Contents

Japanese Game Studies Based on Management Studies

Fumihiko Ikuine

Contents

F. Ikuine et al. (eds.), *Japanese Game Studies*, https://doi.org/10.1007/978-981-95-9857-1_10

10.1 Introduction

As the previous chapters of this book have shown, Japanese games have research materials that are worthy of study. The games themselves are unique and fascinating. Users play them enthusiastically, and they are deeply rooted in society. Moreover, Japanese researchers who are interested in games are as engaged in game research as researchers from other countries and regions. Unfortunately, due to the language barrier, it is not easy for researchers and students from overseas to learn about the results of such research. That is why visiting Japan and observing Japanese games and the surrounding society is worthwhile.

The past 40 years have given rise to a unique Japanese society due to the many fascinating games created in Japan. The entertainment forms familiar to Japanese society, such as manga and animation, have also contributed. In addition, Japanese consumers enjoyed these games. The culture was also influential, including games that developed independently of companies, such as the "Doujin" featured in this book.

What were indispensable, however, were the companies. Numerous companies made games a viable business. They developed the hardware and the software and distributed games one after another. Because of these companies, consumers enjoyed a steady stream of diverse games. Herein lies the management studies' rationale for studying Japanese games. Why and how did so many companies create Japanese games? Answering this question was a significant effort that Japanese researchers have successfully tackled. In this chapter, we would like to introduce them.

The research presented in this chapter is based on Japanese companies such as Nintendo, Sega, Sony Computer Entertainment (Sony), Namco, Capcom, Square Enix, which led the global business of video games. Why did Japan's video game business, which started in the United States, grow so vigorously? Why did both the hardware and the software gain worldwide acclaim? In this chapter, we share with readers the answers to these questions based on the research results of management studies.

In addition, we believe that the research results about the Japanese game business apply to both the past and present. The industry has allowed us to reveal new phenomena from the perspective of management studies (management strategies and organizational forms). Moreover, such phenomena have become common in other countries and industries since the 2000s. For example, Nintendo's strategy and business model, which skillfully utilized platforms are the prototypes of today's Google and Apple business models. The game software business, where many companies coexisted and competed based on platforms, anticipated the so-called ecosystem phenomenon. Furthermore, the geographic concentration of creative personnel and the existence of human networks have also been confirmed and studied, especially in cities such as Tokyo, which anticipated the so-called creative cluster phenomenon.

To sum up, studying Japanese games from the perspective of management studies today is not just a matter of nostalgia; analyzing the past 40 years will yield knowledge that will lead today's advanced management. Moreover, it provides an important insight into contemporary society. This chapter will introduce and recap the results of Japanese game studies from this standpoint and will consider the direction of future research.

We organized this chapter as follows. First, ► Sect. 10.2 reviews how the researchers studied the game business in Japan.[1] Then, ► Sect. 10.3 considers how we connected the study of the game business in Japan to current research in management studies. Then, based on these research trends, we will present a research guide to participation in Japanese game studies from the perspective of management studies in ► Sect. 10.4. Finally, we will consider the future direction of management studies in the game business.

The game business, both in Japan and worldwide will continue to change and incorporate new technologies. How will these advances be incorporated into business and change society? Thinking about this from a management perspective will surely provide stimulating research material.

10.2 Management Studies of Japanese Games

The game business in Japan has attracted people's attention at home and abroad. Existing studies argue that the game software business grew in Japan because many companies entered the business and offered excellent products.

Also, Japanese companies, led by Nintendo, launched the console game (home video game) business. Furthermore, companies exported these home video game consoles and game software overseas and drove the global market. Therefore, early on, Japanese journalists reported on the business of console games.

Until the 1990s, reporting and documentation focused on the corporate behavior of platform folders[2] such as Nintendo. How did a particular platform achieve de facto standards? How did platform folders that achieved de facto standards become highly profitable? The descriptions and studies of the console game business began by answering these questions.

Although these reports and documents are diverse, they can be grouped into two categories. One group reports focusing on Nintendo, Sega, and other platform folders, key players in the 1980s and 1990s. The literature focused on the corporate behavior of platform folders such as Ichikawa (1993), Yamana (1994), and Asakura (1998). The others focus was on game software. It was covered by Yada (1996), Hirabayashi and Akao (1996), and Aida and Ogaki (1997).

---

1 This chapter focuses on the business of console games, given the wealth of research findings in Japan.

2 The platform folder is a concept that is a higher level of Gawer and Cusumano's (2002) platform leader concept. The platform leader is a company that has a leading position in terms of market share and influence within the platform folder.

10.2.1 Research Focused on the Overall Business of Console Games

Among management studies, Kohashi was the earliest to make console games (home video games) a research subject. Kohashi's fundamental question was "Why are Japanese companies leading the world in console games, where software was essential"? She answered this question by conducting research and analysis focused on Nintendo, the leading company in the field of console games.

A series of studies began with Kohashi (1993a) that focused on the relationship between Nintendo, video game software companies, and distributors. It then examined the details of the relationship between the companies. Kohashi named the relationship between Nintendo and other companies an "indirect control type network." She said this relationship among companies differs from corporate conglomerate groups, parent–subsidiary relationships, or manufacturer–subcontractor relationships. In other words, she argued that the relationship between the console game companies differed from the previously observed Japanese interfirm relationships. For Nintendo and the game software companies, the rules and the market established by the rules were essential. She then argued that such an indirect control network contributed to the maintenance of the overall quality of game software, the promotion of competition among companies releasing game software, and the recognition of console games in society. As a result, she concluded that this business has grown in Japan.

Kohashi (1993b) examined the game software's industrial and product characteristics. She then discussed changes in game software development and presented a hypothesis. First, she argued that the growth of game software companies had caused changes in their strategies. That is to say, as game software companies have grown, they have been forced to shift from high-risk, high-return strategies to low-risk, low-return strategies—or at least, to combine them. Then, she categorized the game software development projects from the viewpoint of risks and returns. Therefore, she hypothesized that as game software companies tended to adopt a low-risk, low-return strategy, they changed their development organizations.

Kohashi and Kagono (1995) summarized a series of studies and attempted to comprehensively answer why the console game business was able to develop and succeed in Japan. Their paper first describes Japan's console game history and the basic structure of console games. It then touches on game software development. They further described the development of Nintendo's "Mario Kart" and clarified the characteristics of game software development.

Kohashi and Kagono (1995) then drew two implications from their analysis of console game companies. The first was the role played by ambiguous and implicit images during the development process. In game software development, development team members mutually exchanged their images and gradually implemented them into the product. Next, they examined the relationship between software development and Japanese-style management. Earlier studies suggested that Japan's sociocultural environment and management system were not compatible with software development. However, a case analysis of console games revealed that Japanese employment practices were compatible with the management of game software development. In other words, their research proved that Japanese-style management might be effective depending on the software's characteristics.

Other studies on the overall business of console games and platform folders include those by Baba et al. (1995), Nakama et al. (1996), Kuriki (2008), Fujikawa (1999); Fujita's series of studies; Inoue et al. (2011); and Negoro and Kameda (2011). Among them, Baba et al. (1995), like Kohashi (1993a), found a feature in the industrial structure of the console games business. They called it a "hub structure." Nakama et al. (1996), Kuriki (2008) and Fujikawa (1999) discussed the inter-platform competition between Nintendo and Sony. These three studies analyzed why the leading platform folder (platform leader) changed from Nintendo to Sony. Especially, Fujikawa (1999) analyzed the corporate behavior of platform folders from the perspective of business model competition. Therefore, these studies complemented a series of studies by Kohashi, which focused on Nintendo.

Inoue et al. (2011) analyzed the console game market using the ecosystem as a critical concept. They used game software data in the 2000s and analyzed the relationship between platform folders and game software companies. As a result of their analysis, they found that game software companies can be classified into four types and examined the difference in their behavioral roles. Furthermore, these four types of firms allowed the console game ecosystem to function effectively.

As for computer games other than console games, Fujita (1999a, b, 2006) analyzed the relationship between the arcade[3] and console game businesses. He offers a historical perspective that highlights their close interconnection. In his series of studies, Fujita began by describing the emergence of computer games, followed by the establishment of the arcade game business in the United States, the establishment and collapse of the console game business, and the establishment of the console game business in Japan. Negoro and Kameda (2011) also studied computer-based games as a whole. First, they analyzed how computer games have changed. Next, they focused on the relationship between game hardware and software.

10.2.2 Research Focused on Game Software

Research on the business of game software started later than the research on the overall business of console games. Pioneer Kohashi also shifted her research to game software and its development. In addition to their general interest in the game business, console game software (game software) attracted researchers' attention because it is representative of the Japanese content business.

For example, Kohashi (1997) focused on managing development activities. She then focused on human resource management and game software development (Kohashi 1998). Other early studies dealing with game software include Baba

3 Arcade games are specialized game machines installed in entertainment and commercial facilities.

(1998), Sunagawa (1998), Iino (1998), Shin (2002), Baba and Shibuya (2000a, b), Ohno's series of studies, Hanzawa (2005), and Fujii (2017).

Baba (1998) compared game software development with other software development, which clarified the characteristics of game software development. He discussed two cases, "Final Fantasy" and "Parappa Rapper," and argued that game software development is an "emergent activity."

Sunagawa (1998) studied how both Namco and Sega succeeded in arcade and console games. His discussion focused on building the capability to develop game software. He revealed the capability-building process of the two companies to develop game software from the perspectives of entrepreneurship and technological strategy.

Iino (1998), on the other hand, summarized the author's experiences and thoughts as a game software developer. In addition, Iino (1998) introduced interviews with developers of the excellent game software. Because this book is based on interviews, it is not systematic. However, it is informative about what it means to develop excellent game software.

Shin (2002) conducted a long-term observation concerning software development for one game. He described the activities at the site of game software development and the problem-solving activities that arose. The description is an intensive and highly informative case study.

Ohno (2000) presented a framework for studying genre-based game software development. He also reported on a survey of development activities in which Japanese and foreign companies collaborated (Ohno 2002). He compared the game software business with other entertainment industries, such as movies, and characterized game software as a "sensibility concept-type" software product (Ohno 2004).

Baba and Shibuya (2000a, b) classified game software companies that were located around Tokyo in terms of clusters. The characteristics of each cluster were clarified, and the factors that contribute to the formation of clusters were examined. These two studies were unique in that they analyzed the game software business by focusing on the relationships among firms and their geographic distribution.

Hanzawa (2005) was another study that focused on clusters of game software companies but concentrated on different factors. He focused on the characteristics of the development staff and the game software development process. According to Hanzawa (2005), the development staff want to stay in the Tokyo region. Then, he states that human resources were highly mobile and the propagation of information occurred through this movement of people. The combination of these two factors resulted in the formation of clusters. He also mentioned a division of labor between development and publishing functions within the region.

Fujii (2017) compared Square and Enix through the analytical perspective of entrepreneurs' strategic options. He analyzed the business development of these two companies, albeit in specific categories of the RPG (role-playing game) genre.

Thus, studies on game software initially came from diverse perspectives. Shintaku et al. (2003) comprehensively and multilaterally described and analyzed the console games business. They analyzed the industrial structure established in console games. They examined the platform network externalities. They also analyzed entries and exits from the game software industry and market concentration changes. In addition, they analyzed the characteristic sales patterns of game software and game software development. Finally, they compared the overseas markets and the Japanese market.

Wada followed Shintaku et al. (2003) and examined several research themes in more depth. For example, Wada (2003) analyzed the distribution system of game software and further examined the system's impact on the sales of new products (2007). Moreover, Wada (2011) examined how game software sales changed over time and identified factors that prevented highly novel products from increasing their market presence. Furthermore, Wada (2017) clarified the formation process of the RPG genre (submarket) and revealed the emergence of a tendency among Japanese game software companies to stick to specific genres and series (2019).

Thus, game software business research is still expanding. The studies presented here will provide us with suggestions for future research.

10.2.3 Games as Part of the Content Business

In recent years, many studies have considered the game business to be part of the content industry. These studies compared the game industry with other content industries, such as animation, film, and music, and have attempted to capture their characteristics. Deguchi et al. (2009) and Kawashima (2020) are representative studies. Deguchi et al. (2009) discussed businesses closely related to game software. They then argued that the Japanese model had created a diverse kind of content. Kawashima (2020) comprehensively dealt with the content industry from the standpoint of cultural economics. She then clarified the peculiarities of game software compared with other content.

Underlying these studies is the fact that various types of content have been digitized and have been linked with the game software business. As a result, the game software business has come to be viewed as part of the content business and the creative industry. Hence, there is a possibility of capturing the interactions among content, including games, which can provide new insights.

10.3 An Early Phenomenon in the Japanese Game Business

► Section 10.2 presented management studies of console games in Japan. In many respects, the results of these early studies anticipated those of the 2000s and beyond. That is not surprising. Management studies aim for "global" knowledge—universal research results that are not influenced by the situation in a particular region or country. Therefore, the researchers who investigated the Japanese game business used the same points of view, concepts, and analytical frameworks as their foreign counterparts. They tried to clarify the characteristics of the Japanese game business using these concepts and analytical frameworks. Therefore, the phenomena, factors, and mechanisms found in the studies were primarily applicable to other countries, even if the times or geographies were different. Three main areas of research are described in the following examples.

One example is research on platform-based businesses or ecosystems. For example, in the game business, hardware can be a platform; furthermore, game hardware works as a platform on which various software is provided. Therefore, hardware and software work together to create an ecosystem.

A representative example of hardware that became a platform is Nintendo's Family Computer. Nintendo and Sega used their hardware as a platform to build their business models. Their business models leveraged software, a complementary good to hardware. Nintendo and other companies that provided platforms earned fees by allowing other companies to release software. We call this business model the "semi-open" strategy.

This business model attracted a lot of attention, partly because Nintendo, which had become the platform leader (the leading platform), had generated significant revenues. Therefore, many researchers investigated it. Kohashi's study, Nakama et al. (1996), Fujikawa (1999), and Kuriki (2008) are all representative examples.

Furthermore, the study of platform-based firm behavior, which Nintendo and others have successfully used, provided research materials for empirical studies of network externalities (Shankar and Bayus 2003; Clements and Ohashi 2005; Yamaguchi 2016). Network externalities have been an important concept in contemporary management studies since the pioneering work of Katz and Shapiro (1985). The console game business has the right conditions to verify network externalities in terms of the complementary relationship between hardware and software and the completeness of data. At the same time, it has also inspired research on system diffusion and standards setting (Asaba 1995; Shintaku and Asaba 2014). The gaming business also serves as a compelling empirical example of strategies in two-sided markets, a topic that has drawn increasing academic interest in recent years (Rochet and Tirole 2003; Eisenmann et al. 2006).

Moreover, when a platform is established, and many companies enter the game software business, an ecosystem is established. Inoue et al. (2011) and Negoro and Kameda (2011) also dealt with ecosystems in the game software business.

Since the 1980s, the console game business has provided excellent material for empirical research on platform strategy, network externalities, de facto standards, two-sided market strategies and ecosystem formation. These are hot issues in today's discussions of competitive strategy in management studies, and empirical studies have emerged in other industries.

Second, the creativity of those who developed game software attracts a good deal of attention. Those who develop game software are an issue that researchers have recently addressed in the creative industries. In other words, the game software business is of research interest to clarify the relationship between creative activities and business. There are two representatives research questions. What kind of management fosters creativity? What characteristics does a group or region—a creative class or a creative cluster—have that attract creative people?

The studies by Baba and Shibuya (2000a, b) and Hanzawa (2005), introduced in ► Sect. 10.2, attempted to answer this research question by examining the actual situation in large cities such as Tokyo. Kawashima (2020) also studied the Japanese game business from creative industries and cultural policy perspectives.

The creative activity of game software development is not completed within a single company. Hence, creativity is nurtured and demonstrated by personnel from different companies. In some situations, the work is carried out through personal networks in the same region. Baba and Shibuya (2000a, b), Hanzawa (2005), and Kawashima (2020) addressed frameworks and concepts that captured this. These studies make games relevant to discussing business relationships in specific regions and the personal networks of developers. Studies that focused on game software development and interfirm and inter-personal networks with a similar awareness of the issues include Johns (2006), Izushi and Aoyama (2006), De Vaan et al. (2011), De Vaan et al. (2012), Balland et al. (2013), and Gil and Warzynski (2014).

An example of the third research area is innovation and industry formation. In the 1970s and 1980s, the Japanese game business was an entirely new industry. Therefore, it proved an excellent source for answering the research question, "How do new industries arise?" Among the studies introduced in ▶ Sect. 10.2, Fujita's series of studies and Shintaku et al. (2003) took a historical approach to this research question. In addition, Ikuine (2012) and Uemura et al. (2013) conducted empirical studies of Japanese games and addressed these research questions. Uemura et al. (2013) revealed the rise of the Japanese console game business, with the Family Computer as its centerpiece. Drawing on Abernathy's (1978) research on innovation patterns, Ikuine (2012, 2021) identifies the innovation patterns specific to gaming software and traces the industry's rise and fall.

There are many studies overseas that have addressed similar research questions, including Aoyama and Izushi (2003), Storz (2008), and Subramanian et al. (2011). Schilling (2003) has a pioneering study of industry formation in the US console game business.

In addition, the console game business showed us the emergence of submarkets (genres), and the establishment of these submarkets has led to the growth of the entire market. For example, the RPG genre was born in 1986, and the entire video game business expanded. Yonekura and Ikuine (2005) and Ikuine (2021) pointed out the formation of submarkets in the industry. The same research theme is relevant to recent studies such as Zhao et al. (2018).

As we have seen above, the Japanese game business provided much material for research about the 1980s, including platform businesses, network externalities, ecosystems, industry formation, creative industries and innovations. Therefore, we can learn many new lessons by studying this business.

At the same time, these researchers used the theory of management studies with high universality. In other words, they used "good glasses" to see the phenomenon of the console game business. Hence, the research results concerning the Japanese game business remained valid even after the 2000s. Furthermore, the results could be contrasted and joined with phenomena from countries and regions outside Japan. As a result, we are ready to get more fruitful research results now, both in game studies and management studies.

10.4 How to Conduct Japanese Games Research

Until the 1990s, Japan's game business led the world. However, since the 2000s, it has been overtaken by other countries. American, Korean, and Chinese companies improved their technology and built new capabilities for game software development. As a result, the relative position of Japanese companies and their markets declined. Furthermore, new types of games appeared, such as PC-based online games and mobile games. In other words, companies and markets in other countries grew, and new types of games appeared. Therefore, it is no longer the case that cutting-edge examples and new phenomena are seen only in Japan.

Nevertheless, Japanese companies and markets still occupy a particular global position. The growth of companies and markets in other countries and the emergence of different types of games also mean that new comparisons are possible. By comparing events and research results, it is possible to determine what is universal and what is unique to Japan. Therefore, the knowledge gained today from studying Japanese games is likely to be richer and more accurate than until the 2000s by comparing with other countries' products and business.

Using the theory of management studies with high universality and general concepts is vital in conducting the research. More precisely, you had better learn theories, concepts, analytical frameworks, and empirical approaches of management studies. If you have "good glasses" clear enough to see reality, you can compare phenomena occurring in Japan with those occurring in other countries. Comparisons can provide new insights. That is why it is better to acquire an academic foundation, such as management studies, before starting research on games in Japan.

However, the concepts and analytical framework of management studies are universal. They are not necessarily designed to discuss games and the game business. In order to study Japanese games, we must use highly universal concepts and analytical frameworks. Accordingly, we customize our concepts and frameworks to examine games from the viewpoint of management studies. For example, we may view game consoles as platforms and explain their diffusion through network externalities. We may understand the situation created by various software programs released on the same console as an ecosystem. The emergence of genres may be interpreted as the establishment of a submarket. Game software developers can be regarded as creative people. The geographical connections may be seen as clusters and the human networks of developers as social capital. When we observe new types of games possible with smartphones and VR technologies, it is better to understand these developments as nascent innovations and industries.

The Japanese game business offers many research themes and lessons. The existing research provides you with how to use the concepts of management studies in the context of games. Therefore, they will help you interpret the terms and the theory of management studies differently. Moreover, universities and graduate schools are open to you as a place to learn to do it. These research and educational institutions are staffed by researchers who help you access the research institutions and academic communities described in ► Chaps. 3 and 7.

Researchers working in Japan also want to interact with foreign researchers. The Japanese game research community invites scholars to study the Japanese game business from a new perspective. In addition, international comparative studies can be conducted between Japan and another country. Such international academic exchanges will undoubtedly lead to abundant significant knowledge.

10.5 The Future of Research on Games in Japan

What is the future of Japanese game studies? Several research areas introduced in ▶ Sect. 10.3—platforms and ecosystems, creative industries, and innovation—still hold promise as research topics. However, there is room for research in other areas as well. These possibilities can be considered based on the current state of the game business in Japan and on existing research.

The Japanese game business continues to have a significant global presence. Additionally, Japanese companies continue to develop new hardware and software. Indeed, Japanese games are not as dominant as they were up to the 1990s. However, many users still play games. The Japanese game business also maintains a particular scale as a business. Therefore, it provides sufficient research material.

In this context, Japan is at a high hardware and software technology level. The Nintendo Switch 2 and PlayStation 5 are good examples of this. Therefore, the relationship between advanced technologies and society can be revealed by examining the Japanese game business. Furthermore, such research would answer the research questions for the following questions. How does society accept new technologies? How do they become a part of everyday life? In other words, Japan has excellent materials for research on the social diffusion of technology.

Looking back, 3D CG (Three-dimensional computer graphics) spread rapidly throughout society through the PlayStation. More recently, as Tanaka and Yamaguchi (2015) showed in their empirical studies, cell phones and smartphones were actively used for gaming in Japan. Taken together, these cases illustrate that Japanese companies continue to possess strong technological capabilities and a strong appetite for development. As new technologies continue to emerge, the games that incorporate them will become increasingly valuable as research material. This leads to the following research questions: How will data science, AI, VR/XR, and cybernetic avatars (CAs)—which are expected to spread in the future—be accepted by society, along with the content of games? What factors will shape this process? With this in mind, making the Japanese game business the subject of our research will be exciting.

Second, in Japan, many people have rich game experience and a high level of gaming proficiency. ▶ Chapter 4 of this book introduces the phenomenon of games spreading with other content through animations, manga, music, and movies, for example. In ▶ Chap. 5, we discussed arcade games, where people play games eagerly. In ▶ Chap. 6, we discussed the research on "Doujin," which focuses on users with very rich and unique game experiences. At the foundation of all these phenomena are many users with rich gaming experiences. Therefore, studying how they enjoy games as entertainment and culture is significant. The insight about these users will provide meaningful research material for marketing studies. Of course, the business models and marketing strategies of companies involved with such users will also be research subjects. In the pioneering study, Nojima (2008) analyzed the behavior of users who "buy things that have no form" and companies' business models that respond to consumer behaviors. More than a decade later, how is the relationship between users, user communities, and users and companies about to change? Answering this question will yield new research findings.

Third, since the 1970s, Japan has had a history of creating games and running the business of games. The history of games in Japan has experienced rapid growth, competition among companies, and much trial and error. Rapid technological progress also played a major role. Therefore, phenomena that would have taken decades to observe in other industries can be observed and studied in a short time period. The authors have focused on this point and have started research to preserve the oral history of the game business (Shimizu et al. 2016). However, research on Japanese games from the viewpoint of economic history and management history has just begun. Therefore, there is ample room for further research.

The Japanese game business provides a rich source of research material, some of which can lead to hot issues for management studies. Language is the only obstacle. However, it can be overcome by conducting joint research with researchers who are fluent in other languages. Not collecting materials and data or interviewing people involved in the game business in Japan because of the language barrier will result in missed opportunities to collect important research material.

When researching the game business, there is a significant disadvantage to conducting research without interacting with the Japanese game culture. Therefore, conducting empirical research from the perspective of management studies can be achieved by coming into contact with the actual sites and products of the Japanese game business.

Acknowledgement This work was supported by JSPS KAKENHI Grant Number 21H00753(B), 23K25553(B), 24K05119(C) and JST Moonshot R&D Grant Number JPMJMS2215.

References

Abernathy, William J. 1978. *The Productivity Dilemma: Roadblock to Innovation in the Automobile Industry*. Baltimore, MD: Johns Hopkins University Press.

Aida, Yutaka, and Atsushi Ogaki. 1997. *Sin densi rikkoku 4 bideo ge-mu: kyohu no koubou [The New Electronic Nation 4—Video Games and the Struggle for Great Wealth]*. Tokyo: Nihon housou shuppan kyoukai. (in Japanese).

Aoyama, Yuko, and Hiro Izushi. 2003. Hardware gimmick or cultural innovation? Technological, cultural, and social foundations of the Japanese video game industry. *Research Policy* 32 (3): 423–444. https://www.sciencedirect.com/science/article/pii/S0048733302000161?casa_token=Ba189-lQ4XEAAAAA:UNyzXGSLTcShcRPOdz2KRDg3D3VsZ0RLfi1U9qwFF0ehFb_UeFseD4f-BFMkNW4OlWA3Fv7W; https://journals.sagepub.com/doi/abs/10.1068/a37205

Asaba, Shigeru. 1995. *Kyo-so- to kyo-ryoku no senryaku: Gyo-kai hyoujun wo meguru kigyou koudou [Competitive and Cooperative Strategy: Firm Behavior Toward Industrial Standard]*. Tokyo: Yuhikaku. (in Japanese).

Asakura, Reiji. 1998. *Soni- no kakumei zi tati [Sony's Revolutionaries]*. IDG Communications, Tokyo. (in Japanese).

Baba, Yasunori. 1998. *Dezitaru kati souzou: mirai kara no mono zukuri genron [Digital Value Creation—Monozukuri Theory from the Future]*. Tokyo: NTT Publishing. (in Japanese).

Baba, Yasunori, and Masato Shibuya. 2000a. Toukyou ge-mu sohuto kurasuta- : kigyou no kuukanteki syuuseki no kousatu [Tokyo game-soft cluster: analysis on firm's spatial agglomeration]. *The Journal of Science Policy and Research Management* 14:266–278. (in Japanese).

Baba, Yasunori, and Masato Shibuya. 2000b. Toukyou ge-mu sohuto kurasuta : keisei youin no sougouteki kousatu [Tokyo game-soft cluster: analysis on formation process]. *The Journal of Science Policy and Research Management* 15:33–47. (in Japanese).

Baba, Yasunori, Shinji Takai, and Yuji Mizuta. 1995. The Japanese software industry: the 'hub structure' approach. *Research Policy* 24 (3): 473–486.

Balland, Pierre-Alexandre, Mathijs De Vaan, and Ron Boschma. 2013. The dynamics of interfirm networks along the industry life cycle: the case of the global video game industry, 1987–2007. *Journal of Economic Geography* 13 (5): 741–765.

Clements, Matthew T., and Hiroshi Ohashi. 2005. Indirect network effects and the product cycle: video games in the US, 1994–2002. *The Journal of Industrial Economics* 53 (4): 515–542. https://doi.org/10.1111/j.1467-6451.2005.00268.x.

De Vaan, Mathijs, Balazs Vedres, and David Stark. 2011. Disruptive diversity and recurring cohesion: assembling creative teams in the video game industry, 1979–2009. Working Paper, Institute for Social and Economic Research and Policy at Columbia University.

De Vaan, Mathijs, Ron Boschma, and Koen Frenken. 2012. Clustering and firm performance in project-based industries: the case of the global video game industry, 1972–2007. *Journal of Economic Geography* 13 (6): 965–991. https://doi.org/10.1093/jeg/lbs038.

Deguchi, Hiroshi, Hideyuki Tanaka, and Yusuke Koyama. 2009. *Kontentu sangyou ron: konkou to denpa no nippongata moderu [Content Industry Theory: A Japanese Model of Contamination and Propagation]*. Tokyo: Tokyo University Press. (in Japanese).

Eisenmann, Thomas, Geoff Parker, and M. W. Van Alstyne. 2006. Strategies for two-sided markets. *Harvard Business Review* 84 (10): 92.

Fujii, Daiji. 2017. *Gizyututeki inobe-syon no manezimento: paradaimu kakusin no mekanizumu to senryaku [The Management of Technological Innovation]*. Tokyo: Chuou keizaisha. (in Japanese).

Fujikawa, Yoshinori. 1999. Sohuto kaihatu wo suisin suru dainamizumu no gensen: Nintendou to soni- no bizinesu moderu kan kyousou [The source of dynamism that drives software development—competition between Nintendo and Sony's business models]. In *Era of Marketing Innovation 2—Product Development Innovation*, ed. M. Shimaguchi, H. Takeuchi, H. Katahira, and J. Ishii. Tokyo: Yuhikaku. (in Japanese).

Fujita, Naoki. 1999a. Famikon touzyou mae no nihon no bideo ge-mu sangyou [The Japanese video game industry before the "Famicom": the formation of the modern video game industry]. *Keizai Ronso [Economic Series in Kyoto University]* 163:59–76. https://doi.org/10.14989/45271. (in Japanese).

Fujita, Naoki. 1999b. Famikon kaihatu to bideo ge-mu sangyou keisei katei no sougouteki kousatu [The development of the Family Computer and the formation of the video game industry. *Keizai Ronso [Economic Series in Kyoto University]* 163: 69–86. https://doi.org/10.14989/45282. (in Japanese).

Fujita, Naoki. 2006. Gendai bideo ge-mu sangyou no keisei to hatten: sono gizyutu siteki kousatu [The formation and evolution of the modern video game industry: from the technological history perspective]. Ph.D. Dissertation, Kyoto University. (in Japanese).

Gawer, Annabelle, and Michael A. Cusumano. 2002. *Platform Leadership: How Intel, Microsoft, and Cisco Drive Industry Innovation*. Boston, MA: Harvard Business School Press.

Gil, Ricard, and Frederic Warzynski. 2014. Vertical integration, exclusivity, and game sales performance in the US video game industry. *Journal of Law, Economics, and Organization* 31 (Suppl 1): i143–i168.

Hanzawa, Seiji. 2005. Katei you bideo ge-mu sangyou no bungyou keitai to tiriteki tokusei [Characteristics of the division of labor and geography in the Japanese home video game industry]. *Geographical Review of Japan, Series B* 78:607–633. (in Japanese).

Hirabayashi, Hisakazu, and Koichi Akao. 1996. *Ge-mu no daigaku [The University of Games]*. Tokyo: Media Factory. (in Japanese).

Ichikawa, Koji. 1993. *Konpyu-ta ge-mu: posuto Famikon no hasya ha dare ka [Computer Games—Who Will Be the Post-Famicom Champion?]*. Tokyo: Nihon Keizai Shinbun sha. (in Japanese).

Iino, Kenji. 1998. *Su-pa- hitto ge-mu gaku [Super Hit Gameology]*. Tokyo: Fuho-Sha. (in Japanese).

Ikuine, Fumihiko. 2012. *Kaihatu seisansei no dhirenma [Development Productivity Dilemma: The Innovation Patterns in the Digital Age]*. Tokyo: Yuhikaku. (in Japanese).

Ikuine, Fumihiko. 2021. *The Efficiency and Creativity of Product Development: Lessons from the Game Software Industry in Japan*. Berlin: Springer.

Inoue, Tatsuhiko, Kisuke Maki, and Susumu Nagayama. 2011. Bizinesu eko sisutemu ni okeru nitti no koudou to habu kigyou no senryaku: katei you ge-mu gyoukai ni okeru hukuganteki bunseki [Niches' behaviors and hub-firms' strategies in business ecosystem: multi-perspective analysis for the Japanese video game industry]. *Organizational Science* 44:67–82. https://doi.org/10.11207/soshikikagaku.20220820-84. (in Japanese).

Izushi, Hiro, and Yuko Aoyama. 2006. Industry evolution and cross-sectoral skill transfers: a comparative analysis of the video game industry in Japan, the United States, and the United Kingdom. *Environment and Planning A: Economy and Space* 38:1843–1861. https://doi.org/10.1068/a37205.

Johns, Jennifer. 2006. Video games production networks: value capture, power relations and embeddedness. *Journal of Economic Geography* 6 (2): 151–180.

Katz, Michael L., and Carl Shapiro. 1985. Network externalities, competition, and compatibility. *The American Economic Review* 75 (3): 424–440. http://www.jstor.org/stable/1814809.

Kawashima, Nnobuko. 2020. *Kontentu sangyou ron dai 2 han: bunka souzou no Keizai, hou, manezimento [Content Industry: Economy, Law, and Management of Cultural Creation 2nd edition]*. Kyoto: Minerva Shobo. (in Japanese). https://researchmap.jp/read0059346/books_etc/12678872; https://researchmap.jp/read0059346/books_etc/41074076

Kohashi, Reika. 1993a. Kansetu seigyo gata nettowa-ku to hukakuzitusei: katei you terebi ge-mu sangyou ni okeru kigyou kan sisutemu [Rule-regulated networks and uncertainty: inter-corporative systems in Japanese consumer video-game industry.]. *The Rokkodai Ronshu* 41:114–125. (in Japanese).

Kohashi, Reika. 1993b. Katei you terebi ge-mu sangyou no senryaku to sosiki [Strategy and organization of the home video game industry]. *Business Insight, Autumn*74–87. (in Japanese).

Kohashi, Reika. 1997. Nihon ni okeru katei you terebi ge-mu sohutowhea no kaihatu [The mechanism of the development processes of Japanese video game software companies]. *OIU Journal of International Studies* 10:81–107. (in Japanese).

Kohashi, Reika. 1998. Nihon no ge-mu sohuto gaisya no zinzai manezimento [Management of development engineers in Japanese video game software companies]. *OIU Journal of International Studies* 12:1–22. (in Japanese).

Kohashi, Reika, and Tadao Kagono. 1995. The exchange and development of images: a study of the Japanese video game industry. In *Paper presented at the Hitotsubashi-Organization Science Conference on Asian Research in Organizations: Emerging Paradigms in Organization Studies*. Tokyo: Kunitachi.

Kuriki, Kei. 2008. Katei you terebi ge-mu sangyou ni okeru bizinesu sisutemu no hukugou kyousou [Multi-dimensional competition by business systems in video game industry]. *Hitotsubashi Business Review* 56 (1): 46–60. (in Japanese). https://researchmap.jp/kuriki/published_papers/23213731?lang=en

Nakama, Masahiko, Yosuke Fuimoto, Yoshiyuki Eto, and Fumihiko Ikuine. 1996. Katei you ge-mu ki sizyou no itikousatu: soni-konpyu-ta entateinmento no zirei yori [A study of the home video game console market: a case study of Sony Computer Entertainment Inc.]. The University of Tokyo Takahiro Fujimoto Seminar Collection. (in Japanese).

10

Negoro, Tatsuyuki, Naoki Kameda. 2011 Ge-mu sangyou ni okeru 「ge-mu moderu」 no henka [The "Game Model" transformation in the gaming industry]. Research Institute of IT & Management Working paper No. 38 (2011_RIIM-WP-38), Waseda University. (in Japanese).
Nojima, Miho. 2008. *Hito ha naze katati no nai mono wo ka u no ka: kasou sekai no bizinesu moderu [Why People Buy Things That Don't Have a Form: Business Models in the Virtual World]*. Tokyo: NTT Publishing. (in Japanese).
Ohno, Mitsuhide. 2000. Seihin kaihatu no siten kara mi ta ge-mu sohutouea no taikei ka ni kan suru itikousatu [A study of video game software in terms of product development]. *Doshisha University Worldwide Business Review* 1:139–163. (in Japanese).
Ohno, Mitsuhide. 2002. Nihon ni okeru ge-mu sohuto kaihatu purosesu to kaigai kyoudou kaihatu seisaku no zyoukyou [Engineering process of video games and foreign coproduction in Japan]. *Doshisha University World Wide Business Review* 4:13–27. (in Japanese).
Ohno, Mitsuhide. 2004. Kansei konseputo gata sohutouea purodakuto no kaihatu seisaku moderu to kadai [Development model of software products, which allows sensible concepts to be embodied and related issues]. *Doshisha University World Wide Business Review* 5:94–110. (in Japanese).
Rochet, Jean-Charle, and Jean Tirole. 2003. Platform competition in two-sided markets. *Journal of the European Economic Association* 1(4):990–1029. https://doi.org/10.1162/154247603322493212
Schilling, Melissa A. 2003. Technological leapfrogging: lessons from the US video game console industry. *California Management Review* 45 (3): 6–32.
Shankar, Venkatesh, and Barry Bayus. 2003. Network effects and competition: an empirical analysis of the home video game industry. *Strategic Management Journal* 24 (4): 375–384.
Shimizu, Hiroshi, Megumi Kimura, Mmabu Eto, Fumihiko Ikuine. 2016. Aso bi kara bizinesu he : nihon to amerika ni okeru ge-mu no sangyou ka [From fun to business: the industrialization of computer games]. In *2nd Kyoto Game Conference, Amusement and Innovation: Toward the History of the Game Industry, 17th March 2016*, Ritsumeikan University, Kyoto (in Japanese).
Shin, Kiyoshi. 2002. *Ge-mu kaihatu saizensen 『Samurai』 ha kou si te tuku ra re ta - aku waia seisaku 2 ka no 660 niti sensou [This is How the Samurai Was Created: Acquire Development Section 2 660-day]*. Tokyo: Shin Kigen sha. (in Japanese).
Shintaku, Junjiro, and Shigeru Asaba. 2014. Intergenerational competitive strategies for industry standards. *Annals of Business Administrative Science* 13 (1): 47–66.
Shintaku, Junjiro. Noriyuki Yanagawa, Tatsuo Tanaka. (eds.) 2003. Ge-mu sangyou no keizai bunseki- kontentu sangyouhatten no kouzou to senryaku [Economic Analysis on Game Industry.] Toyo Keizai Shimpo-sha, Tokyo. (in Japanese).
Storz, Cornelia. 2008. Dynamics in innovation systems: evidence from Japan's game software industry. *Research Policy* 37 (9): 1480–1491.
Subramanian, Annapoornima M., K.-H. Chai, and S. Mu. 2011. Capability reconfiguration of incumbent firms: Nintendo in the video game industry. *Technovation* 31 (5): 228–239.
Sunagawa, Kazunori. 1998. Nihon ge-mu sangyou ni miru kigyousya katudou no keiki to gizyutu senryaku : - sega to namuko ni okeru sohutowhea kaihatu sosiki no keisei [Continuous entrepreneurial behaviors and their strategic innovations in Japanese computer game industry: the development of 'Software Factories' at SEGA and Namco]. *Japan Business History Review* 32:1–27. (in Japanese).
Tanaka, Tatsuo, and Shinichi Yamaguchi. 2015. *So-syaru ge-mu no bizinesu moderu : huri-miamu no keizai bunseki [The Business Model of Social Games: An Economic Analysis of Freemium]*. Tokyo: Keiso Shobo. (in Japanese).
Uemura, Masayuki, Koichi Hosoi, and Akinori Nakamura. 2013. *Famikon to Sono Jidai [The Life and Times of the Nintendo Famicom: The Birth of TV Games]*. Tokyo: NTT Shuppan. (in Japanese).
Wada, Takeaki. 2003. Katei you terebi ge-mu sohuto no ryuutuu — risuku to rita-n no kouzou to sizyou he no eikyou [Video game console software distribution: risk/return structure and market impact]. *Amamon Management Review* 2:563–580. https://doi.org/10.14955/amr.021101. (in Japanese).
Wada, Takeaki. 2007. Katei you ge-mu sohuto sizyou ni okeru ryuutuu dankai de no sinseihin no sizyou kikai isitu [Failure of new product introduction and selling chance loss by distributor: case of the Japanese TV game software market]. *Organizational Science* 40:93–102. (in Japanese).

Wada, Takeaki. 2011. Exploitation reduces novelty: an empirical analysis of the Japanese video game industry. *Annals of Business Administrative Science* 10:1–12. https://doi.org/10.7880/abas.10.1.
Wada, Takeaki. 2017. History of Japanese role-playing games. *Annals of Business Administrative Science* 16:137–147. https://doi.org/10.7880/abas.0170228a.
Wada, Takeaki. 2019. The core rigidity of Japanese home video game companies. *Annals of Business Administrative Science* 18:195–208. https://doi.org/10.7880/abas.0190921a.
Yada, Mari. 1996. *Ge-mu rikkoku no miraizou [The Future of a Game Nation]*. Tokyo: Nikkei BP. (in Japanese).
Yamaguchi, Shinichi. 2016. Nettowa-ku gaibu sei no zikan keika ni yoru kouka gensyou to hukyuu senryaku : ge-mu sangyou no zissyou bunseki [An empirical analysis of the game industry to demonstrate decreased impact of network externalities over time]. *Organizational Science* 49 (3): 60–71. https://doi.org/10.11207/soshikikagaku.49.3_60. (in Japanese).
Yamana, Ichiro. 1994. *Kingu obu ge-mu no mirai sen [The Future of the King of Games]*. Tokyo: Nihon Jitsugyo Shuppan. (in Japanese).
Yonekura, Seiichiro, and Fumihiko Ikuine. 2005. Nihon no ge-mu sohuto sangyou - siri-zu senryaku no wana [Japanese Game Software Industry: Series Strategy Trap]. *Hitotsubashi Business Review* 53 (3): 52–69. (in Japanese).
Zhao, Eric Yanfei, Masakazu Ishihara, P. Devereaux Jennings, and Michael Lounsbury. 2018. Optimal distinctiveness in the console video game industry: an exemplar-based model of proto-category evolution. *Organization Science* 29 (4): 588–611.

Reconstruction of Japanese Game History in the 1980s: Reconsidering Game as a Narrative Medium

Hiroshi Yoshida

Contents

F. Ikuine et al. (eds.), *Japanese Game Studies*, https://doi.org/10.1007/978-981-95-9857-1_11

11.1 Introduction

The purpose of this paper is to reconstruct the history of games in Japan in the 1980s while restoring the contemporary cultural contexts, thereby placing digital games within a broader cultural ecology. The 1980s are known as the first golden age of digital games in Japan, but if we examine the discourse of that time closely, we can see that there was a context in which board games and TRPGs were considered superior to digital games, and digital games were considered postmodern narrative devices.

This paper consists of three parts. Firstly, I analyze the discourse of Hitoshi Yasuda, a translator and introducer of Western tabletop RPGs, to clarify the position of computer RPGs within the gaming culture of the time. Secondly, through an analysis of Genichiro Takahashi's novels and critical essays, we examine how avant-garde writers saw the potential for a "new type of literature" in digital games. Thirdly and at last, through an analysis of game critiques by religion scholar and cultural anthropologist Shin'ichi Nakazawa, we understand that he viewed digital games as postmodern narrative devices and players who play with bugs as post-capitalist subjects.

The three authors discussed in this paper were leading intellectuals and cultural figures in Japan at the time, but what is interesting is that they were complete contemporaries: Yasuda and Nakazawa were born in 1950, and Takahashi in 1951. Yasuda and Takahashi were also classmates in the same high school. Although they worked in different fields, they all had a deep connection to games in their own contexts and have written about games. However, with the exception of Nakazawa, their discourse has received little attention in game studies to date. As this paper will show, their texts are the best key to understanding the cultural and social significance of digital games in Japan at that time. What becomes clear from this examination is that at the time, games were primarily appreciated in relation to stories and literature, far beyond what we might expect today.

11.2 Computer RPGs as a Subgenre of SF Fantasy Games: Hitoshi Yasuda

Hitoshi Yasuda (1950–) was one of the central figures in building Japan's gaming culture in the 1980s. He began his career as an introducer and translator of English and American science fictions, during which he played a key role in introducing simulation games such as *Triolanetray* (1973) and *Starforce* (1974) as well as role-playing games such as *Dungeons & Dragons* (1974) and *Tunnels & Trolls* (1975) to the Japanese public. In 1987, he founded a company called Group SNE, which began translating and producing tabletop role-playing games (hereafter abbreviated as TPRGs) and trading card games (hereafter as TCGs). Yasuda is also known as an avid player of early computer games such as *Zork* (1980) and *Wizardry* (1981), and has commented on them from his own unique perspective.

Yasuda's view on games can be understood from his two earliest books, *The World of SF Fantasy Games* (1986) and *Myth-Making Machines* (1987). Let us explore these works to find out what he thought about the diversity of contemporary gaming culture and the position of digital games within it. According to him, computer games cannot compete with original role-playing games or adventure games that do not use computers, either in terms of game systems or the appeal of the stories they provide.

> Of course, there are some excellent pieces of software available at present, but whether it be role-playing games (programming capabilities that allow players to create new stories) or adventure games (freedom of input/output options, i.e. volume and inference), we have not yet reached the stage where they can fully replicate the original. But above all, computer games save you a lot of effort, are perfect when you don't have anyone to play against, and have the added benefit of sound and graphics. (Yasuda 1986, p. 64; here and hereafter, unless otherwise noted, the author's translation)

However, as stated here, Yasuda does not forget to point out that one of the benefits of computer games is that they can be played alone. Role-playing games are originally party games played by multiple people. However, unlike in the West, party culture has not taken root in daily life in Japan. This has hindered the spread of games in Japan. However, he thought that computer games that can be played alone would provide good practice for Japanese players to get used to RPGs.

> The only problem is that you can't play *D&D* or *Traveler* by yourself. In the West, parties are popular, so even people who don't know each other often gather on some occasion, and "games" are the traditional foundation (another reason is that there is a foundation for family games, where these games are played as a form of communication between parents and children). I believe that these party-style and family games will become more popular in Japan in the future, but for the time being, it is undeniable that the difficulty of gathering a large number of people is one of the obstacles to enjoying such attractive games. However, computer role-playing games are originally designed to be played by one person, so there is no need to worry about this aspect. If you want to know what role-playing games are like, but are stuck on the number of people, it would be best to get used to them with these games first. (Yasuda 1986, pp. 229–230)

He explains the appeal of the computer RPGs *Wizardry* and *Ultima* in this way. However, Yasuda believes that RPGs are games that are played by multiple people, and that single-player games cannot replace them. This applies not only to computer games, but also to adventure gamebooks published in book form. Yasuda, who has translated and introduced gamebooks to Japanese readers in the same way as TRPGs, says the following:

> Whether it's *Sorcery* or *Fantasy*, the appeal of the original role-playing games, "immersion into the character" and "adventure in the narrative world," is impeccable. However, the original versions of *D&D* and *Traveler* have an appeal that goes beyond that. "World creation"—in other words, the rules themselves have a function

added that allows the gamemaster's imagination to create as many adventure worlds as possible. And the correlation (communication) between the gamemaster who creates this world and the players. For now, this is the only aspect that can only be enjoyed in the original role-playing games. (Yasuda 1987, pp. 34–35)

Yasuda describes the characteristics of the gamebook *Sorcery* (1983–1985) and the CPRG *Fantasy* (1985) as above. With books for single-player and computer programs, the player can enjoy "immersion in the character" and "adventure in the narrative world," but they cannot experience the original appeal of RPGs, which is the free creation and expansion of the world through the gamemaster's imagination, and the negotiations through conversations between the players and the gamemaster. Computer RPGs cannot beat TRPGs for two reasons: technical and communication constraints.

Thus, if it seems surprising today that TRPGs were more highly regarded than digital games in Japan in the 1980s, this is also the effect of the *digital fallacy*. As Jaakko Stenros and Annika Waern point out, digital games are merely "a special case of games," and their features are not always "characteristic of games in general" (Stenros and Waern 2011, p. 12). If we forget this and have an unconscious bias that places digital games at the center of game culture, it will only cloud our view. Reexamining Yasuda's discourse will help us distance ourselves from the *digital fallacy*.

Yasuda's text also teaches us that what has come to be considered characteristic of Japanese digital games actually existed before that time. One of these is the emphasis on characters. In discussing the board game based on *The Lord of the Rings*, Yasuda points out that such "character games" based on original works were seen early on in Japan.

» By the way, what's interesting is that SF games in Japan have followed this trend of character (original) games from the very beginning. Tsukuda Hobby and Bandai have been working on domestic SF games since the end of 1981, and both of them started out by focusing on games based on original works. Tsukuda Hobby's first game was *Jabro: The Game of Ground Fighting in Gundam*, a tactical game based on a part of the anime *Mobile Suit Gundam*, and since then they have focused on anime such as the *Gundam* series, *Space Runaway Ideon*, *Macross*, and *Combat Mecha Xabungle*. Bandai's first game was a game based on a science fiction novel called *The Sinking of the Japanese Archipelago*, but they also tend to make games based on special effects movies such as *Mothra vs. Godzilla* and *Ultraman*, as well as anime such as *Space Battleship Yamato*. (Yasuda 1986, pp. 46–48)

As he states, toy manufacturers such as Tsukuda Hobby and Bandai released board games based on anime such as *Mobile Suit Gundam* and *Space Battleship Yamato*, and special effects films such as *Mothra vs. Godzilla* and *Ultraman*. In order to consider the origin of "transmedia storytelling" that traverses the boundaries between films, comics, and games, we must go back to the era before digital games.

11.3 Computer Games as "New Literature" That Deconstructs the Narrative: Genichiro Takahashi

In order to understand the presence and significance of digital games in the intellectual context of Japan in the 1980s, it is impossible to leave out the novelist and literary critic Genichiro Takahashi (1951–). Takahashi was a classmate of Yasuda at Nada High School, Japan's top elite boys' school in Kobe, and the two could be said to be complete contemporaries in terms of generation and culture. To understand Takahashi's interests and commitment to games, one must look at both his work as a writer and as a critic.

First, let's look at his work as a novelist. Takahashi has a series of works that can be "game novels." Among these are included "Reports on the Adventures, Love, Daily Life, etc. of Nameless  s," which were published in two parts in the magazine *Bungei* in 1986.[1] The protagonist of this novel is a boy called "Kimi" (You) and printed in the text with a specific icon shown in ◘ Fig. 11.1. One night, he finds a game disc in his room with no label or instructions, inserts it into the machine, and switches it on.

The scene is described as follows:

> Kimi (You) turn it on and insert the disc. A human-like figure appears on the display. PLAY IT ON!
>
> 
>
>  woke up, but felt like  was still half asleep, because  had no memory of the previous day. (Takahashi 1986, p. 165)

In this novel, the protagonist relives his life over and over again, just like in a game. During the game, the protagonist asks himself the following question:

> Is there one , or many? If there are many, is there no relationship between the first  and the second  ? If there is only one , then what is the relationship between the first  and the second  ? (Takahashi 1986, p. 169)

Takahashi's novel puts the experiences of game players into the format of a novel, anticipating the trend that Hiroki Azuma would call "game-like realism" (Azuma 2007) 20 years later. As a novelist, Takahashi deconstructed traditional narrative forms to explore new possibilities for fiction. The forms of computer

◘ **Fig. 11.1** An icon of the protagonist in Genichiro Takahashi's novel

1 "Reports" were published in *Bungei* in May and August 1986 as the fourth and fifth installments of his serialized novel, *Japanese Baseball: Elegant and Sentimental* [*Yuga de kansho-teki na Nippon-yakyuu*].

games were of great help to Takahashi in this endeavor. And it was not long before that avant-garde novelists had adopted forms suggested by computers. And even before that, avant-garde novelists had adopted computer-inspired forms.

For example, Argentine novelist Julio Cortázar's *Rayuela* [English: *Hopscotch*] (1963) can be read in two different ways (Cortázar 1963). The book is made up of chapters numbered 1–155, with the end of each chapter indicating which chapter it leads to next. The "first book" is read in the normal way from chapter 1 to 56. The "second book," on the other hand, begins with chapter 73, then jumps to the chapters numbered at the end of each chapter, eventually looping between chapters 131 and 58 forever.

Similarly, French author Philippe Sollers's work *Nombres* [English: *Numbers*] (1968) is composed of 100 chapters, each numbered from 1 to 4 to indicate its sequence (Sollers 1968). The sequences from 1 through 3 are written in the past tense, while the sequence 4 is written in the present tense. This means that different tenses are mixed together. So the reader is required to work through the sequences as if assembling a "device."

Takahashi's works can be placed in the lineage of avant-garde novels from the 1960s onwards. What he rejected was the "linear story with a fixed beginning and end." Takahashi attempted to deconstruct the linear story by making a game character the protagonist, who can be revived no matter how many times he dies. Takahashi claims that we can now easily experience "metafictions" comparable to the works of Jorge Luis Borges and Michel Butor in video games. In his literary criticism collection, *Is It Okay to Understand Literature This Well?* (1989), he writes:

> » The Famicom [Family Computer, the original Japanese of version of the Nintendo Entertainment System (NES)] can be used to easily create labyrinth structures that would envy even Borges. It's no wonder that Michel Butor lamented, "Writers have to get used to computers, too." It's like a work of art with the same structure as the one that metafiction writers put their wisdom into creating can now be bought right away at a toy store. (Takahashi 1992, p. 20)

Takahashi's "game novels" spawned many followers in contemporary Japanese literary circles. Like Takahashi's "Reports," Chiaki Kawamata's *You Died* [Japanese: *Anata wa shinimashita*] (1987), and Masato Takeno's *Yamada-san's Diary* [Japanese: *Yamada-san nikki*] (1988) are novels that depict the perspectives and experiences of game players, and they demonstrate the great impact that games had on literature in the 1980s.

For Takahashi, computer games were a device for deconstructing "stories." This is also evident in his work as a critic. In his literary critiques, Takahashi often referred to contemporary games such as *Dragon Quest*. His basic stance was that "games do not need stories."

> » The world is so filled with stories that it's almost tiring. It's no wonder they want to say, "There's no way games even have stories." (Takahashi 1992, p. 18)

His rejection of stories is consistent in his game criticism. In his review of *Dragon Quest III* (Enix 1988), he criticizes the game for abandoning the "excess" of its predecessor, *Dragon Quest II* (Enix 1987), and instead introducing an "easy-to-understand story." He points out that *Dragon Quest III* adds stories of mothers and children, fathers and children, and men and women to a simple role-playing game of defeating monsters.

> In any case, there is certainly an unconventional, otherworldly, unrestrained element to *Dragon Quest II*, and even when I was thoroughly exhausted and finally cried out, "Damn it! I can't take this anymore," I would clutch the controller, half-consciously pressing the A and B buttons like a phoenix, and before I knew it, I found myself slipping between life and death, crossing a wall that seemed insurmountable. *Dragon Quest III* has abandoned this excess of *Dragon Quest II* in order to achieve perfection. So we who journey through *Dragon Quest III* no longer suffer from meaninglessness. The method the creators used to banish excess from *Dragon Quest II* was to fill the gaps with a "story." (...) *Dragon Quest III* adds stories of "mothers and children," "fathers and children," and "men and women" to a simple role-playing game of defeating monsters. What an easy-to-understand, smooth-flowing story it is. The incomprehensible and the fearless are banished, and I hate to say it, but without any trouble, if we just let ourselves go, *Dragon Quest III* automatically kidnaps us and carries us to the climax. But was it really the "story" that we were looking for in the *Dragon Quest* series? (Takahashi 1992, pp. 305–306)

What Takahashi wanted from a game was not a "story," but an experience that was unique to games: excess, the incomprehensible, fear, and looseness. He continues:

> So we must say that what we need is not a story full of good intentions (although it would be no different if it was bad intentions), but a game with a bottomless void from which a cold wind blows. (Takahashi 1992, p. 307)

Takahashi's sharp contrast between story and game anticipates the discourse of 1990s *ludologists* who sought to find the values of game in areas other than narrative.[2] As is well known, since *Dragon Quest III* and *Final Fantasy II* (Square 1988), Japanese RPGs have gradually become more "story-oriented," a trend that would later become associated with the term *JRPG*. It is interesting to note that criticism of this tendency was raised as early as the 1980s by an avant-garde novelist.

11.4 *Game Freak* as a Postmodern, Postcapitalist Subject: Shin'ichi Nakazawa

Shin'ichi Nakazawa, a scholar of religion and cultural anthropology, was one of Japan's leading postmodern intellectuals in the 1980s. He is also known as the founder of game criticism in Japan. His 1984 article "The *Game Freaks* Who Play with Bugs: In Praise of the Video Game *Xevious*," published in the magazine

2 For more on how *ludologists* such as Gonzalo Frasca, Markku Eskelinen and Jesper Juul vigorously condemned the "story" or "narrative" as the enemy of *ludology*, see Aarseth (2014).

Gendai Shisou, is known as a monumental essay that describes the encounter between an academic intellectual with a background in postmodern thought and video game culture.

What is noteworthy for the present discussion is that story or narrative is also a keyword in Nakazawa's argument. He traces the history of arcade equipment's from pinball machines such as *Shangri-la* (Williams 1967) to video games, and emphasizes the discontinuity between pinball and video games. Relying on the arguments of anthropologist Michael Oppitz, Nakazawa sees in pinball machines a reflection of "capitalism based on the principle of competition" and "the dream of capitalism during the period of high economic growth."

» It is immediately clear that the enjoyment of pinball lies in the enjoyment of a kind of competition through battling the machine. The player controls the balls, which the machine shoots out in seemingly random directions, by using the left and right flippers. The machine is designed so that the player's control skill is immediately displayed in decimal notation on the scoreboard in front of the machine. Anthropologist Oppitz believes that this type of enjoyment of pinball machines cleverly reflects the dreams of capitalism during the period of high economic growth. (Nakazawa 1984, pp. 191–192)

» The pinball machine *Shangri-la* epitomises the popular spirit of the era when electro-mechanical gaming machines were at their peak, a time when capitalism based on the principle of competition had not yet shown any significant signs of decline. (Nakazawa 1984, p. 193)

Pinball machines and electromechanical games are entertainment devices that embody the principles and desires of capitalism. In contrast, the video games that appeared in the 1970s show "the major changes that were taking place within capitalism." Nakazawa traces the history of video games from Atari's *Pong* (1972) through *Breakout* (1976) to Taito's *Space Invaders* (1978), focusing on what *Space Invaders* added.

» *Space Invaders* succeeds in transforming the "paddle and ball" format into something completely new by injecting new kinetics and mythical imagination. (...) The game is set against the background of a truly classic (almost old-fashioned) science fiction mythological structure that manipulates the dualistic opposition between the Earth and hostile invaders from outside it. (Nakazawa 1984, p. 196)

» Compared to "capitalist games" like pinball, where the skill to control probabilistic factors such as contingency and chance is immediately converted into numerical values and displayed on a scoreboard, *Space Invaders* is a game that has a background of a "pre-capitalist cosmology," in which the destruction caused by the invaders is immediately converted into numerical values and displayed on a screen. (...) In that the introduction of new kinetics occurred in tandem with the injection of old mythical imagination; *Space Invaders* has something in common with the character of the "techno culture" that followed. (Nakazawa 1984, pp. 196–197)

According to Nakazawa, *Space Invaders* overcomes capitalism by combining a "pre-capitalist" mythical imagination with the "new kinetics" on the display. In other words, he sees in video games a revival of "pre-modern mythology" that replaces "modern stories." This trend was furthered by *Xevious* (Namco 1983), which introduced stories linked to mythological imagination into video games.

> *Xevious* has succeeded in taking the stimulation of kinetics and imagination that *Space Invaders* introduced to video games to an even higher level. (...) The biggest difference between *Space Invaders* and *Xevious* is the presence or absence of a narrative development. *Space Invaders*, even if you get high scores, can be monotonous and unbearable when played for long periods of time. (...) However, players of *Xevious* can continue to "dialogue" with the machine for hours. This is because the "dialogue" continues to develop and expand. Players are driven by the intuition that there is some great narrative hidden behind the scrolling development of *Xevious*. (Nakazawa 1984, p. 198)

"The evocation of narrative in *Xevious* is done in two main ways" (Nakazawa 1984, p. 198), Nakazawa says. The two are quotations and background stories. *Xevious* is full of quotations from science fiction movies and anime, which connect the game to "another larger story" and create "profound signification."

> [Being reminiscent of the monoliths in *2001: A Space Odyssey* and the Nazca Lines] the scrolling development of *Xevious* is full of "quotations" from movies, anime, science fiction, and other things that are common to both the game's creator (the person in charge of planning *Xevious* is a young man in his early twenties named Endo) and the players. Therefore, as soon as a "quoted character" appears, that scene is connected to another larger story, and acquires a profound signification. (Nakazawa 1984, p. 199)

The second way *Xevious* evokes narrative is through its background story. It is well known among fans that Masanobu Endo, the developer of *Xevious*, prepared a full-length science fiction novel as the background for the game. This allows players to sense "the grand narrative behind the video game *Xevious*" (Nakazawa 1984, p. 199) and instills in them a desire to learn more about the world.

> The narrative that players sense behind *Xevious* is in fact nothing other than this inseparable, indestructible energy body that permeates and dominates the entire game. In other words, what players sense in this game is not the narrative of a novel realized in a concrete form, but the existence of a field of flow of energy that encourages the generation of a story. By being able to come into contact with the field of energy that encourages the generation of a story, *Xevious* leaves a mysterious impression on those who experience it, as if their *mythopoetics* had been stimulated. (Nakazawa 1984, p. 200)

The "energy to encourage the generation of a story" that Nakazawa sensed in *Xevious* also has an affinity with what Henry Jenkins would later call *environmental storytelling*. Jenkins has called the design technique used in theme parks such as Disneyland, where "the story element is infused into the physical space a guest walks or rides through" (Jenkins 2004, p. 123) and "players can define their own goals and write their own stories" (Jenkins 2004, p. 128), *environmental storytelling*, and the stories experienced by players of *Xevious* can be said to be similar to this.

Unlike novels, the story of *Xevious* is one that the player actively reads as he participates in the game's world. Furthermore, *Xevious* was epoch-making in that it taught players a new way of playing video games, by discovering *kakure characters* (easter eggs) and bugs. For *Game Freaks*, "the enemy" is no longer the Xevious army, but "the computer programs that run video games" themselves.

> Through the masterpiece that is *Xevious*, a new generation of *Game Freaks* are discovering new ways of enjoying video games that had never been seen before. For children who have now become able to achieve high scores, the "enemy" is no longer the Xevious army. The next battle for the new *Game Freaks* is unfolding against the very computer programs that run the video games. In other words, *Game Freaks*' interest has shifted to discovering *kakure characters* (easter eggs), bugs in programs, and strange or unusual phenomena that sometimes occur during the process of transferring data between CPUs. (Nakazawa 1984, p. 201)

Game Freaks, which *Xevious* brought to the forefront, became the prototype of the gamer community in Japan. As is well known, the booklet *Xevious: The Solution to 10 Million Points*, written by Urusei Anzu (the pen name of Yasuhiro Ohori) as a strategy guide for the game, gave birth to the *doujinshi* culture among Japanese gamers. According to Nakazawa, these *Game Freaks* are "post-capitalist" subjects. He says that *Game Freaks* communicate with computers and even with "the consciousness of the universe itself."

> *Game Freaks* are now moving beyond the capitalistic pleasure of simply getting a high score and into a new stage of "dialogue" with computers, or even with the consciousness of the universe itself (and through combat). (Nakazawa 1984, p. 203)

Furthermore, Nakazawa's perspective on *Game Freaks* is noteworthy in that it anticipated the theory of *narrative consumption* that would later be proposed by Eiji Otsuka (1989). The word *otaku* was first used by Akio Nakamori in 1983, the same year that *Xevious* was released.

11.5 Conclusion

Over the course of three chapters, we have examined discourses on digital games in Japan in the 1980s. All three, Hitoshi Yasuda, Genichiro Takahashi, and Shin'ichi Nakazawa, appreciated digital games in relation to literature and narrative. Takahashi was ahead of his time in the perspective of *ludology*, while Nakazawa was ahead of his time in the perspective of *environmental storytelling*. Furthermore, the fact that Yasuda's argument was still centered on tabletop RPGs in the mid-1980s, which could be said to be the golden age of digital games in Japan, gives us an opportunity to correct the *digital fallacy* in the study of game history, that is, the overvaluation of digital games.

Understanding the history of games in Japan in the 1980s in its cultural context will force us to update the framework and common sense of game studies.

References

Aarseth, Espen. 2014. Ludology. In *The Routledge Companion to Video Game Studies*, ed. Mark J. P. Wolf and Bernard Perron, 185–189. New York & London: Routledge.

Azuma, Hiroki. 2007. *The Birth of Game-Like Realism: Animalizing Postmodern 2 [Gēmu-teki riarizumu no tanjō: Dōbutsukasuru posutomodan 2]*. Tokyo: Kōdansha.

Cortázar, Julio. 1963. *Rayuela*. Buenos Aires: Editorial Sudamericana.

Jenkins, Henry. 2004. Game Design as Narrative Architecture. In *First Person: New Media as Story, Performance, and Game*, ed. Noah Wardrip-Fruin and Pat Harrigan, 118–130. Cambridge, MA: The MIT Press.

Nakazawa, Shin'ichi 1984. The *Game Freaks* Who Play with Bugs: In Praise of the Video Game *Xevious* [Gēmu-furīku ha bagu to tawamureru: Telebi gēmu Zebiusu san]. In *Gendai Shisou*, vol. 12(6), 190–203. Tokyo: Seidousha.

Otsuka, Eiji. 1989. *A Theory of Narrative Consumption [Monogatari shōhiron]*. Tokyo: Shinyōsha.

Sollers, Philippe. 1968. *Nombres*. Paris: Éditions du Seuil.

Stenros, Jaakko, and Annika Waern. 2011. Games as Activity: Correcting the Digital Fallacy. In *Videogame Studies: Concepts, Cultures, and Communication*, ed. Monica Evans, 11–22. Oxford: Inter-Disciplinary Press.

Takahashi, Genichiro. 1986. Japanese Baseball: Elegant and Sentimental [4]: Reports on the Adventures, Love, Daily Life, etc. of Nameless ☎ s. [Yuga de kansho-teki na Nippon-yakyuu [4]: Mumei no ☎ tachi ga tadoru bōken, ai, nichijō nado ni kansuru hōkokusho]. In *Bungei*, vol. 25(2), 164–174. Tokyo: Kawade Shobō Shinsha.

Takahashi, Genichiro. 1992. *Is It Okay to Understand Literature This Well? [Bungaku ga konna ni wakatte ii kashira]*. Tokyo: Fukutake Shoten. (First edition, 1989).

Yasuda, Hitoshi. 1986. *The World of SF Fantasy Games [Esuefu fuantajī gēmu no sekai]*. Osaka: Seishinsha.

Yasuda, Hitoshi. 1987. *Myth-Making Machines [Shinwa seisaku kikairon]*. Tokyo: BNN, Inc.

Imagining Future Pathways for Japanese Game Studies

Martin Roth

Contents

F. Ikuine et al. (eds.), *Japanese Game Studies*, https://doi.org/10.1007/978-981-95-9857-1_12

12.1 Introduction

At a point in time when an increasing number of scholars from all over the world are taking an interest in the variously defined field referred to as "Japanese video-games," it seems crucial to ask how the attribute "Japanese" figures in and bears on the diverse range of research projects it is applied to. This chapter takes stock of some of the tendencies in the research that speak to or are motivated in Japanese Game Studies, and imagines future pathways for the field.

If, as Wolf and others assert, the local is eroding as a context for game production and game cultures in our contemporary, globalized times (Wolf 2015), one might think that losing the national or regional attribution altogether could be a solution. However, there is an important difference between a global condition under which the world is widely connected—a condition most of us most certainly live in—and the ways in which globalizations in plural play out in particular places (Middell 2018). The local is far from irrelevant today (Swalwell 2021a, b; Svelch 2018; Liboriussen and Martin 2016). Instead of denying the attribute "Japanese" any value from the start, I thus want to ask how it may be made productive in Game Studies to replace the dichotomy of global vs. local with a more detailed inquiry of diverse, multilayered game cultural spatialities.

To be clear, this chapter is not advocating for a notion of Japanese Game Studies as a national project that is meant to be undertaken by scholars located in Japan or operating in Japanese. On the contrary, it aims to imagine an inclusive and contextually aware version of Japanese Game Studies that is not simply characterized by a critical and self-reflected attitude about each participating researcher's individual position, but actively strives toward the discomfort of dislocation.

In order to ground such imagination, this chapter exposes some of the challenges Japanese Game Studies faces, asking how invoking Japan and Japaneseness succeeds or fails to capture game cultural objects, phenomena, and processes. Such inquiry necessarily requires reflecting on the (power) relation between game research discussed and published in the Japanese language space and Japan-focused research in other language spaces, predominantly English. I use language space here deliberately to include not only the language itself, but also the affordances and limitations that structure and direct knowledge circulation in any language. As such, my reference to the English language is a crude simplification, considering the diverse local contexts within which English is used in academic knowledge transfer.

This chapter cannot cover all situations in which "Japaneseness" is entangled in knowledge production with elevating or detrimental effects, or the historical, cultural, and structural factors leading to such entanglement, comprehensively. Yet, I do hope that the following observations can open a pathway toward a version of Japanese Game Studies that withstands the test of criticality, reflexivity, and transgression. Criticality is used here to designate a transparently normatively grounded engagement aimed at a structural understanding and betterment of the social and cultural situation we find ourselves in; reflexivity implies a conscious effort toward situating the researchers perspective and the research explicitly within a broader context; transgression designates the intent to break out of the confinements indicated by reflexivity, for example by connecting to discourse outside of the comfort zone, perhaps accepting the risk of what Brian Massumi (2014, 27) refers to as "double deterritorialization" in his complicated text on animal politics: "In the movement of play, existential territories enactively intersect and mutually modulate, across their difference, swept in the direction of novel expressions of their dynamic forms, each new play-move having the value of a fight-move in improvisational potential. Play becomes combatesquely, as combat becomes ludically. It is a question of a reciprocal deterritorialization, each arena stretched differentially into the other." Without pretending to capture the core of Massumi's argument here—not least because he emphasizes the need for abandoning the kind of normativity I have listed among the features of a potential future version of Japanese Game Studies above—I draw on his notion of play as an operation on the territory it presupposes (Massumi 2014, 21) to imagine a play-based deterritorialization of Game Studies.

The following sections focus on games as objects, game contents, and games as a discursive research field, asking how Japaneseness is involved in, interferes with and can be made productive for investigating game cultures in each.

12.2 Japaneseness and Game Objects

Games are produced, distributed, and consumed as material or digital objects, even if they nowadays often remain incomplete and are subjected to frequent updates. If Japanese Game Studies are concerned with Japaneseness on this level, they tend to consider games as produced in or originating from Japan, as part of the Japanese market. Japaneseness may appear most straightforward here, considering how the material territory at play coincides not only with the state borders, but also with those of the market defined by the Japan release region. Japaneseness in this sense is relevant as it determines the legal—and, maybe less distinctly, the historical, social, and cultural—underpinnings of local production, distribution, and reception.

On the level of production, labor laws, government support and subsidies, regional creative clusters, work ethical norms and expectations, and local education systems are examples of such factors. Game production has always unfolded across multiple sites located in more than one country (Consalvo 2016; Picard 2013). However, that does not mean that local production does not exist anymore, nor does it untie such production from the aforementioned legal and cultural conditions. Consequentially, a critical perspective on Japaneseness should motivate us to take a closer look at these sites and territories and understand their interplay in detail, rather than generalizing and homogenizing descriptions of production by relying on Japan, Asia, or "the global." As I show elsewhere, Japaneseness is frequently more complicated than such labels can convey, with as much diversity within domestic spaces as we might expect from transregional collaborations (Roth 2025). Japanese Game Studies is in a unique position to shed light on these complexities if Japaneseness is used as a question mark rather than a given—or abandoned in favor of detailed inquiries into production processes (Hartzheim 2023).

A similar argument can be made for the domain of distribution, in which child protection acts and the various regulations concerning game shops, game rental, and piracy constitute a domestic, Japanese territory of circulation, in concert with historical and cultural developments that bear on the place games have in department stores, secondhand shops, and convenience stores. The most visible and widely discussed agents of national regulation in the domain of distribution are the Computer Entertainment Rating Organization (CERO) and, trailing far behind due to its relative niche domain, the Ethics Organization of Computer Software (EOCS), also known as Sofurin. Very generally put, CERO is mandatory for almost all games released on dedicated gaming platforms because the platform makers only license games that the organization has approved of for specified age ranges. EOCS makes sure the games their members produce meet ethical standards and, most importantly, national legal requirements for media representation, in particular with regard to sexually explicit content.

This story is complicated in several ways. While CERO can certainly be considered as a nationally operating organization with substantial coverage, it is not based in Japanese law, but in the absence of clear regulations. As Kelly (2010, 2020) shows, CERO ratings and with them the preemptive measures taken by game publishers and developers are intended to reflect nationally shared cultural conventions and norms. In addition, circulation is also in part regulated by the prefectures, which have diverging approaches to child protection when it comes to games (Kawasaki 2022). Add to this the fact that resellers tend to reflect cultural norms in their own regulations, sometimes refusing to sell certain types of games on their own accord. What emerges is thus a mosaic that is far more complex than any general account of game distribution in "the Japanese market" might offer.

The other side of the coin is that of the distribution of Japanese games—and in some cases of "Japaneseness" outside of Japan. Regardless of the aforementioned issues that arise when we try to capture production nationally, Japanese games have certainly been exported and localized as such to other regions around the world, be it via official, sanctioned channels, or in semi-sanctioned or non-sanctioned ways. The fact that many of these games emerged centrally from a transnationally entangled Japanese game industry or are marketed as such elsewhere should be acknowledged. In fact, localizers and publishers outspokenly rely on or actively promote stereotypical Japaneseness (Schules 2015; Carlson and Corliss 2011). Localization thus needs to be questioned in detail with regard to its effects on the material object and its position within the local game cultural space. Such work involves technical differences (Newman 2019), language differences and market dynamics (Consalvo 2013; Liang 2018), and game cultural contexts (Hutchinson 2019; Navarro-Remesal and Zapata 2022). As Pelletier-Gagnon and Picard (2015) show, such differences are both subject to globalizing currents and to attempts to counteract such currents, in particular in fields that are grounded in locally particular game cultures and their sensitivities. Future pathways for Japanese Game Studies thus may lead away further from exoticizing Japaneseness or subsuming recent developments under the label of globalization, toward more detailed questions, particularities of circulation, effects of diverging regulations on game production and distribution, or social norms and cultural dynamics that influence game circulation and, by extension, production, and consumption even in early stages. Considering that games are, today, created within the global condition and with more or less transregional awareness as a presupposition rather than a result of domestic success, it may be time to stop thinking in unidirectional models in which something travels from Japan to elsewhere, and instead assume a multi-territorial playing field from the start.

The existing research already exposes two challenges these pathways present. The first is the instability of game objects—a term I adopt from Newman (2012; see also Roth 2025). Considering the diversity and abundance of dedicated gaming platforms in Japan, the strong tendency toward media mix, characters, transmedia storytelling and transmedia franchising strategies (Tosca and Klastrup 2019; Blom 2023), and the ways in which game objects lend themselves to porting, re-releasing and re-packaging, remakes, and modding, Japanese Game Studies has an opportunity to cover important ground with regard to mapping videogame objects and their diverse instantiation as a process of deterritorialization. Such task implies a transregional perspective as much as it needs to cope with the instability of the territory that is the individual game object.

The second is the diversity of game platforms and their relatively short life cycles and thus availability for research. We have yet to understand better how videogame platforms outside of the scope of Nintendo, Sega, Sony, and Microsoft have influenced videogame cultures in Japan, and how respective processes are embedded in regional media and gaming cultures in Asia. While some research on less prominent platforms and developments exists (Picard 2013; Therrien 2019), it may be time—or in fact, considering degrading hard- and software, too late—to take a closer look at the wide range of game related computers and dedicated platforms that, over decades, have shaped the material basis upon which local gaming cultures in Japan are built.

Given the diversity of game objects and gaming platforms in Japan, Japanese Game Studies are in a unique position to see past the usual suspects, and beyond the geographical boundaries of Japan, to ask how, where, by whom and for whom the instability of game objects is created and how it underpins game culture. A closer look at production and distribution in this broad sense of the word may help us understand not only gaming culture in Japan, but some of the tendencies shared with other local videogame and media cultures. Many of these pathways would benefit from less reluctance and less secrecy on the part of game industrial actors. The type of deterritorialization I imagine here hinges, to some extent, on their answer to the following question: When will you start playing?

12.3 Japaneseness in Game Contents

When it comes to game contents, taking Japaneseness seriously means to engage with the ways in which historical, social and cultural processes and experiences in Japan are reflected in content production, distribution, and reception, and with the ways in which they are produced, distributed, and received as representations of Japaneseness. A critical perspective on Japaneseness needs to ask how these two dimensions are conflated or otherwise converge, and reflect on the ways in which research is involved in such convergence.

On the level of production, the former approach that centers on experiences in and of Japan tries to understand game contents as expressions of historically changing everyday life, structures, or traditions. Significance is often derived from the fact that there is a local or regional distinctiveness to these expressions, and that they can be used to understand the local. For example, Hutchinson (2019) considers specific game titles as reflections of and critical engagements with relevant discourses, beliefs, and social imagination in Japan. Herfs (2020, 2021) exposes the complexity with which Japanese identity is constructed in selected games such as *Zelda: Breath of the Wild* (Nintendo 2017) or *Persona V* (Atlus 2016), drawing attention to the importance of designer intention in this process. Whaley (2023) focuses on Japanese representations of disaster and trauma in video games. Fujita (2025) grounds Hideo Kojima's game creation in his experience of postwar Japan and his perception of Japanese subcultures.

The abovementioned authors connect in-depth analyses of game contents with methodological questions of regionality and positionality in productive ways. Nevertheless, invoking the label of Japan or Japaneseness always risks superimposing specific cases or particular media expressions onto representations of Japan, thus contributing generalizing notions of Japaneseness. This risk emerges from two co-occurring strategies: Attaching nation-wide significance to particular characteristics or representations—and thus generalizing them—, and reducing the complexity of a field by positioning a subset of elements that can then be examined in terms of commonalities as representational. Equating specific representations with expressions of or commentary on Japan, equating particular subdomains of video-game culture, such as genre, with the wider domain, or artificially separating particular expressions or subdomains from a wider context, turns Japan into the central frame of reference for understanding and evaluation.

Both strategies—extrapolating from individual cases and isolating a part of the research field—are common and necessary research practice. However, if used without sufficient attention to the limitations of such practice in terms of scope and diversity, either strategy is prone to constructing what might be called a synecdochic representation of Japanese gaming cultures and of Japan: A part of the domain is used to describe the entire domain or even stands in for the much wider national culture, or vice-versa. The open question a critical version of Japanese Game Studies needs to address more forcefully is whether and in what ways synecdochic operations lead to valid and adequate descriptions of game cultural territories, which connections to the outside of each territory are severed in the operation, and how such operation relates to or constitute the nation and national identity. In the same way in which the variety of gaming contexts and practices in Japan is not addressed by references to "Japanese games," the common signifier of "Japan" and its positioning as an actor that speaks through, is constructed by or represented in games remains superficial at best. In this respect, Japanese Game Studies are challenged to surpass the limitations of homogenizing and generalizing. In the face of territorializing currents in both Area Studies (to cling onto "Japan") and Game Studies (to cling onto "games"), individual scholars and institutions are asked: Can you/will you play?

In the domain of distribution, content analysis is most centrally concerned with the distribution of content across or through diverse media (Tosca and Klastrup 2019; Picard and Pelletier-Gagnon 2015; Steinberg 2015; Nakamura and Tosca 2021), and with the localization of Japanese content outside of Japan—both in the broader sense of transregional distribution and marketing of a gaming culture originating in Japan, and in the sense of translation and cultural translation of gaming contents. Such research has developed a series of stimulating perspectives on localization practices and their effects on regional gaming cultures and players (O'Hagan and Mangiron 2013; Schules 2015; Mandiberg 2015, 2021; Fiadotau 2021).

A future version of Japanese Game Studies can expand on such achievements in several ways. First, it may consider in more detail the significance and character of the Japaneseness subject to localization. Doing so requires understanding the function particular representations of Japan or Japaneseness have within the game work, both in regard to the game world and its narrative and goal, and in regard to Japan and Japanese identity. We might ask if Japaneseness is themable and thus superficial, or has an "odor," meaning with Iwabuchi (2002, 27) that "cultural features of a country of origin and images or ideas of its national, in most cases stereotyped, way of life are associated *positively* with a particular product in the consumption process." Such analysis does not need to be limited to localization outside of Japan. It may, instead, also question the smelliness of video game representations aimed at the domestic market. Such inquiry might take a closer look at representations of national and cultural identity, and respective appeals to such identity, as can be found in military shooters, historical games and other contents that play with nationalist rhetorics, generic traditions or common tropes (Picard and Roth 2022). It may also consider how games promote political agency or, convey a sense of complacency in the face of global crises by offering fantastic fictional worlds and embracing a game cultural language that is largely detached from its former subcultural and thus inherently political posture. One question that remains largely underexamined is how representational experiences in all the abovementioned meanings are constructed not only via narratives and references, but in terms of gameplay and player experiences. Japanese Game Studies has yet to develop a better understanding of the procedural arguments (Bogost 2007) made about Japan or Japaneseness in games. Schules' (2015) work on JRPG and Kawaii makes an important step in this direction, as it succeeds in relating questions about the Japaneseness of games with questions about the Japaneseness in games, while also attending to the specificity of gamic expression and representation, and remaining conscious of the particularity of the representations or sites of representation analyzed.

A critical inquiry in the domain of content is thus concerned with the representation of Japanese culture and Japaneseness in videogame content and its experience both toward domestic and international playership, including the ways in which such representation is constructed, elevated, orientalized or mitigated by marketing and localization considerations, as well as distribution geographies. It requires asking what Japaneseness refers to in any specific context beyond stereotypical cultural references. Iwabuchi's work on the "odor" of Japanese popular culture addresses this challenge only vaguely, but in doing so, it invites us to replace superficial references to representational "Japaneseness" with a more far-reaching discourse on the ideological underpinnings encoded in games in various regional and historical contexts.

Both "Japanese" productions of contents and the circulation and marketing of "Japanese" content directly bear on the domain of consumption, in which content is interpreted and appropriated in myriad ways within diverse contexts during what Apperley (2010) calls situated play. Internationally, the reception of Japanese games has been studied to some extent, with results suggesting a specific appeal of what is perceived as Japanese design and Japanese experiences to players (Consalvo 2016; Goto-Jones 2015; Hutchinson and Pelletier-Gagnon 2022). Recent research is consequently extending its understanding of playing to include both fan communities that collect data about games and create walkthroughs, modding practices, and video streaming and sharing culture (Roth 2022). Questions of Japan and Japaneseness in these fields are yet to be asked more comprehensively and beyond asserting the geographical or cultural origin of game titles in particular case studies.

They also need to be considered in the domestic domain. Research on the ways in which Japanese culture and Japaneseness are reflected on and engaged with by players in Japan is scarce to date. Future Japanese Game Studies might start here, by reconsidering the significance of cultural and gamic literacy to decode national cultural references among players, the importance of irony and cynicism, which have been identified as tendencies in Japanese otaku online communication already in the early 2000s (Kitada 2005) and are under scrutiny once again in recent years, in particular in the context of the political situation in the United States (Bogost 2016). The diversity of voices negotiating games on a wide range of digital platforms today should further motivate us to investigate the ways in which Japaneseness is not only constructed and experienced in game worlds, but also in interconnected digital spaces outside of or beyond the game.

To summarize, scrutinizing game contents from the perspective of critical Japanese Game Studies means to ask both how Japan features in production, distribution, and reception of games, but also how Japaneseness is the result of various practices of encoding and decoding that unfold across these three domains, both in Japan and beyond, and are negotiated not only at play, but also on a wide range of digital platforms. Given how game designers and localizers mention their intent to cater to the expectations of Japaneseness in their target audiences, or how they intent to expose foreign audiences to the Otherness of Japan (Herfs 2021; Carlson and Corliss 2011), such inquiry also has to leave the theoretical territory and ask what representations of Japaneseness are representative of for the actors/players involved in particular situations and against the background of political stirrings.

12.4 Videogames as Discursive Research Field

Given my imaginary of Japanese Game Studies thus far, foregrounding a Japanese version of Game Studies or the need to study Japanese Games specifically—as this edited volume does—should feel counter-intuitive and perhaps problematic. That said, it is important to recognize that this emphasis reflects a perceived need to overcome a divergence in the research community dedicated to studying games, first and foremost between researchers mostly operating in the Japanese language space and those operating in other language spaces, most centrally the English, and, secondly, between researchers focusing on "Japanese games," and those focusing on other regions. This divide is further amplified by the central position English-language Game Studies have occupied within the field of Game Studies. Granted that the regions most directly attached to it are far from homogeneous themselves (Swalwell 2021a), this position has resulted in implicit or explicit claims to "general," "global," or "abstract" perspectives on video games perpetuated in research drawing on such perspectives. What is at stake here is the ideal of abstract, contextless theory vs. the recognition that any knowledge production is necessarily grounded in locally or regionally limited perceptions, processes and structures. Accompanying and amplifying such dichotomy is the binary of West vs. the rest, in particular the tendency toward orientalism, exemplified by practices that apply a Western theoretical model to oriental phenomena.

Emphasizing the "local" does not necessarily solve this problem. As Maitra and Chow (2016, 18) suggest, "an unqualified emphasis on the local or the regional often gives rise to ethnoculturalist approaches that, while resisting technoculturalism, tend to overlook differences *within* these apparently homogeneous spaces." In the context of videogames, this tendency is apparent in the aforementioned case in which a specific subset of games is equated with "Japanese games." Moreover, Maitra and Chow (2016, 20) remind us that phrases like "in Asia"—and, I would add, "in Japan"—tend to inherit "forms of techno-orientalism and self-orientalization spawned by the East/West binary." These two tendencies, by which "Japan" and "Japaneseness" are rendered a homogeneous "other" (to be known and thus conquered) or "self" (to distinguish and safeguard from the outside), are amplified by the degree to which the label is used in an unspecific and uncritical way. Such use of "Japanese Games" renders researches not only compatible but also complicit with the political strategies and nationalist discourses. In the case of Japan and Japaneseness, these discourses and political strategies are most notably related to cyber-orientalism, Japan bashing, "nihonjin-ron," and the nation branding strategy known as "Cool Japan" (Iwabuchi 2016; Oyama 2016).

A number of scholars successfully connect or challenge both spaces. Nevertheless, circumstantial evidence suggests that this divide results in at least two, if not more, discursively more or less disconnected spheres that each follow their own logic and political economy. For example, the list of academic articles published in English in journals such as Replaying Japan that flag their intent to discuss "Japanese videogames" in their title, only to then focus on a small subfield of this domain, is rather long. Out of 48 English-language articles published in

Replaying Japan between 2019 and 2024, 24 include some general and often also generalizing reference to Japan or Japaneseness, such as “Japanese digital games”, “Japan-related videogames,” or “games in Japan.” In contrast, out of the 14 Japanese-language articles, only one makes a reference to a specific geographical or geopolitical area, suggesting that it deals predominantly with South Korea.

One possible explanation for this difference may be that the flagging on the English-language side is founded in the perceived need to highlight the respective article’s relevance to the journal and its readership, while the perception on the part of the authors of Japanese-language articles might be that their scope is self-explanatory. However, even if attention economical reasons and other strategic considerations may play a superficial role in these choices, I would argue that the difference in titles also hints at differences in the approach to the field of games in both language spaces. Crudely put, English-language scholarship on Japanese games or gaming culture in Japan is the result of a deliberate choice to study an area or territory. Such a choice is, today, made in most cases against the background of the self-reflection and criticism toward the Area Studies and its inherent orientalist tendency, voiced by scholars such as Said (2012) or Sakai and Harootunian (1999). While thus often conscious about the implications of this choice, the aforementioned risk of creating a synecdochic representation remains acute. Japanese-language scholarship, where it does not also engage in abstract or generalizing discussions of games and play, on the other hand, tends to either foreground or take the national field for granted, at risk of falling into the trap of methodical nationalism—artificially and inadequately limiting the scope of research to the national space. These risks on both sides are currently largely unchecked, as scholarship that engages critically with or self-reflects on existing research either within the same language space or across the language barriers remains scarce. Overall, these tendencies contribute to the emergence of two quite different ecosystems, connected only tentatively by translations (which then become part of the representation of the “other” space), dedicated conferences and journals, and individual relations and efforts. Importantly, both ecosystems produce decisively different territories, despite their superficial overlap. With Massumi, the question once again is: will we start playing and: what does that mean?

Game Studies are not the first field to experience a divide between what is widely—in a somewhat carelessly generalizing fashion—referred to as “the West” and Japan or other “areas.” On the contrary, the situation of Japanese Game Studies seems to resemble that of media studies, where, according to Steinberg and Zahlten (2017, 3), the invisibility of “Japanese theory” in the English language space is points towards “a larger and by now familiar structural imbalance in knowledge production itself [...] between a West that is figured as the site of Theory, and the Rest as the site of history or raw materials (‘texts’)”?[1] This imbal-

1 In Japan Studies, Sakai and Harootunian (1999) have criticized the Western perspective and its then predominantly colonialist and paternalist attitude towards to East, which was seen as raw material to be understood and evaluated in detail.

ance results in “a perception that visual media cultures are practiced in Japan—film, art, architecture—but understood or thought elsewhere” (Mizuta Lippit 2017, xi).

Arguing against this current, Steinberg and Zahlten (2017, 10–11) suggest that Japanese media theories are important due to their embeddedness in Japanese experiences and everyday practices, which provide a rich basis for local or embedded knowledge about the world. Other scholars have also highlighted the importance of vernacular or regional game cultures in their relation to the global condition, as well as vernacular theorizing (Swalwell 2021a, b). Most explicitly, Liboriussen and Martin (2016) emphasize the need for “regional game studies,” which they characterize as a “growing body of research that investigates games and gaming cultures at a range of geocultural scales, identifies connections across and between these scales, highlights and addresses unequal global power relations within gaming culture and within the academic study of games, and enriches the field with new perspectives drawn from regional cultural contexts.”

These arguments are understandably focused on highlighting the value of local or regional perspectives and theories. For Liboriussen and Martin, regional knowledge is valuable if it feeds back into and thus enriches a vaguely defined, potentially “global,” knowledge. Given the hegemony of the English language in many academic fields, including Game Studies, feeding back also implies a potentially one-directional translation process. As such, Liboriussen and Martin’s approach risks maintaining or amplifying the hierarchy between center and periphery the authors take issue with.[2] Zahlen and Steinberg suggest that regionally embedded knowledge is not necessarily about the region, but about the world as it is perceived specifically in and via this region. It is this embedded perspective which then contributes to “globally situated media theorization,” characterized by a diversity of perspectives on the world which “stand alongside” each other, connected by the intent to theorize (Steinberg and Zahlten 2017, 26). Ignoring the problem of theory for a moment, the centrality of which has itself been identified as a characteristic of “Western” knowledge production, this positioning implies a coincidental existence of multiple perspectives on the world. It argues for their necessity in the face of today’s “geographically situated but constantly intra-acting media infrastructures” (Steinberg and Zahlten 2017, 26).

The question that remains open in this account is how diverse perspectives are expected to interact or resonate with each other, and why they should matter to the situated individual. A basic answer is that new knowledge contributes to a better

2 This risk also transpires from the article. Despite the authors’ awareness of the ways in which the term “regional game studies” serves to validate the center-periphery model, the language and attitude of the proposal nonetheless perpetuate the idea of an empirical periphery and a theoretical center. This is most explicit in the examples chosen in order to illustrate the idea of regional concepts, which the authors highlight as the contribution that regional game studies can make to the core of game studies. By selecting the US American anthropologist Clifford Geertz’s ethnographic work and his considerations of the Balinese cockfight as an inspiration for the broader field or core of game studies, the authors replicate the abovementioned structure of Western theory—Eastern material (Liboriussen and Martin 2016).

understanding of the world and, in our case, video games and gaming culture. However, considering the structural severity of the divide of the field described at the outset of this section, such a general vision may not suffice to generate scholarly discourse that can bridge it. As Yoshimoto (1991, 250–251) argues for the case of cinema, "[t]he studies of non-Western national cinemas based on the axiomatics of self/Other opposition cannot but reproduce the hegemonic ideology of Western neocolonialism. It can produce knowledge on non-Western national cinemas only for those who can put themselves into the position of the subject (i.e., Western theorists)." Sakai and Harootunian (1999) observe already in the 1990s that this structure is one of mutual complicity: "Once again we find complicity between Japanese studies in the United States and Japanese studies in Japan. These two are continuous and complicit precisely because they share the task of erecting an imaginary culturalist divide between the two; they intimately collaborate with one another to create a convenient myth that they are far apart—the West never meets the East—because of 'the cultural difference.'"

Riffing on Steinberg and Zahlten's notion of a globally situated media theorization, I would like to consider the possibility of a transregionally situated media theorization or, more broadly, knowledge production, that is measured not only in terms of its specificity or distinctness, but in terms of its contribution to mutual deterritorialization. Such deterritorialization requires imagining Japanese Game Studies as an intersection of more than one territory, an intent to position any inquiry in each of them and a willingness to play and thereby risk the discomfort of uncertainty and exposition. This might mean giving up agency and instead seeking allies where individual limitations suggest it, and it involves pushing back against territorial claims made both from within and outside of the Japanese language space.

In the concrete context of the divide between Japanese-language and English-language scholarship foregrounded above, this could mean to engage with the problem of connectivity to other regional discourse and relevance for them actively, and in two directions: (a) Research is challenged to consider in what ways perspectives on videogames from within Japan speak to issues discussed in the English-language space—and, of course, beyond—, other than by being about Japan or in Japanese; (b) It needs to consider in what ways English-language scholarship on Japan speaks to domestic perspectives on videogames and how adequately it captures the domestic empirical situation if intended to do so. This double challenge, I would suggest, needs to be taken on by both sides of the divide in both dimensions. In the context of Japanese-language scholarship, it requires an intent to situate knowledge not only domestically, but transregionally and theoretically, as well as an active engagement with Japan in English and other languages—Chinese, Korean or French come to mind immediately. Continued emphasis of the early stages of Game Studies in Japan does not contribute to such endeavor.

In the context of English-language scholarship, it demands an intent to situate knowledge production not only in the English-language sphere, but also in the Japanese and beyond, as well as recognizing, making transparent, and overcoming individual limitations with regard to regional knowledge and language proficiency. In other words, expertise on Japanese Games would strive to withstand scrutiny anywhere, including in Japan.

If scholarship is, as Said and many others have argued, always situated, such a regionally grounded version of Japanese Game Studies further benefits from reflecting on a structural level about its position and structural significance within the wider spaces of regionally embedded knowledge production. Simply put, neither the version of Japanese Game Studies outlined above, nor domestic research on videogames published in Japan can escape its Japaneseness. Studying Japanese Games should be recognized as inevitably political, insofar as it singles out a particular region, domestic or foreign, depending on the researcher's position, attaching significance or distinctiveness to that region—in line with soft power campaigns such as Cool Japan. At the same time, studying "Japanese games" is frequently pitted against the mainstream, as it intervenes with the Western-centric tendency of Game Studies, even though Japanese games are themselves perceived as part of this mainstream by scholars operating in other vernacular spaces (Swalwell 2021a, 14). Beyond the dynamics of orientalism, it may help to advance our awareness and understanding of structural regional differences in the academic landscape in detail, instead of invoking the general and somewhat outdated reference to the novelty or exotism of the field. This means to both ask how domestic and Japanese-language Game Studies are positioned within the Japanese academic landscape, and to ask how Game Studies focusing on Japan elsewhere are related to their respective academic contexts—Game Studies and Area Studies in particular. It might further include conscious attention to differences within the English language space, which itself should be considered a region.[3] The problem of Japaneseness and the ways we play with it may serve as a reference point for such questions.

Finally, a shared discourse benefits from transparency regarding the researcher's position within the multilayered and fragmented space that is Japanese Game Studies. This is particularly important in the context of critical inquiry and the normative basis it requires. Such normative positions may be directly related to perceptions of Japan, or they may originate elsewhere. Critical inquiries, to paraphrase Heath (2018), are only successful to the extent to which they succeed in exposing their normative basis, and developing an argument for their position rather than assuming it implicitly. Instead of relying on and thus constructing either a "Japan-centered" or a "universal" position from within or without, critical scholarship dealing with Japanese games, Japanese representations, or representations of Japaneseness may benefit substantially from such exposition, combined with the abovementioned understanding of the researcher's own limitations. In other words, it may be useful to be explicit about the territories we presuppose when playing Japanese Game Studies.

3 As has been commented regularly, the Digital Games Research Association (Digra) does not feature a US Chapter, whereas many "local chapters" do exist, including the Japanese.

12.5 Potential Next Steps

In this chapter, I have discussed some of the challenges Japanese Game Studies faces when dealing with game objects, game contents, and academic discourse. Inferring or constructing Japaneseness from objects, from contents and in the shape of discursive spaces implicitly or explicitly risks establishing synecdochic representations that conflate parts with a whole or vice versa, and thereby call into existence a whole that didn't exist to begin with. Japaneseness can serve as a signpost for this risk, and a starting point for imagining new pathways. The consequentially regional and deterritorializing version of playing Japanese Game Studies proposed above as a potential future pathway is invested in transregional discursive relatedness and mutual resonance instead of separation and hierarchical positioning.

With Yoshimoto (1991, 252), this extends to the relation between theory and the empirical. In his analysis of scholarship on Japanese film, he suggests that the divide between the West and Japan is complicated by a divide between theoretical work that tends to decontextualize regional research subjects due to the authority of theory and historical work aimed at a contextualized understanding based on the cultural expertise of the scholar in question. Against this background, Yoshimoto (1991, 252) suggests that "we need to reexamine how the differentiation of empirical history from abstract theory creates an illusion that different critical approaches could democratically coexist side by side without any interference. What is at stake in the end is not a specific problem debated in the field of Japanese film studies but the question of how Japanese film studies is constructed as an academic sub-discipline." Adopted to Japanese Game Studies, this means not only to reflect on the historical, structural, or empirical distinctness of Japanese Games, but on the necessity of Japanese Game Studies as a sub-discipline with a distinct methodology. Instead of presuming such distinctness in both cases from the outset, Japanese Game Studies can benefit from a critical self-reflection of its current state and take a more active role in defining its purpose, tasks, perspective and methodology, including a recognition of the vastly different structural conditions that provide the basis for the actors involved in shaping the field.

A first step in this direction may be to ask and make explicit what is gained by invoking the label of "Japanese Games" or "Japanese Game Studies", and what kind of representational status is claimed by it in any particular context. Recent trends in AI-based translations and localizations suggest that this question may become even more important in the future. Another important path forward might lie in strengthening and expanding on collaborations across different regional contexts. Such collaborations have already proven fruitful in many cases in the context of Japanese Game Studies (Rockwell and Amano 2015, 2019; Nakamura and Tosca 2021).

A third step is to foster academic exchange that is invested in mutual dialogue and critique. The importance of exchange and discourse has already been noted by some of the aforementioned scholars. Sakai and Harootunian (1999) suggest that *zadankai* or *taidan*, two forms of intellectual dialogue prominent in Japan, are one possible pathway towards narrowing the various divides in research. Yoshimoto (1991, 243) outlines a similar direction, asking us to construct "a new position of knowledge through a careful negotiation between the self and the Other".

However, all these steps are only possible if we recognize our own regional perspectives and positions. As such, instead of removing the regional and thereby potentially inheriting it implicitly, it should be foregrounded critically and scrutinized for its limitations. Along those lines, this chapter has emphasized the need to reflect on how scholarship approaches or avoids questions of self and other in the case of Japanese Game Studies and Game Studies focused on Japan, and to expose the structural conditions of such scholarship. Instead of aspiring toward a "global," "general," or "abstract" version of Game Studies, the challenge is to methodologically work toward the imagination and thus likely impossible notion of playful deterritorialization (Massumi 2014) or center-less play (Derrida 1978), while remaining conscious and self-reflective of the fact that no network is entirely without hierarchy (Ingold 2008). Overcoming this challenge may threaten the "Japaneseness" of Japanese Game Studies, but I am convinced that it will provide for a more nuanced, discursive and collaborative approach to games and game cultures. Our success in developing such academic field may be measured by the extent to which we are willing and able to risk playing at deterritorialization.

Acknowledgement This work was supported by JSPS KAKENHI Grant Number JP22 K18155.

References

Apperley, Thomas. 2010. *Gaming Rhythms: Play and Counterplay from the Situated to the Global*, Theory on Demand 6. Amsterdam: Institute of Network Cultures.

Atlus. 2016. Persona V. Sony PlayStation 3 & PlayStation 4.

Blom, Joleen. 2023. *Video Game Characters and Transmedia Storytelling*. Amsterdam: Amsterdam University Press.

Bogost, Ian. 2007. *Persuasive Games: The Expressive Power of Videogames*. Cambridge, MA: The MIT Press.

Bogost, Ian. 2016. *Play Anything: The Pleasure of Limits, the Uses of Boredom, and the Secret of Games*. New York, NY: Basic Books.

Carlson, Rebecca, and Jonathan Corliss. 2011. Imagined Commodities: Video Game Localization and Mythologies of Cultural Difference. *Games and Culture* 6 (1): 61–82.

Consalvo, Mia. 2013. Unintended Travel: ROM Hackers and Fan Translations of Japanese Video Games. In *Gaming Globally: Production, Play, and Place*, ed. Nina B. Huntemann and Ben Aslinger, 119–138. New York: Palgrave Macmillan.

Consalvo, Mia. 2016. *Atari to Zelda: Japan's Videogames in Global Contexts*. Cambridge, MA: The MIT Press.

Derrida, Jacques. 1978. Structure, Sign and Play in the Discourse of the Human Sciences. In *Writing and Difference*, ed. Jacques Derrida, 278–294. Chicago: University of Chicago Press.

Fiadotau, Mikhail. 2021. Isolated Connectedness: Applying the Concept of Transinsularity to Japan's Game History. *Replaying Japan* 3:33–41.

Fujita, Naoya. 2025. *Gēmu Kurieitā Kojima Hideo Ron*. Tokyo: Sakuhinsha.

Goto-Jones, Chris. 2015. Playing with Being in Digital Asia: Gamic Orientalism and the Virtual Dōjō. *Asiascape: Digital Asia* 2 (1–2): 20–56.

Hartzheim, Bryan Hikari. 2023. *Hideo Kojima: Progressive Game Design from Metal Gear to Death Stranding*. New York/London: Bloomsbury.

Heath, Joseph. 2018. The Problem with 'Critical' Studies. A Canadian Public Affairs Blog. *In Due Course* (blog). http://induecourse.ca/the-problem-with-critical-studies/.

Herfs, Laurence. 2020. Dreams of the Japanese Self in The Legend of Zelda: Breath of the Wild. *REPLAYING JAPAN* 2:33–47.

Herfs, Laurence. 2021. 'We Will Take Your Heart': Japanese Cultural Identity in Persona V.

Hutchinson, Rachael. 2019. *Japanese Culture Through Videogames*. London: Routledge.

Hutchinson, Rachael, and Jérémie Pelletier-Gagnon, eds. 2022. *Japanese Role-Playing Games: Genre, Representation, and Liminality in the JRPG*. Lanham, MD: Lexington Books.

Ingold, Tim. 2008. When ANT Meets SPIDER: Social Theory for Arthropods. In *Material Agency*, ed. Carl Knappett and Lambros Malafouris, 209–215. Boston, MA: Springer US.

Iwabuchi, Kōichi. 2002. *Recentering Globalization. Popular Culture and Japanese Transnationalism*. Durham, NC: Duke University Press.

Iwabuchi, Koichi. 2016. Creative Industries and Cool Japan. In *Global Game Industries and Cultural Policy*, ed. Anthony Fung, 33–52. Cham: Palgrave Macmillan.

Kawasaki, Yasuo. 2022. *Nihon no gemu sentashi: goraku shisetsu to shite no hensen to shakaiteki ichizuke [The History of "Game Centers" in Japan: Historical Changing and Social Positioning as Entertainment Facilities]*. Tokyo: Fukumurashuppan.

Kelly, William H. 2010. Censoring Violence in Virtual Dystopia: Issues in the Rating of Video Games in Japan and of Japanese Video Game Outside Japan. In *Utopic Dreams and Apocalyptic Fantasies: Critical Approaches to Researching Video Game Play*, ed. Talmadge Wright, David G. Embrick, and András Lukács, 143–160. Lanham/Plymouth: Lexington Books.

Kelly, William H. 2020. Hands with Four Digits: An Issue in the Rating and Censorship of Video Games in Japan? *Replaying Japan* 2:61–71.

Kitada, Akihiro. 2005. *Warau nihon no "nashonarizumu"*. Tokyo: Nihon Hōsō Shuppan Kyōkai.

Liang, Yuxi. 2018. Nihon No Gēmu Taitoru No Chūgokugoyaku Ni Tsuite No Ichikōsatsu: Hiseikishijō Ni Okeru Gēmu No Denpa 日本のゲームタイトルの中国語訳についての一考察: 非正規市場におけるゲームの伝播 [A Study on Chinese Translations of Japanese Game Titles: Propagation of Video Games in Unofficial Market in China]. *Core Ethics* 14:247–259.

Liboriussen, Bjarke, and Paul Martin. 2016. Regional Game Studies. *Game Studies* 16 (1).

Maitra, Ani, and Rey Chow. 2016. What's 'in'? Disaggregating Asia Through New Media Actants. In *Routledge Handbook of New Media in Asia*, ed. Larissa Hjorth and Olivia Khoo, 17–27. London: Routledge.

Mandiberg, Stephen. 2015. Playing (with) the Trace: Localized Culture in Phoenix Wright. *Kinephanos* 5:112–141.

Mandiberg, Stephen. 2021. Video Games Have Never Been Global: Resituating Video Game Localization History. In *Game History and the Local*, Palgrave Games in Context, ed. Melanie Swalwell, 177–198. Cham: Palgrave Macmillan.

Massumi, Brian. 2014. *What Animals Teach Us About Politics*. Durham: Duke University Press.

Middell, Matthias. 2018. Narratives About Globalization: International Studies and Global Studies. In *The Routledge Handbook of Transregional Studies*, ed. Matthias Middell, 1st ed., 659–666. Abingdon, Oxon/New York, NY: Routledge.

Mizuta Lippit, Akira. 2017. Preface (Interface). In *Media Theory in Japan*, ed. Marc Steinberg and Alexander Zahlten, xi–xv. Durham/London: Duke University Press.

Nakamura, Akinori, and Susana Tosca. 2021. The Mobile Suit Gundam Franchise: A Case Study of Transmedia Storytelling Practices and Ludo Mix in Japan. *Transactions of the Digital Games Research Association* 5 (2).

Navarro-Remesal, Víctor, and Beatriz Pérez Zapata. 2022. Taiko vs Bongo: Taiko No Tatsujin, Donkey Konga, and Japaneseness in Their European Distribution. *Replaying Japan* 4:63–74.

Newman, James. 2012. Ports and Patches: Digital Games as Unstable Objects—James Newman, 2012. *Convergence* 18 (2): 135–142.

Newman, James. 2019. Slower, Squashed and Six Months Late: Japanese Videogames in the UK, 1991-2019. *REPLAYING JAPAN* 1:5–28.

Nintendo. 2017. The Legend of Zelda: *Breath of the Wild*. Nintendo WiiU & Switch.

O'Hagan, Minako, and Carmen Mangiron. 2013. *Game Localization: Translating for the Global Digital Entertainment Industry*. Benjamins Translation Library, Volume 106. Amsterdam: John Benjamins Publishing Company.
Oyama, Shinji. 2016. Japanese Creative Industries in Globalization. In *Routledge Handbook of New Media in Asia*, ed. Larissa Hjorth and Olivia Khoo, 322–332. New York/London: Routledge.
Pelletier-Gagnon, Jérémie, and Martin Picard. 2015. Beyond Rapelay: Self-Regulation in the Japanese Erotic Video Game Industry. In *Rated M for Mature*, ed. Matthew Wysocki and Evan W. Lauteria, 28–41. New York/London: Bloomsbury Academic.
Picard, Martin. 2013. The Foundation of Geemu: A Brief History of Early Japanese Video Games. *Game Studies* 13 (2).
Picard, Martin, and Jérémie Pelletier-Gagnon. 2015. Introduction: Geemu, Media Mix, and the State of Japanese Video Game Studies. *Kinephanos* 5 (1): 1–19.
Picard, Martin, and Martin Roth. 2022. The 'Last Japanese Soldier': Putting the Nation into Play. In *Capture Japan: Visual Culture and the Global Imagination from 1952 to the Present*, ed. Marco Bohr, 87–106. London/New York: Bloomsbury Visual Arts.
Rockwell, Geoffrey, and Keiji Amano. 2015. Pachinko: A game studies perspective | Kinephanos. *Kinephanos* 5 (1). https://www.kinephanos.ca/2015/pachinko-a-game-studies-perspective/.
Rockwell, Geoffrey, and Keiji Amano. 2019. Pachinko: A Case Study in Hybrid Physical and Virtual Interface. *Journal of the Japanese Association for Digital Humanities* 4 (1): 72–89.
Roth, Martin. 2022. Reclaiming Everydayness and Japanese Cultural Routines in Animal Crossing: New Horizons. *Journal of Intercultural Studies* 43 (6): 722–739.
Roth, Martin. 2025. *Unboxing Japanese Videogames*. Cambridge, MA: MIT Press.
Said, Edward W. 2012. *Orientalismus*. Frankfurt (Main): S. Fischer Verlag.
Sakai, Naoki, and Harry D. Harootunian. 1999. Japan Studies and Cultural Studies. *Positions: East Asia Cultures Critique* 7 (2): 593–647.
Schules, Douglas. 2015. *Kawaii* Japan: Defining JRPGs Through the Cultural Media Mix. *Kinephanos* 5:53–76.
Steinberg, Marc. 2015. 8-Bit Manga: Kadokawa's Madara, or The Gameic Media Mix. *Kinephanos: Journal of Media Studies and Popular Culture* 5:40–52.
Steinberg, Marc, and Alexander Zahlten. 2017. Introduction. In *Media Theory in Japan*, ed. Marc Steinberg and Alexander Zahlten, 1–29. Durham/London: Duke University Press.
Svelch, Jaroslav. 2018. *Gaming the Iron Curtain: How Teenagers and Amateurs in Communist Czechoslovakia Claimed the Medium of Computer Games*. Cambridge, MA: The MIT Press.
Swalwell, Melanie. 2021a. *Homebrew Gaming and the Beginnings of Vernacular Digitality*. Cambridge, MA: The MIT Press.
Swalwell, Melanie. 2021b. Introduction: Game History and the Local. In *Game History and the Local*, Palgrave Games in Context, ed. Melanie Swalwell, 1–15. Cham: Palgrave Macmillan.
Therrien, Carl. 2019. *The Media Snatcher: PC/CORE/TURBO/ENGINE/GRAFX/16/CDROM2/SUPER/DUO/ARCADE/RX*. Cambridge, MA: MIT Press.
Tosca, Susana, and Lisbeth Klastrup. 2019. *Transmedial Worlds in Everyday Life*. New York/London: Routledge.
Whaley, Ben. 2023. *Toward a Gameic World: New Rules of Engagement from Japanese Video Games*. Ann Arbor, MI: University of Michigan Press.
Wolf, Mark, ed. 2015. *Videogames Around the World*. Cambridge, MA: MIT Press.
Yoshimoto, Mitsuhiro. 1991. The Difficulty of Being Radical: The Discipline of Film Studies and the Postcolonial World Order. *Boundary 2* 18 (3): 242.

13

Expectations for Japanese Game Study Participants

Akito Inoue, Kazufumi Fukuda, and Fumihiko Ikuine

Contents

F. Ikuine et al. (eds.), *Japanese Game Studies*, https://doi.org/10.1007/978-981-95-9857-1_13

This book traces the history, scope, and defining features of Japanese game studies. It is intended as a guide for current and aspiring researchers who are either engaged in game studies in Japan or interested in exploring Japanese game literature.

- What new possibilities might Japanese game studies open with your participation?
- How might it help you transcend current limitations?
- In what ways can it contribute to your success in and influence on global game studies?

With these questions in mind, consider the many new perspectives that may illuminate your future direction, including opportunities in entertainment and game informatics, management studies of the game industry, the humanities, web and service informatics, library and information science, and humanistic and social informatics.

13.1 On the "Opacity" of Japanese Research

Broadly speaking, humanities research in Japan has two spheres. One is the sphere of criticism, in which figures such as Hiroki Azuma and Kōjin Karatani are active. The other is the academic research community. The two overlap philosophically to some degree, but each has its own history and constituency, and they do not necessarily share participants. However, their boundaries are permeable; hence, people can move back and forth between the two. For example, one of our editors, Inoue, came from the criticism-oriented sphere and joined the academic sphere.

For readers outside Japan, this situation can be difficult to parse, and it lends itself to the perception that Japanese humanities research is opaque to some degree. However, Japan's multilayered cultural contexts, with their deep historical roots, continue to influence both spheres discussed. When overseas researchers discuss Japan's game culture, covering topics such as religion and gender, misunderstandings are difficult to avoid. Even scholars familiar with Japanese studies and well versed in "Orientalism" often do not see the cultural machinery at work behind the empirical lens. Japanese is rich in culturally specific nuances and shared meanings that often do not translate easily into English or other Western languages. Hence, there are limits to what can be understood by reading only English-language materials that discuss the Japanese humanities. The same challenge often arises when Japanese people attempt to understand Western studies. It is therefore crucial for scholars and all readers to visit Japan, talk with Japanese writers and researchers, and work together to identify whether opacity exists, and, if it does, how to illuminate our understanding.

At the Ritsumeikan Center for Game Studies (RCGS), inquiries from abroad have steadily increased. At times, they exceed what we can reasonably manage, and in those cases, we emphasize that Japan has many excellent experts and research groups. For example, fan communities can provide a wealth of answers, and we intend with this book to guide readers to connect to a broader range of Japanese humanities groups. Doing so should help make the network of game studies in Japan and worldwide more diverse and vibrant.

Our hope is that this book will serve as a fresh entry point for readers who are interested in Japanese game criticism and research, and that it will bridge perceived gaps in understanding among specialists in Japan and worldwide.

13.2 The Future of Game Business Management Studies

The outlook for research on Japanese games from the perspectives of management studies and economics is promising for two main reasons. First, games and the game industry provide rich opportunities for empirical research on topics central to both fields. Consequently, a substantial body of prior research already exists.

You will see in ► Chap. 10 themes such as platforming and ecosystem development, network externalities, and the cultivation of creative industries. Indeed, academic research in management studies and economics related to the game business is also connected to the research of innovation. We expect that game studies are likely to play an important role as a testing ground or sandbox for the practical application of advanced information and communication technologies (ICTs), including artificial intelligence (AI) applications. Researchers interested in how technology diffuses into society, drives innovation, and shapes new industries will increasingly turn to games and the game business. This is known as the "digital humanities" (DH). Moreover, given the continued growth of companies in the United States, Europe, South Korea, and China, Japanese companies and markets are likely to maintain a presence, making Japanese games an enduring research subject.

Second, management studies and economics are fields in which international research and cooperation are highly active, and with continued collaboration, findings readily cross language barriers, helping eliminate any sense of opacity. Corporate behavior and economic phenomena can be quantified with metrics such as sales, market size, product counts, and firm numbers, enabling cross-country and regional comparisons. Hence, valid empirical interpretations can be made and shared.

In recent years, the quantification of games as measurable content has advanced significantly. There are even ways to measure enjoyment and the scale and impact of a genre. The game research domain has its own typology, including ratings for entertainment value, classification based on genre or franchise, and databases cataloging both ideas and individuals involved in game production and enjoyment. These data enable empirical research on the aforementioned phenomena, social, and cultural effects of games—particularly hypothesis-driven work.

Most management studies today aim for journal publication, and editors of academic journals value quantitative empirical research. As such, research in management studies and economics related to the game business offers strong opportunities for young scholars. In short, games and the game industry are subjects rich in quantitative data, and the size and scope of the domains covered by the two spheres of interest in this field are growing fast…particularly in Japan.

When closely examining the quantifiability of gaming experiences and studies, another aspect of opacity arises. Given that many observable—and experiential—phenomena can be and are being quantified, certain social dimensions still resist full quantitative measurement. These include the enjoyment of play, the intentions and creativity of developers, and the passion of users. Although measuring and understanding such elements are valuable, there remains a vast and unexplored realm in which we strive to understand the *meanings* behind the numbers, including comprehending the social and cultural dynamics that exist behind the observed phenomena.

We hope that the research guide in this volume will serve as a foundation for making the promising future of this field even more fruitful. As mentioned, we feel that the continued research conducted in Japan will provide meaningful insights into Japanese society today as well as help guide its future transformations.

13.3 The Horizon of Game Studies: AI and DH

Both social science researchers and critics often sense that the traditional humanities are showing signs of stagnation. As mentioned, DH has emerged as a field full of growth and vitality. Indeed, it is rapidly transforming under the influence of generative AI, particularly large language models (LLMs).

Pioneering DH projects in game studies are underway, such as the Historical Arcade Game Studies Project (HACS n.d.), which encodes the promotional discourse of magazines, and the Japanese Visual Media Graph Project (Japanese Visual Media Graph n.d.), which aims to build a research database for Japanese visual media, including anime, manga, games, and visual novels. Important to the readers of this book, this field is still in its early stages.

There is a strong natural affinity between DH, AI, and game studies. Games are "born-digital" media, created as data from the outset, meaning that their programs and extensive log data are directly available for computational analysis. In addition, vast paratexts (e.g., strategy wikis, gameplay videos, and social media discussions) offer rich resources for study. We are in a genuinely "hot" period of research and development, in which years of archival work may blossom at once, causing a magnitude shift in our capabilities and understanding.

LLMs have made academic writing and data analysis more efficient, while also enabling researchers to discover new problems while solving existing ones. However, many of us are realizing that the AI capabilities we are putting to use are making things less "easy" than more "endless." The ability to sustain ongoing dialogue with an LLM—whether in the lab, at home, or on the train—is both stimulating and boundless. This welcome development nevertheless calls for a fundamental reconsideration of what research itself should be, both pragmatically and culturally.

To illustrate how daily interaction with AI is reshaping research, I can draw on my own recent experience of using LLMs in my daily work. My applications range from research support and implementation to archive management, public relations, language learning, and ideation. The following list, adapted from ChatGPT's summaries of activity across chats, illustrates these uses:

1. Research support and academic writing:
   (a) Proofreading and editing texts for research projects.
   (b) Improving the structure and phrasing of research proposals.
   (c) Summarizing content to draft abstracts for presentations.
   (d) Assisting with statistical analysis and generating code to interpret and visualize results.

2. Technical development and implementation:
   (a) Text classification and clustering using paratext classification and narrative extraction (e.g., bidirectional encoding and transformer-powered LLMs).
   (b) Drafting architectural proposals for web services.
   (c) Generating Python code for image and text processing.
   (d) Designing user interface/experience concepts for data visualization and business intelligence tools.

3. Archive management and collection support:
   (a) Formulating collection policies for analog game museums.
   (b) Proposing classification schemes and conversion policies for borderline materials.
   (c) Advising on digitization setups (e.g., lighting, scanners, and acrylic plates).
   (d) Creating digitization specifications and glossary entries.

4. Event management and public relations:
   (a) Planning events for board game museums and archives; analyzing user surveys.
   (b) Refining calls for papers and social media posts for submissions.
   (c) Proposing structures for exhibitions and seminars.

These capabilities have already exceeded the "life hack" motif; they are also powerful indicators of a fundamental shift in our civilization. Compared with the pre-generative AI era, the current situation can feel almost like cheating. Such wide-ranging use shows that the integration of AI and DH is already operating at a practical level, reshaping not only individual skills but the research mindset as a whole. Of course, as is well-known, generative AI poses risks such as hallucination and plagiarism, making its use potentially hazardous in scholarly work. But then again, human authors possess the same risks. Nevertheless, for the time being, LLMs should remain assistants, with manuscripts fully authored and overseen by the human researcher, who retains full responsibility.

Gaming culture consists not only of vast content but also of immense paratexts. This is why DH methodologies (e.g., "distant reading," which surveys large datasets for patterns rather than focusing on individual works) are well-suited to game studies. However, because games have a shorter history than traditional books, relatively few works are available in the public domain. Research methods must therefore be developed through trial and error with this limitation in mind. In particular, building datasets in collaboration with rights holders and deepening discussions of fair use in the context of game studies will be essential.

The future of game studies lies in exploring new methodologies built on collaboration between AI and DH. This future research environment will be more open, more agile, and above all, one that preserves the spirit of play. I encourage researchers to venture into this evolving field.

13.4 Closing Remarks

Japanese game studies—and the very activity of research—is currently undergoing a profound transformation. This shift is driven by generative AI, particularly LLMs, which now enable computers to perform recognition and inference once considered uniquely human.

We are now compelled to reexamine the meaning and methods of research in ways unprecedented for our predecessors, envisioning new forms of inquiry that incorporate generative AI. Among academic domains, game studies may be among the most urgently called to adapt. Games are inherently digital, and their environments are saturated with digitized information, which is naturally heavily influenced by culture and language.

Because games are composed of digital data—including content, text, images, and audio—they can be "shared" between humans and AI, and subjected to analysis and interpretation. This digital nature makes game research more susceptible to transformation than other cultural, economic, or social domains where non-digitizable elements remain central.

The evolving research environment shaped by generative AI may lower language barriers and blur disciplinary boundaries. In such an era, what constraints will remain? How will past critiques and achievements in the humanities and social sciences be carried forward? At present, uncertainties outnumber certainties. Yet it is reasonable to expect that games will continue to serve as shared objects of inquiry, enabling experts to engage in cross-disciplinary—and at times, cross-community—dialog. Through such studies, we may uncover new insights into society, culture, technology, and the human–machine relationship in entirely new ways.

Amid these changes, Japanese games, with their rich history and distinctive character, will undoubtedly remain central. We envision a future in which research transcends national, regional, disciplinary, and institutional boundaries, with Japanese games as a focal point. To that end, we hope that this book will serve as a guide, synthesizing accumulated academic knowledge on Japanese games.

References

HACS. n.d.. https://gamexperience.ludov.ca/visualizations. Accessed August 13, 2025.
Japanese Visual Media Graph. n.d.. https://jvmg.iuk.hdm-stuttgart.de/. Accessed August 13, 2025.

Supplementary Information

F. Ikuine et al. (eds.), *Japanese Game Studies*, https://doi.org/10.1007/978-981-95-9857-1

Corporate Bodies Index

Game Works / Game Series / Product Names Index

S

T

U

W

Y

Institutions / Organizations Index

Person Names Index

Topics / Concepts / Subject Index

Q

R

S

T

V

W

GPSR Compliance

The European Union's (EU) General Product Safety Regulation (GPSR) is a set of rules that requires consumer products to be safe and our obligations to ensure this.

If you have any concerns about our products, you can contact us on ProductSafety@springernature.com

In case Publisher is established outside the EU, the EU authorized representative is:

Springer Nature Customer Service Center GmbH
Europaplatz 3
69115 Heidelberg, Germany

Batch number: 10703869

Printed by Printforce, the Netherlands